P9-DTD-567

GREAT CAMPAIGNS

THE WATERLOO CAMPAIGN

Napoleon I, Emperor of the French.

GREAT CAMPAIGN SERIES

The Atlanta Campaign
The Chancellorsville Campaign
The Gettysburg Campaign
The Little Bighorn Campaign
The Peninsula Campaign
The Petersburg Campaign
The Philadelphia Campaign
The Waterloo Campaign
The Wilderness Campaign

GREAT CAMPAIGNS

THE WATERLOO CAMPAIGN

June 1815

Albert A. Nofi

COMBINED BOOKS
Pennsylvania

PUBLISHER'S NOTE

Combined Books, Inc., is dedicated to publishing books of distinction in history and military history. We are proud of the quality of writing and the quantity of information found in our books. Our books are manufactured with style and durability and are printed on acid-free paper. We like to think of our books as soldiers: not infantry grunts, but well dressed and well equipped avant garde. Our logo reflects our commitment to the modern and yet historic art of bookmaking.

We would like to hear from our readers and invite you to write to us at our offices in Pennsylvania with your reactions, queries, comments, even complaints.

We encourage all of our readers to purchase our books from their local booksellers, and we hope that you let us know of booksellers in your area that might be interested in carrying our books. If you are unable to find a book in your area, please write to us.

For information, address:
COMBINED BOOKS, INC.
151 East 10th Avenue
Conshohocken, PA 19428

Copyright © 1993 by Albert A. Nofi
All rights reserved. No part of this publication may be reproduced, stored in a retrieval system or transmitted in any form or by any means, electrical, mechanical or otherwise, without first seeking the written permission of the publisher.

ISBN 0-938289-29-2

First published in the USA in 1993 by Combined Books
and distributed in North America by
Stackpole Books, Inc., 5067 Ritter Road, Mechanicsburg, PA 17055

Printed in the United States of America

Maps by Christopher J. Couch

*For Marilyn J. Spencer
and Lori Fawcett
In Loving Memory*

Acknowledgments

As always in an undertaking of this nature, several people were of great help in the production of the final text. Among the many who were of assistance, special thanks are in order to Daniel Scott Palter and the staff of *West End Games* for access to their extensive Napoleonics library; Daniel David of *Sky Books International* in New York, for assistance in locating a number of unusual volumes; James F. Dunnigan, author and former editor of *Strategy & Tactics*, for suggestions and advice on several Napoleonic projects, and with whom, along with Bill Owen and the Millenium of Mayhem Tour, I walked the field; Prof. Richard L. DiNardo, for some helpful tips and suggestions; David C. Isby, for some useful suggestions; John E. Koontz, for many years of interesting correspondence on Waterloo and related subjects, as well as for a look at his impressive research into the French and Prussian order of battle; Dennis Casey for providing advice, references and access to his collection of Napoleonic literature; Professor John Boardman for his advice on time; Wilbur E. Gray, who kindly pointed out a number of errors in an early version of one portion of the manuscript; William Keyser, for assistance elucidating the order of battle; Kenneth S. Gallagher and Edward Wimble for reading the last stage of the manuscript and raising important issues; and Dr. Jay Stone for some useful advice and the loan of several valuable reference works. Dan Kilbert, of New York's The Complete Strategist, and Richard Berg, publisher of *Richard Berg's Review of Games*, were immensely helpful in sorting through the enormous number of wargames dealing with the campaign. John E. Johnston, Robin D. Roberts, Mark Hennessey, Sam Belcher and Phil Feller were kind enough to read the manuscript and make some useful suggestions. As always, the staff of the New York Public Library and the Mina Rees Library of the Graduate School of the City University of New York were of enormous help in tracking down odd items.

Particular thanks are in order to Bob Pigeon, Lizbeth Nauta, Toni Bauer and John Cannan, of *Combined Books*, for making this volume possible, and to Christopher J. Couch, who produced the maps from my rough sketches.

Very special thanks are reserved for my wife, Mary S. Nofi, and my daughter, Marilyn J. Spencer, who suffered through the writing.

Albert A. Nofi
Brooklyn, N.Y.

Stylistic Note

To simplify matters several ahistorical conventions have been adopted in this work:
1. The identities of French units are in *italics*.
2. Times have been rendered on a 24-hour basis.

CONTENTS

Maps

Sidebars

Preface to the Series

*J*onathan Swift termed war "that mad game the world so loves to play." He had a point. Universally condemned, it has nevertheless been almost as universally practiced. For good or ill, war has played a significant role in the shaping of history. Indeed, there is hardly a human institution which has not in some fashion been influenced and molded by war, even as it helped shape and mold war in turn. Yet the study of war has been as remarkably neglected as its practice commonplace. With a few outstanding exceptions, the history of wars and of military operations has until quite recently been largely the province of the inspired patriot or the regimental polemicist. Only in our times have serious, detailed and objective accounts come to be considered the norm in the treatment of military history and related matters.

Yet there still remains a gap in the literature, for there are two types of military history. One type is written from a very serious, highly technical, professional perspective and presupposes that the reader is deeply familiar with the background, technology and general situation. The other is perhaps less dry, but merely lightly reviews the events with the intention of informing and entertaining the layman. The qualitative gap between the last two is vast. Moreover, there are professionals in both the military and academia whose credentials are limited to particular moments in the long, sad history of war, and there are laymen who have more than a passing understanding of the field; and then there is the concerned citizen, interested in understanding the phenomena in an age of unusual violence and unprecedented armaments. It is to bridge the gap between the two types of military history, and to reach the professional and the serious amateur and the concerned citizen alike, that this series, GREAT CAMPAIGNS, is designed. Each volume in GREAT CAMPAIGNS is thus not merely an account of a particular military operation, but is a unique reference to the theory and practice of war in the period in question.

The GREAT CAMPAIGNS series is a distinctive contribution to the study of war and of military history, which will remain of value for many years to come.

CHAPTER I

France, Napoleon and Europe

1814-1815

On 6 April 1814, at his palace of Fontainebleu, Napoleon, Emperor of the French, arbiter of Europe, greatest soldier of the age, at once hero and villain to millions, abdicated. Faced with a coalition hitherto unparalleled in history, defeated on all sides, abandoned by his most talented subordinates, deserted by his family, alienated from his people, Napoleon, the "Corsican Ogre," bowed to the inevitable. Within a month, he was established on Elba, sole master of the tiny island between Italy and Corsica, granted him in pension by the triumphant Great Powers. It marked the end of a momentous quarter-century which had opened with the storming of the Bastille on 14 July 1789, an event that touched off the French Revolution, the great wars and the rise of Napoleon to the mastery of Europe.

After 25 years of almost incessant revolution and war, most people, even most Frenchmen, greeted Napoleon's downfall with considerable relief. In the first flush of peace, Louis XVIII, the representative of the newly re-stored Bourbon monarchy, found himself a relatively popular king. Indeed, all over Europe returning exiles also

Napoleon Bonaparte

Napoleon Bonaparte, Emperor of the French and King of Italy (1769-1821), was born to an impoverished Corsican noble family. Sent to the military school at Brienne in France at an early age, he entered the Royal Army and trained as an artilleryman. Embracing the Revolution, the young officer soon rose rapidly through connections with the most radical elements, the Jacobins. An outstanding job of directing the artillery at the siege of Toulon in 1793 secured him rapid promotion and a series of important administrative and staff appointments. Although he barely survived the purge of the Jacobins, in 1796 he was appointed commander of the *Armee d'Italie*. Napoleon led his army to a spectacular series of victories which drove the Austrians entirely out of Northern Italy and precipitated the Peace of Campo Formio in October of 1797, which brought the War of the First Coalition to an end on terms highly favorable to France. The following year Napoleon led an army to Egypt as the first step in a war to deprive Britain of India. Napoleon's Egyptian campaign resulted in a major strategic defeat, but he emerged covered with glory and abandoned his army to its fate to escape to France, where he staged a coup d'etat and installed himself as First Consul of the Republic in 1799.

War having in the meanwhile broken out again, with the Republic suffering reverses on all fronts, Napoleon led an army once more into Italy, where he defeated the Austrians at Marengo (14 June 1800) before returning to Paris to direct successful operations on France's other fronts. By early 1801 France was again at peace, save with England. Over the next three years Napoleon converted the Republic into an Empire with himself at its head, while building the *Grand Armee*, a thoroughly professional fighting force. This he led to victory after victory in a series of wars against Austria and Russia in 1805, Prussia and Russia in 1806-1807 and Austria again in 1809, after each of which he expanded French territory and control, and imposed reform and tyranny simultaneously on Europe.

Despite his victories, however, Napoleon proved unable to inflict serious injury on his principal foe, Britain. In his efforts to defeat Britain Napoleon made a series of politi-

gained a measure of public support. After all, at least the wars, with their insatiable appetite for manpower and their gross consumption of monies, were over. But that popularity did not long endure. In France, though Louis XVIII was inclined to forgive and forget, and, indeed, even

cal, strategic and military errors. An invasion of Spain resulted in a protracted and highly unsuccessful guerrilla war which proved an enormous drain on his resources. And in 1812 he invaded Russia in an effort to force that country to comply with his embargo on trade with England. The disastrous campaign which followed resulted in the virtual destruction of an army of nearly 600,000 men. This signaled a general uprising against Napoleon's empire. In the two years which followed Napoleon attempted to restore his authority, twice spurning offers of peace on terms very favorable to France. Finally defeated in the spring of 1814, he was exiled to Elba, from where he attempted a comeback the following spring, only to meet final defeat at Waterloo. Napoleon lived out his final years in exile on St. Helena.

Napoleon's private life was as acrimonious and ultimately unhappy as was his public life. His numerous brothers and sisters all more or less proved unwilling or unable to assist him in his dream of empire. His first wife, the rather older Josephine de Beauharnais, brought him useful political contacts, two fine step children, but no heir, causing him to divorce her to marry Marie Louise of Hapsburg in an attempt to forge a strong link to the Austrian monarchy. The young princess—some 25 years his junior—did produce an heir, but promptly abandoned Napoleon in his misfortune. By 1815 she was living openly with her lover the Austrian general Count Adam Albrecht von Neipperg.

Napoleon was about 5'6" tall, not particularly shorter than most contemporary Frenchmen. In his youth he was quite slender and boyish looking and had tremendous energy. As he grew older he grew rather stout, was plagued by various ailments and became somewhat lethargic. Napoleon's personal habits alternated between extremes, being sometimes totally overdressed and overly meticulous about meals and the like, and at others being totally indifferent. Thus at the *Champ du Mai*, the grand review and ceremony at which he presented his revised Constitution to France, he wore a wholly ridiculous Renaissance costume, while at Waterloo, despite the heat, he donned once more his old threadbare gray greatcoat over his old green uniform.

A genuinely great man brought low by his faults.

to leave most of the reforms of the Revolutionary and Napoleonic Eras in place, his supporters were not. The voices of reaction were strong, advocating total abolition of anything having the taint of "Jacobinism." Thus, many useful and proper laws were overturned, loyal and experi-

Napoleon's residence in Porto Ferraio, Elba. Modest as it was, the house was one of the most elaborate on the island.

enced civil servants were turned out of their posts in favor of some functionaries who had last served a generation earlier. Some sought to cancel land reform, others to abolish the metric system. So extreme were some that they sought even a return to the clothing styles of the *ancien regime*, a measure which actually was adopted in some smaller states! As if such foolishness was not enough, there was the army.

The army which Louis XVIII inherited was steeped in the glories of the Revolutionary and Napoleonic eras. A hard, seasoned force, it had time and again proven itself in the test of fire. Though war weary, to a man it had pride in the glory and the honor gained in the name of France on hundreds of far flung fields. With Napoleon gone, the army had no choice but to give its loyalty to the crown, a loyalty which might well have stood the test of time had it not been abused. Unfortunately, men with no qualifications beyond their Royalist sympathies were placed in positions of command; men who often knew far less about war than those whom they replaced. Worse yet, the new regime handed out the coveted *Legion of Honor*—under the Empire a reward for heroic or exceptional service—indiscriminately and for the most trivial reasons, frequently to men who had stood with France's enemies in the glorious days of yore. The troops grumbled, and kept their old badges and insignia and eagles well concealed. So there was uneasiness in the army, and, indeed, in all France, an uneasiness which grew as the abuses of the restored regime grew. And as it was in France, so too it seemed in all of Europe.

Whatever his faults—and he had many—Napoleon had been a faithful son of the Revolution in many ways. Wherever his armies had trod he wiped out the vestiges of feudalism, imposed reform, sparked nationalist and even republican sentiments. Now, with the wars over, the Great Powers—save only liberal Britain—were everywhere intent on the restoration of ancient privilege. Thus, whether in Italy or in Germany or in Belgium or in Poland, nationalist sentiments were brutally crushed, reforms stamped out. In the lands of the victors—Austria, Prussia and Russia—reforms engendered by the necessity of sparking resistance to Napoleon were abolished. Internal tensions rose. Moreover, having united solidly to defeat Napoleon, the Great Powers began falling out over the division of the spoils.

In November of 1814 the Great Powers convened an international congress at Vienna to reshape the map. There, amid the parties and the parades and the platitudes it soon became evident that the wartime unity of the Allies was gone. Britain, and to some extent France, represented a liberal view, Russia and Prussia a reactionary one, with Austria trimming from one side to the other depending upon its interests. Each of the powers sought advantage for itself. Only Britain had any understanding of the

causes of the generation of upheaval and sought to preserve as much as possible of the progressive reforms of the
Revolutionary and Napoleonic periods. Clashes were inevitable: Russia, Austria and Prussia quarreled over the
division of Poland; Austria and Prussia over that of Saxony
and over hegemony in Germany; France and Austria
disputed control of Italy, where Britain sought to preserve
more liberal institutions; and Britain, France and Russia
fell out over the distribution of a rich colonial booty. And
the weaker states—Spain, Portugal, Bavaria, Piedmont,
Naples, Denmark, Sweden—sought security and advantage in the face of the overwhelming strength and influence of the Great Powers. As 1814 turned into 1815
tensions seemed to be rising.

An extensive network of agents, sympathizers and relatives enabled Napoleon to observe all of this from the quiet
of his Elban "Empire." Although he had thrown himself
into the management of the tiny island's economy, resources, government, educational system, intellectual life
and military forces with characteristic energy, it was
hardly to be expected that a man whose talents and
ambitions could scarcely be confined to Europe would
long be satisfied with little Elba. So he waited and he
watched and he planned. Napoleon's situation on Elba
was by no means secure. Though the island was guaran-
teed to him by the Great Powers, the Bourbons and the
Prussians would have preferred to see him dead. Louis
XVIII reneged on his pledged word to provide Napoleon
an annual subsidy. Without it Napoleon could not afford to
protect himself. As early as December of 1814 he had been
forced to make economies in the tiny armed forces which
constituted his bodyguard, little more than 1,200 men at
the onset. Soon his agents provided information that the
Bourbons were willing to pay well for his death. Even if
such a plot should fail, more direct action, such as the
landing of some thousands of troops, would most certainly
succeed. Thus, early in 1815, cognizant of the rising

tensions among the Great Powers, aware of the increasing disenchantment of the French towards the Restoration government, assured of the secret support of many throughout France, bankrolled by his sister Pauline's impressive collection of jewelry and determined to follow his star, he resolved upon a desperate gamble. He had once promised that he would "return with the violets." It was almost spring and the violets were in bloom. It was time. He would make one last bid for power. On 26 February 1815 everything was in readiness. With a tiny army and a small band of close advisers, Napoleon, "Emperor of Elba," embarked for France and his destiny on the brig *Inconstant*.

The Empire of Elba

As part of the general settlement of European affairs proposed after Napoleon's abdication in April of 1814, he was granted the right to select from among the islands of Corsica, Corfu and Elba as a place of exile, which would be his in full sovereignty, with the title "Emperor." For some reason he selected Elba, a small island between Italy and his native Corsica. He arrived at Porto Ferraio, the capital of the island, aboard the British frigate HMS *Undaunted* on 3 May 1814, accompanied by a small staff and representatives of the various Allied powers. Napoleon's new domain was quite small, little more than 90 square miles with perhaps 12,000 inhabitants, including a number of nearby tiny islets, among them the later fictionally famous Monte Cristo. Almost as soon as he settled in, requisitioning a modest residence for himself, Napoleon set about managing his new empire.

Displaying his characteristic energy and curiosity, Napoleon made personal inspections of the famous iron mines and salt works which provided most of the island's revenues, and proposed various improvements. He also laid plans for the establishment of a number of model farms on which he would settle some of his veterans, proposed the introduction of several new industries (notably orchards, silk and horse breeding), and thoroughly reformed the island's finances. These measures led to increased prosperity for the island, not in the least because Napoleon's arrival brought a good deal of new money into the local economy; he had about 5,000,000 francs when he landed. The Emperor's arrival also wrought a considerable change in the social life of the sleepy little island, notably so after he was joined by his sister Pauline (subject of the famous nude by Canova), and still later by his mother. His most loyal lover, Madam Walewska, showed up for a short visit, bringing with her their "love child." There were regular balls, receptions were held by foreign representatives, visiting dignitaries were feted and the Royal Navy made it a point to make regular port calls, just to keep an eye on the Exile.

Napoleon paid particular attention to the state of his defenses, being concerned on the one hand that his enemies in Europe might attempt a coup against him, and on the other hand, that the Barbary pirates, who had become increasingly active again during the wars, might raid the island as they had so often in the past. He directed that existing fortifications be improved and selected sites for new ones, including several on the outlying islet of Pianosa. He also began to acquire a small fleet, so that he eventually had eight vessels, of which three were armed and suitable for coast defense and anti-piracy patrol, two were small merchant vessels, and three were oared barges suitable for pleasure outings.

It was on his army, however, that Napoleon lavished the most attention. The powers permitted him

The Imperial Elban Navy			
Ship	Type	Tons	Guns
Caroline	aviso	26	1
Etoile	sloop	83	6
Inconstant	brig	300	18

to have an army of 300 men, provided he could afford it, but Napoleon paid no attention to this limitation. He began with about 800 veterans of the *Garde Imperial*, who arrived on Elba at the end of May with Vicomte Pierre Cambronne at their head (he later attained undying fame for his defiance of an Allied call to surrender at Waterloo). These troops, veterans all, formed the core around which Napoleon built his army that was under the immediate command of Comte Antoine Drouot, who commanded the *Garde* during the Waterloo campaign.

Order of Battle
The Imperial Elban Army
Battalion Napoleon (607):
   Chasseurs (300 in 3 Coys)
   Grenadiers (300 in 3 Coys)
Battalion Corse (400 in 4 Coys)
Battalion Elba (400 in 4 Coys)
Light Cavalry (460 in 6 Sqns)
Chasseurs (380 in 5 Sqns)
Polish Lancers (76 in 1 Sqn)
Artillery (100)
Engineers (25)

The Corsican and Elban battalions were supposed to be recruited from local personnel, who were essentially militiamen. Aside from two or three regularly trained officers, all of the engineers were locally recruited, primarily as a fire brigade. Including these units, the total paper strength of the army was nearly 2,000 men. However, the militia units were never properly organized, so that in practical terms the army did not exceed 1,200. Moreover, since he had a shortage of horses, and in any case Elba was very rugged and unsuited to cavalry, Napoleon dismounted most of his cavalrymen, turning them into fortress artillerymen, retaining only 22 Polish lancers as a mounted escort.

By the winter of 1814-1815 Napoleon was well settled on Elba. Superficially he appeared happy. As one of his staff observed, "The Emperor lives very contentedly on his island. He seems to have forgotten the past." But Napoleon was growing restless. The island was too small to occupy his energies, too confining for his ambitions and too exposed to his enemies. Moreover, he was slowly going broke. Although his resources were now severely limited, Napoleon could not break the habit of lavish spending which he had acquired while master of Europe, so that, for example, Henri Bertrand, former chief marshal of the Imperial household and now head of the civil government of Elba, had a salary of 80,000 francs a year! His personal fortune was diminishing rapidly, as was the money which his sister Pauline brought to him, and the Elban revenues were insufficient to make up the difference. Moreover, the Bourbons were showing signs of reneging on their pledge to provide him an allowance of a million francs a year. Napoleon was soon making various economies in his lifestyle and his development projects. With his usual attention to detail, he even specified the amounts to spend on chairs to be purchased for his dining suite, noting that the price ought not to exceed five francs apiece and quibbled about 280 francs requested by his Stores Department for petty cash. This sort of penny-pinching saved some money, but not enough, and finally he had to make reductions in his armed forces, not a good idea in view of the fact that the Bourbons were quietly offering considerable sums for his head.

All through his exile Napoleon had been in constant touch with events in France and Europe through a complex web of agents, friends and family members. By winter he sensed that the time was ripe to return to power. So on 26 February he took ship with his little army for France.

CHAPTER II

"The Grand Disturber"

Winter 1815

Napoleon sailed from Elba with 1,100 men, 80 horses and 4 cannon distributed among eight vessels. As soon as the flotilla was away it split up, each ship going its own way, the better to evade British and French naval patrols. The voyage was uneventful. On the afternoon of 1 March the little squadron rendezvoused in the Gulf of Jouan, near Cannes in Provence. By 1700 hours the Emperor and his tiny army were ashore. There, by chance, shortly after Napoleon debarked he encountered Colonel Honore Grimaldi, the Prince of Monaco, riding through town with a small entourage. The Emperor asked the Prince, who had commanded a regiment with great distinction during Napoleon's later campaigns, to join his great venture. When the Prince replied, "But sire, I'm going home!" Napoleon rejoined with "So am I!" But the Emperor's jaunty response must have concealed considerable disappointment. He had already noticed that the local populace was less than overwhelmed by his return. Nevertheless, he had to press on and he prepared to march on Paris. Since the regular route—along the coast through Toulon and Marseilles and then up the valley of the Rhone—lay through territory of Royalist sentiments, he led his little army across the mountains striking directly for Grenoble,

"Soldiers of the 5th! Behold me! If there be one among you who wishes to kill his Emperor, he can! I come to offer myself to your assaults!" Grenoble, 7 March 1815.

in the anti-Royalist region of Dauphiné. In the first two days the column advanced nearly 60 kilometers through snow and freezing temperatures, crossing a ridge which in places reached 12,000 feet. Though supplies were plentiful and the peasantry friendly, recruits were few, four men only coming forward: two old soldiers, a tanner and a gendarme. The small local garrisons were unenthusiastic about committing themselves to the Emperor, yet equally unwilling to oppose him. The entire enterprise hung in the balance. The tiny expedition pressed on. The critical moment came on 7 March.

On 7 March, having advanced nearly 300 kilometers in a week, Napoleon's column reached the hamlet of Laffray, not 15 kilometers from Grenoble. There Napoleon encountered a small detachment of infantry from the *5th Regiment of the Line*, supported by a few lancers. The two little forces faced each other across a stretch of road. Tension filled the air. Napoleon appeared at the head of his men, wearing his battered old gray-green coat and his cocked hat sporting a tricolor cockade.

A Royalist officer called out, "There he is! Fire!" And nothing happened.

As the troops hesitated Napoleon walked slowly forward. "Soldiers of the *5th*!" he cried, "Behold me!" He advanced a few more steps, opening his coat to reveal the familiar uniform beneath, on which he sported the ribbon of the *Legion d'honneur*. "If there be one among you who wishes to kill his Emperor, he can! I come to offer myself to your assaults!"

In an instant all semblance of order among the Royal troops vanished. The men crowded about Napoleon, crying out his name, weeping, clutching at his garments, kissing his hands. Escorted by the *5th of the Line,* led by its commander, Colonel Charles de la Bedoyere, Napoleon marched into Grenoble to the enthusiastic cheers of its garrison. On 9 March he set out once more on the road to Paris at the head of 7,000 men. As he put it, "As far as Grenoble, I was an adventurer; at Grenoble, I was a prince once more!"

Napoleon's little army began to grow. Regiment after regiment was set in his path, only to desert to him at the earliest opportunity, the men bringing their tricolor cockades out of their knapsacks, unfurling once more the long-hidden battleflags and remounting the carefully guarded eagles. As he advanced, Napoleon sent agents and emissaries throughout France and disseminated propaganda asserting that he returned with the consent of the Great Powers. He issued proclamations, overturning acts of the Bourbons, restoring old reforms, banishing Royalist sycophants. The growing army pressed on. Advancing another 400 kilometers over the next 9 days, he won Lyons, Macon, Chalons-sur-Saone, Autun and Auxerre to his cause without a shot. On 18 March at Auxerre,

Field Marshal Sir Arthur Wellesley, the Duke of Wellington

Field Marshal Sir Arthur Wellesley, the Duke of Wellington (1769-1852), was a younger son of an impoverished Irish peer who nevertheless managed to send the boy to Eton and then a military school at Angers, in France. Wellesley entered the British Army by purchasing a commission as an ensign at the age of 16. His rise through the ranks was rapid; by means of a series of exchanges and promotions he ended up serving in seven different regiments over the next six-and-a-half years, so that by the age of 24 he was a lieutenant colonel commanding the 33rd Foot, and had found time to be elected to the Irish Parliament. He commanded his regiment in the brief Netherlands campaign of 1793, but then languished in garrison and politics for some years until his brother, Lord Mornington, was appointed governor of Bengal in 1798, at a time when the 33rd had just been ordered out to India as well.

In India young Wellesley commanded in a series of successful campaigns against various local potentates, the most notable of which was Assaye in 1803, a battle which he later referred to as the most difficult of his career. Meanwhile he had risen to major general, so that by his return to Europe he had gained some measure of fame: Lord Nelson knew of his accomplishments and on the one occasion that the two actually met went out of his way to discuss military affairs with him. (Not knowing who the young major general was, Nelson, having little patience with sycophants, had at first snubbed him, only to seek him out when he shortly afterwards learned his identity.) Back in Britain, Wellesley was elected to Parliament and served in various political posts, occasionally being recalled to duty, notably against the Danes in 1807 and the French in Portugal in 1808, where his victory at Vimiero resulted in the surrender of the French Army. Wellesley was able to weather the political storm which resulted when his inept superiors in Portugal allowed the French to return home in British ships. Surprisingly, this brief touch of disgrace-by-association probably saved his career, since it prevented him from being sent on the disastrously mismanaged Walcheren Expedition. So far Wellesley's career had been impressive, but hardly spectacular. All that was to change

he encountered Marshal Michel Ney, formerly the greatest of his paladins, now in Royal service. Some days before, as he left Paris at the head of a substantial corps, Ney had

in 1809, when he was sent to Portugal once again.

From 1809 to 1814 Wellesley conducted a series of campaigns in Portugal and Spain in cooperation with Portuguese regular troops and Spanish irregulars, giving Napoleon what has been called the "Spanish ulcer," an unwinnable war which consumed men and treasure and reputations in endless amounts. These operations honed Wellesley's skills to a fine edge, while serving to train his troops to a superb degree of expertise. Ending the war with an impressive victory at Toulouse, in the south of France, Wellesley, who was created the Duke of Wellington as a result of his victories, was subsequently the British ambassador to Bourbon France and a delegate to the Congress of Vienna. With the return of Napoleon from Elba, he was put in command of the Anglo-Allied Army concentrating in Belgium, in which capacity he won the battle of Waterloo, which was his biggest and last battle.

After the wars, Wellington served for many years as commander in chief of the British Army, became a prominent diplomat and conservative politician. He served a term as prime minister, (1828-1830), during which he reluctantly moved Catholic Emancipation through Parliament. He fell from power as a result of his disastrous policies regarding the Near Eastern Crisis of 1829.

Wellington was a rather tall man, who might have been considered handsome but for his rather prominent nose. He was casual about his dress, and during the Waterloo campaign affected a neat, but wholly civilian outfit, carrying a blue cape, which he put on and off several times during the battle as the weather changed. Aside from his general's sash and the four national cockades—Britain, Portugal, Spain and the Netherlands—on his hat, the only thing military about him was the telescope with which he alternately surveyed the field and fidgeted throughout the day (his "indifference" towards dress was quickly adopted by many of his subordinates, a matter which made the British officers a rather motley looking lot). Personally he could be quite charming, and he was rather a ladies' man. However, he frequently appeared somewhat aloof, perhaps because he tended to become focused on whatever was occupying his mind at the time; on one occasion he was so involved in a conversation that he failed to notice that an egg which he was eating was spoiled. A truly great captain, one of the unanswerable questions of history will ever be how well would Wellington have done had he met Napoleon in his prime.

sworn to Louis XVIII that he would bring the usurper back "in an iron cage." For some days Ney had been bombarded by messages and emissaries from his erstwhile Emperor.

Field Marshal Sir Arthur Wellesley, the Duke of Wellington. One of the best commanders in history, Wellington had never met Napoleon before Waterloo, which was to be his last battle, as it was also Napoleon's and Blucher's.

His loyalties were already in doubt. When the two finally met, Napoleon said, "Embrace me, my dear marshal! I am glad to see you, and want neither explanations nor justifications." Ney and all his troops went over. The way to Paris was open.

The final days of Napoleon's advance on Paris were more of a triumphal procession than a military operation. A wag posted a placard on the railing around the Vendome Column in the Place Vendome that read: "Napoleon to Louis XVIII. My good Brother, it is useless to send me more troops; I have enough." Louis XVIII fled the capital on 19 March. And at 2100 Hours on 20 March Napoleon's traveling carriage pulled up in front of the Tuileries Palace. He had won France almost without a shot.

News of Napoleon's escape reached Vienna on 7 March, even as he was encountering the *5th of the Line* and making his triumphal entry into Grenoble. The delegates to the congress were stunned. The British delegate, Field Marshal Sir Arthur Wellesley, the Duke of Wellington, was the first to learn of it. He passed the word on to the others. Many disbelieved it at first, until confirmation was received. Most, including Wellington himself, thought that Napoleon might attempt to flee to Italy or even America, but none believed he would once more seek the throne of France. None, that is, save Tsar Alexander I of Russia, once one of Napoleon's greatest admirers and now counted among his most implacable foes. Placing a hand on Wellington's shoulder, he said softly, "It is for you to save the world again."

The political and diplomatic consequences of Napoleon's return to power were interesting, though not overly complex. Regaining the throne had proven surprisingly easy. Keeping it would certainly prove more difficult. Domestically, Napoleon realized that he could not rule with such sweeping disregard for individual rights and public opinion as had hitherto marked his style. The restoration of the Empire would have to be accomplished on firmly constitutional grounds. This would be the only way to unite all the anti-Bourbon factions in the country, thereby creating a stable internal political situation for the inevitable clash of arms with the Great Powers. The problem was how to accomplish this and still retain the degree of control necessary to permit him to recreate a great army and lead it to victory. Napoleon believed that he had the answer. Almost as soon as he landed in France Napoleon began proclaiming a new order. He represented the restored Empire as a nationalistic and democratic institution. Confirming the abolition of conscription—one of the few popular measures taken by Louis XVIII—he spoke of "unrestricted discussion, public trials, emancipated elections, responsible ministers, and all the paraphernalia of constitutional government." He appointed a cabinet on the very day that he arrived in Paris. It was what might be termed a "government of national unity," a sort of *union sacré* of all the anti-Bourbon factions in France, including even a few die-hard Jacobins left over from the days of the Revolution. To this body he entrusted the formulation of a new constitution for France. The work was swiftly done. On 23 April the new constitution was promulgated.

The "Additional Act," as the document was termed, extended the franchise, abolished Catholicism as the state religion, confirmed freedom of conscience and swept away the reactionary legislation of the Bourbon Restoration. The new government would have a two-house legislature, one of peers appointed by the Emperor and one of the people elected indirectly by a collegiate system. It was a relatively liberal document in a rather reactionary age. But it received only marginal support. When offered for public approval, only 1,300,000 votes were cast in its favor, less than half the number given Napoleon in 1800 when he established the Consulate, or in 1804 when he secured the Imperial dignity. There appeared to be less enthusiasm for Napoleon than he believed. As if to confirm that fact, in some parts of France the opposition to Napoleon was resorting to bullets rather than ballots.

Even as Napoleon reached Paris, Royalists throughout France began to organize, particularly in the west and the south, and in the Calais area. There were a few contingents of troops who held out for the king, as well as some peasants and bourgeoisie elements. A brief civil war ensued during late March and early April, as Bonapartist troops clashed with Bourbon sympathizers. The flight of Louis greatly hampered the efforts of his supporters to develop a serious opposition to Napoleon, but in the Vendee, the peasantry united with the bourgeoisie and aristocracy to put up a sustained resistance, aided by arms and officers thoughtfully landed from British warships. Though the Vendee was exceptional in its Royalist sentiments, several other areas had to be heavily patrolled, and such ongoing resistance represented a repudiation of the

Empire. Moreover, this unrest was symptomatic of a general malaise which afflicted France, as underscored by the disappointing results of the plebiscite. The people of France wanted peace above all and Napoleon hardly represented that. Indeed, France—or rather Napoleon—was already at war with the Great Powers, for on 18 March the diplomatic representatives of the powers had declared him an "outlaw."

During his dramatic return from Elba, Napoleon had more than once asserted that he was in diplomatic contact with several of the Great Powers, and even stated flatly that he returned with their consent. It was a complete fabrication. The monarchs and statesmen and generals had immediately suspended their division of the spoils at Vienna to take up the question of Napoleon and no one suggested treating with him. Therein lay the key diplomatic problem confronting Napoleon: in order to survive on the throne of France, Napoleon had to have the cooperation of at least one of the Great Powers. He had counted on the divisions among them being so great that he would be able to secure such support without difficulty, possibly from his estranged father-in-law, the Emperor Francis I of Austria. But none of the issues dividing the Allies were as important as that which united them, a universal opposition to Napoleon. In the face of the common foe, the divisions among the powers evaporated, at least for the duration. On 25 March the Seventh Coalition was concluded in Vienna among Britain, Prussia, Russia, Austria and a whole galaxy of lesser states. The signatories pledged not to negotiate with Napoleon, who was declared an outlaw, and, financed by Britain, committed themselves to mobilizing 600,000 men for a general offensive in June. There would be no peace with Napoleon.

CHAPTER III

The Armies Gather

Spring 1815

As spring began to run its course, the pace of military activity in Europe began to intensify. Armies had to be readied, plans made for the inevitable clash of arms and wills.

Mobilization

By 1815 the physical task of creating and fielding an army had become quite sophisticated. All European countries had elaborate mechanisms for recruiting, organizing, training and equipping large bodies of men in relatively short order. Moreover, as a result of the generation of wars which had followed the French Revolution, all had considerable numbers of furloughed, time-expired and discharged veterans, not to mention significant forces still under arms. As a result, though there were some notable exceptions, many of the troops who marched and fought and died during the Waterloo campaign were seasoned veterans.

The French Armies

Napoleon had a remarkable talent for improvising armies, and France had the resources to enable him to do so. In the short time available he made tremendous efforts to

Napoleon and his secretaries at work, in a sketch from several years before the Hundred Days. Napoleon would sometimes work with as many as six secretaries at a time, dictating several letters, messages, and memoranda simultaneously; this was particularly easy when he was writing to his wife and mistresses, as the letters were often virtually identical.

recreate a strong, effective army with which to try conclusions with the Allies one more time. Despite the drain of manpower which France had experienced during the long wars, there still remained a considerable pool available. Nevertheless, he was unable to tap this vast mass of potential soldiery due to the abolition of conscription.

Despite this handicap, he made rapid progress. Between 20 March and 15 June he managed to create an army of over 600,000 men, a goodly proportion of whom were battle-hardened campaigners.

Louis XVIII's army had about 180,000 effective men under arms when Napoleon resumed the throne. The Emperor immediately recalled some 50,000 whom that parsimonious—and impecunious—king had sent on extended leave. He procured a further 80,000 by going after the 100,000 men who had deserted during the campaign of 1814. This gave him 310,000 men, all of whom had seen some regular service, and many of whom were old campaigners, such as his *Imperial Guardsmen*. Yet another 90,000 were taken from the ranks of the 150,000 men of the class of 1815, who had been called up during 1814 and never properly discharged. By combing through the *National Guard*—a bourgeois militia force—for the best men and units, by encouraging discharged veterans to re-enlist, and by actively promoting volunteering among liberal and republican elements of the populace, he was able to raise a further 200,000, and thus attained a total of nearly 615,000 men under arms by 15 June. Of these, 215,000 were immediately assigned to the field armies, while 285,000 went to garrison the most critical fortresses, and the remaining 115,000 were assigned as reserves or were still in the depots. Nor did Napoleon's efforts to beef up his forces end there, for he believed that with a little luck he could have some 800,000 men available by the end of September.

Equipping this host was not difficult. There were available in arsenals and depots throughout France sufficient muskets and more than enough cannon for the forces on hand in June. By stepping up production, any anticipated needs would be readily met. The only real problem was a severe shortage of horseflesh, the loss of horses during previous wars having been proportionally far greater than that of men. As a result, the planned grand army would be relatively short of cavalry. Despite this deficiency, however, Napoleon was still confident that he could win. But the forces which could be committed against him were far greater than his own, more so even than his hoped-for 800,000-man army.

The Allied Armies

The Allied mobilization was rapid. Their recruiting presented relatively few problems. Indeed, the Russian Army was still on the march home from the Campaign of 1814 and subsequent occupation duty in France when the renewed call to arms came. It almost immediately turned around. The other powers had considerable forces in being, though their quality was uneven. The British had lost some fine, seasoned manpower in the ill-fated assault on New Orleans on 8 January 1815, and many of the regiments on occupation duty in Belgium had discharged numerous veterans and were filled with new men, who, however well trained were nevertheless green. As a result, only about half of the British troops present were veterans, who, together with the veterans of the King's German Legion and the veteran cadres of some Hanoverian units, amounted to only about a third of the army of the Duke of Wellington. The Prussian Army had a larger core of battle-hardened veterans, but was in the process of absorbing thousands of recruits from newly annexed territories. Most of the minor Allied powers had manpower which was unreliable to say the least, many of the troops having but recently been in the service of France. But the numbers involved were enormous. On 31 March the Allies had agreed to have some 600,000 men available for operations by 1 June. In fact, their efforts exceeded these goals. Between 4 April, the day set for the start of mobilization, and 15 June they managed to place over 750,000 men on the frontiers of France, all well equipped, well supplied and more or less adequately led. Given three more months they expected to have over a quarter of a million more men in the field. Against such superior numbers not even a commander of Napoleon's caliber could long endure. Although Napoleon was aware of the odds against him, his confidence in his abilities blinded him to their implications.

Planning

The military situation confronting Napoleon in the spring of 1815 was a difficult one, but one in which he saw certain possibilities. To be sure, his enemies would outnumber him. However, he would be operating on interior lines, able to strike out at any one of the enemy's many armies, which would be dispersed around the frontiers of France. With a little luck he would be able to engage each of the enemy's forces individually in sequence, thus permitting him to defeat each of them in isolation. Deciding which of the enemy armies would be the first to feel his wrath was not difficult: he would fall upon the most threatening. The enemy was strong on three fronts. On the Italian front the enemy would have upwards of 120,000 men available by June. However, the distance from the Alps to the heartland of France was great, there were numerous small fortresses and the terrain was favorable to a fighting withdrawal by small forces: a field force of about 30,000 men would be enough to support the local garrisons until a decision could be reached elsewhere. Along the Rhine was where the greatest concentration of enemy strength was to be expected, at least 300,000 Austrians, Russians and Germans by June. But these forces were not led by the boldest of generals nor were they likely to move with any great speed: any threat from this direction could be delayed by the numerous fortresses, supported by a small field army of some 32,000 men. In the light of these calculations, it was clear from where would come the most serious threat to France—from the north, in Belgium.

The Allies would have some 245,000 men in Belgium by June, divided into two ably led armies. There would be

Napoleon and his entourage in travel order, from a sketch made some time before 1815. Note the traveling coach, which was fitted as a mobile office, with several compartments, book shelves, folding desks, and even a foldaway bed, so that the Emperor could sleep or work while he traveled.

about 130,000 Prussians under Generalfeldmarschall Gebhard von Blucher, an aggressive and determined septuagenarian with a passionate hatred for France. Cooperating with Blucher would be the skilled and tenacious British Field Marshal Sir Arthur Wellesley, the Duke of Wellington, with a force running to about 120,000 men. Wellington's army was a truly Allied force, speaking nearly a half-dozen languages and containing men from a dozen countries. Although the Prussian and Anglo-Allied forces each contained many inexperienced or unreliable troops, both were built around a core of veterans. More importantly, they were commanded by good men, whose talents were complementary, for the cool, cautious Wellington was a good yoke-mate for the daring, impetuous Blucher. With their strong armies, these two represented the best the Allies had, and they were concentrating not

Napoleon at work, from an early sketch. His favorite method of studying maps was to stand or even lie on them, indicating the positions of the troops with pins of various colors, taking measurements with his dividers and dictating instructions to his staff.

240 kilometers north of Paris. Thus it would be in the north that Napoleon would make his move.

Belgium was unfamiliar territory to Napoleon. However, though he himself had never campaigned in Belgium, some of the most critical operations in the early days of the Revolution had taken place there and the region had been part of France for nearly a decade. As a result, there was a great deal of information available. In the weeks before operations began he sifted through this information, analyzing it in conjunction with the military intelligence brought in by his numerous agents. He laid his plans on the basis of the geography and nature of the theater of operations, on the information available as to the strength and dispositions of the enemy and on what he knew about the personalities, character and abilities of the enemy commanders. He sought not merely to understand the material resources of his foe and the nature of the theater of operations, but also to comprehend the character of the enemy, from the lowest soldier to the highest commander, realizing that war is not merely a clash of physical resources, but also one of character and will.

Napoleon's favorite strategic ploy was the *manoeuvre sur les derrieres*, which involved getting the bulk of his army into the enemy's rear area. Unfortunately, in the circumstances of 1815 he would be unable to execute this maneuver, for it required superior numbers, a concentrated enemy and a favorable geographic environment. At best he would have on hand an army of perhaps half the strength of the combined enemy force, though the latter was widely dispersed. Thus, his basic scheme for the campaign was the Strategy of the Central Position. This was his "strategy of inferiority." It was useful in situations where the army was weaker than its enemy, but the latter were dispersed in two or more rather widely separated concentrations. Napoleon had used this strategy several times, most notably in the opening phases of his Italian campaign of 1796 and even more spectacularly in the face of overwhelming odds in 1814, culminating in the triple victories of Champaubert, Montmiral and Vauchamps. It was just such a situation which confronted Napoleon in 1815. This strategy necessitated bold leadership, careful timing and aggressive movement, for it required the army to get between the two enemy concentrations, thereby preventing them from uniting. By moving swiftly into the area between the two enemy forces, Napoleon could concentrate the bulk of his army against the more threatening enemy contingent and seek a decisive battle, while a corps or two undertook to hold off the other enemy contingent for as long as possible. When the first enemy army was defeated, a corps or two would be sent in pursuit, while he would shift the attentions of the rest of the army to the support of the probably hard-pressed screening forces before the balance of the enemy. A second decisive engagement, a second pursuit and the campaign would be well on the road to a successful conclusion. Things could go wrong, of course. The enemy could discern the French intentions and withdraw, as occurred in April of 1809 leading to a protracted and bloody campaign, or a battle might not turn out as decisively as expected or the pursuit might be poorly handled, allowing a defeated contingent to march to the support of its comrades. Nevertheless, Napoleon believed that this was the way to conduct the campaign. His analysis of the character of the two enemy commanders led him to conclude that Blucher was the more aggressive, while the cautious Wellington would never abandon his line of retreat to the sea. As he put it, "Blucher...would have hastened to support Wellington, though he had but two battalions," while Wellington "would not come up to [Blucher's] assistance." Thus, the pattern of the coming campaign became clear. Napoleon would deliver a crushing blow against Blucher, followed by yet another against Wellington, thereby eliminating both of his most dangerous foes in one quick campaign. Then he would conduct a rapid shift of front, and, marching to the Rhine, would deal with the Austrians and the Russians and everyone else. With a little luck, France would be saved and his throne secured.

By 1815 Napoleon's enemies knew him well. They had suffered defeat at his hands often enough, and they had learned how to avoid those defeats. None of his opponents could compare with him as either a strategist or a tactician. Most of them were more or less able, but unspectacular. The Duke of Wellington was the one exception, being able to comprehend the overall strategic picture superbly, having some skill at executing the indirect approach and being a master of retreat, always one of the truest tests of generalship. The best strategy Napoleon's opponents were able to come up with was the Trachenberg Plan (15 August 1813), which envisioned a concentric advance against Napoleon, that is moving several armies simultaneously against him from different directions. Given the vastly superior resources which the Allies commanded, this strategy was a workable one, particularly since the Allies had also agreed to avoid actually coming to battle with Napoleon, concentrating instead on defeating his subordinates. It was this plan which had led directly to Napoleon's defeat in 1813 in Germany and again in 1814 in France. Although this strategy enabled Napoleon to win numerous tactical victories using the central position, which it conceded to him, his outnumbered forces could not win every battle. If the concentric advance was an uninspired strategy, it was one in which his foes had confidence, for though Napoleon might win some battles, he could not be everywhere at once. As a result, in the end they would surely win the war. Thus, in 1815, the Allies envisioned a simultaneous invasion of France from the North Sea to the Mediterranean with upwards of 800,000 men to begin on 1 June. For the Allies, the eventual outcome of the campaign did not seem in doubt.

Slowly the armies concentrated.

The Bigger Battalions: Manpower Considerations in the Campaign of 1815

Although a great commander can sometimes achieve spectacular results with inferior resources, that's not usually the way wars are won. As the old saying has it, "God is on the side of the bigger battalions," particularly in a protracted war.

The campaign of 1815 was decided in less than a week. However, both sides had expected a longer struggle and both made strenuous efforts to ensure that they would have sufficient manpower to maintain the

Front	Contingent	15 June	1 October
		(Thousands of Men)	
Northern	British	40.0	60.0
	Danish	0.0	12.0
	Dutch-Belgian	25.0	40.0
	French Royalists	2.1	10.0
	North Germans	60.0	65.0
	Portuguese	0.0	14.0
	Prussian	120.0	150.0
	Sub Total	*247.1*	*344.0*
Rhine	Austrian	150.0	200.0
	Bavarian	50.0	60.0
	Russian	80.0	150.0
	Saxon	16.0	16.0
	Swiss	35.0	35.0
	Wurttemberger	20.0	20.0
	Others	20.0	20.0
	Sub Total	*371.0*	*501.0*
Italian	Austrian	100.0	150.0
	Piedmontese	15.0	35.0
	Other	5.0	10.0
	Sub Total	*120.0*	*195.0*
Iberian	Spanish	24.0	36.0
	Portuguese	0.0	6.0
	Sub Total	*24.0*	*42.0*
Total		758.1	1,081.0

fight for as long as necessary to achieve a decision.

The Allies. When the representatives of the Allied powers met in Vienna on 25 March to renew their alliance—the Seventh Coalition—they pledged to undertake the offensive in June with a total of 600,000 men. In addition, the powers pledged to mobilize as much manpower as would be necessary to put a definitive end to Napoleon's ambitions. They were remarkably successful in their efforts to concentrate manpower, actually exceeding their projected goal for June, and would probably have had no difficulties meeting the goal for October had the war lasted that long.

It's important to note that on the table on page 43 the figures given represent troops available in the "front" areas, not all of which necessarily would have gotten into action. There were, in addition, considerable forces in the Allied rear which are not included here.

Also, note that Allied figures for October do not account for casualties.

The French. Napoleon's manpower problems were far more serious than those of the Allies. He calculated the odds against him with a fair degree of accuracy. He was thus able to estimate that he would need about 600,000 men under arms by June and at least 800,000 by October. He then undertook strenuous efforts to attain these numbers, a feat at which he proved rather successful.

These sources of manpower gave Napoleon about 600,000 troops by June of 1815 (see table below left). Logistical duties, training establishments, the recruiting service, internal security, coast defense and fortress duty required about 285,000 of these troops. Another 115,000 were still in training or had not yet joined their assigned army corps by this time, which left Napoleon with only 215,000 men in his field armies, 122,000 of them with the *Armee du Nord* and the rest scattered

Manpower	Source
210,000	Active forces of the Royal Army on 20 March 1815.
30,000	Gendarmes, unfit personnel, and so forth.
80,000	Deserters form the campaign of 1814.
90,000	Conscripts of the Class of 1815 who had enrolled and trained, but never formally discharged at the end of the campaign of 1814.
185,000	Elite National Guards.
15,000	'Federals,' nationalist volunteers

Manpower	Source
-60,000	Anticipated 'wastage' between mid-June and October, virtually all of it in the field armies.
60,000	Conscripts of the Class of 1815 who had been called in 1814, but never enrolled.
70,000	Naval personnel transferred to fortress duty, thereby relieving army personnel for field service.
150,000	Improperly discharged veterans of prior years.
30,000	Limited service volunteers.
15,000	Special volunteers for the Young Guard.

about the frontiers. Napoleon's calculations did not stop here, as he projected his manpower to October (see bottom right table on page 44).

These deletions and accessions would give Napoleon about 865,000 men by the beginning of October, at least on paper. Since most of the new manpower would be available for field service, by 1 October Napoleon expected to have a field force of about 550,000 men. However, these figures were probably optimistic. And even had he attained them,

they would still not have been sufficient: by October the odds in the field against Napoleon would have grown more favorable than the 3-to-1 prevailing in June, but would still have been an unhealthy 2-to-1. Having himself once observed "Against greatly superior forces it is possible to win a campaign, but hardly a war," the ultimate outcome would not have been so very different, save that there would have been far more death and suffering and destruction.

The Armies of the Waterloo Campaign

The armies which met in Belgium in June of 1815 were in many ways remarkably similar in character. Each was composed mostly of infantry with substantial cavalry and artillery forces in attendance, and small contingents of engineers and other services as well. The organization of each of these arms was quite similar, as was, indeed, the very weapons and tactics employed. But there were interesting technical differences and many doctrinal ones as well.

Each of the armies had a different ratio among the principal arms, with the French being substantially stronger in cavalry, artillery and engineers. This can best be seen in the accompanying table on the following page.

This table compares the ratio among the various arms in each of the armies at the onset of the Waterloo campaign. Figures for Men are in thousands. Other includes engineers, trains, medical, and staffs.

Virtually the entire French Army was composed of veterans. About 57 percent of the Prussian Army consisted of regular troops, many of whom had been recruited in provinces of dubious loyalty and some of whom had seen no real regular service. The balance of the Prussian Army was composed of militiamen—Landwehr—many of whom had seen active duty in the cam-

The Armies of the Waterloo Campaign						
	French		Prussian		Anglo-Allied	
	Men	%	Men	%	Men	%
Total	122.6	100.0	130.2	100.0	112.0	100.0
Infantry	88.4	72.1	106.2	81.5	87.1	77 8
Cavalry	21.6	17.6	16.7	12.8	16.2	14.5
Artillery	9.6	7.8	6.4	5.1	8.5	7.6
Other	3.0	2.5	0.9	0.6	1.2	1.1

paigns of 1813 and 1814. About 40 percent of the Anglo-Allied Army was composed of British or King's German Legion men; while only about 60 percent of the Britons were veterans, all of the KGL were. Most of the rest of the Anglo-Allied Army was composed of relatively unseasoned men, save for a few battalions in each of the various national contingents.

The Infantry. There were several varieties of infantry in most armies. Line infantry was supposed to do all the serious fighting. In addition, most armies had light infantry—called variously voltigeurs, chasseurs, jagers, rifles, flanquers—who were supposed to be trained for special operations, flank protection, skirmishing and so forth. In practice most light infantry was operationally indistinguishable from line infantry, even carrying the same musket. Some, however, did continue a tradition of special service. In the British Army most light infantrymen were equipped with rifles, which made them particularly effective skirmishers. All armies had some heavy infantry, usually in the form of one company of grenadiers

in each battalion, albeit that they had long ago discarded the use of the hand grenade. Heavy infantry was an elite arm composed of the biggest, bravest and most seasoned men, who were supposed to be ready for any particularly hazardous duty, such as storming parties or desperate charges. The French Garde Imperial had several whole regiments of heavy infantry, called grenadiers and tirailleurs. Most armies also had guards, special contingents originally raised for the protection of the sovereign but eventually evolving into an elite tactical force. Napoleon's Garde Imperial was enormous, comprising a substantial portion of his army, indeed virtually an army corps, with an unusually large proportion of heavy infantrymen. While he received excellent service from these troops, one wonders what improvements might have occurred in the overall quality of the regular forces if the superior manpower and equipment of the *Garde Imperial* had been distributed among the line troops.

The principal infantry tactical unit was the battalion, usually comprising a mix of line, light and

Infantry Battalion Oraganization					
Army	Type	Number of Companies (Men)			
		Light	Heavy	Line	Total	Note
British	Regular	1 (112)	1 (112)	8 (86)	10 = 952	A
	KGL	1 (112)	1 (112)	4 (112)	6 = 672	B
	Brunswicker			6 (112)	6 = 672	C
Dutch-Belgian		1 (129)	1 (129)	4 (129)	6 = 788	D
Hanover				4 (170)	4 = 700	E
French	Guard			4 (150)	4= 600	F
	Line	1 (100)	1 (100)	4 (100)	6 = 600	F
Nassauer		1 (260)	1 (260)	4 (260)	6 = 900	G
Prussian				4 (201)	4 = 830	H

heavy companies. Light companies and heavy—grenadier—companies were elite formations composed of the bravest and sturdiest men and were supposed to undertake particularly hazardous tasks. In the Prussian, French and Nassauer armies, battalions were grouped into regiments which usually fought as a unit. Regiments existed on paper in the British Army, but the individual battalions rarely served on the same field, and never operated together as a unit. In the other armies involved in the campign the highest formation was the separate battalion. Operationally, all armies grouped battalions into brigades. Since Prussian regiments consisted of three battalions, the brigade was the highest tactical formation of the Prussian infantry, roughly equal in manpower to the divisions of two or three brigades which everyone else formed.

In the table above, figures in parentheses are for the number of men in each company, while that under total is for the entire battalion. These figures are ideal ones, and include battalion staffs, bandsmen and medical personnel, the numbers of whom have in some instances been estimated. In practice, battalions were rarely at full strength due to the exigencies of war, recruiting difficulties, and the effects of disease. The 175 French infantry battalions involved in the Waterloo campaign averaged 505 men apiece, the 136 Prussian ones ran some 780 men, and the 129.5 British and Allied ones about 670. Letters in the right hand column refer to the following notes:

A. Battalion structure was substantially the same for line, light, rifle, or Guards. However, it was not unheard of for units to be overstrength, particularly Guard units, in which companies as strong as 154 men were sometimes found.

During the Waterloo campaign all four Guards battalions were somewhat over strength, while the 52nd Foot had at least 1,050 and possibly as many as 1,175 men.

B. Light and line units had the same battalion organization.

C. Minor differences existed between the Guard and the line and light battalions.

D. In practice militia battalions were mostly 450 to 650 strong, while regular ones actually varied from about 400 to over 650, with only one approaching paper strength.

E. Most Hanoverian battalions had a cadre of KGL veterans.

F. Napoleon had ordered *Guard* companies to recruit to 200 men as soon as possible, and line companies to 140 men, but none approached this figure. On paper, a regiment had four war battalions and one depot, for a field strength of about 2,400 for line regiments and 3,600 for the *Guard*. However, in practice most regiments took the field with but two battalions, so that at full strength they ran about only about 1,215 men, including staff.

G. Of the three Nassau regiments present for the campaign, one was composed of two line battalions, one of three line battalions, and one of two line battalions and a landwehr battalion, the latter comprising only three line companies.

H. In regular Prussian regiments, one battalion consisted of light infantry, designated fusiliers, while the other two were termed musketeers. Landwehr regiments had three musketeer battalions only. At full strength both types ran about 2,500 men.

The Cavalry. Like the infantry, the cavalry was divided into several distinct types, with a confusing array of titles which often told one little about the type of cavalry in question. Light cavalry—variously designated hussars, light dragoons, dragoons, uhlans, lancers, chasseurs—were designed for reconnaissance, foraging, patrolling, screening and pursuit, though they could be used in shock action. Heavy cavalry—variously designated horse grenadiers, dragoons, carabiniers, cuirassiers, and so on—had heavier mounts and equipment, some even wearing breastplates, and were designed for shock action, although they were sometimes used for other duties as well. Regardless of type, cavalry equipment differed little. All troopers carried a sword of some sort, usually a light saber in the light regiments and a heavier, straighter weapon in the heavy ones. In addition, all carried a carbine or short musket and frequently a pistol or two as well. Lancers and uhlans carried a light lance, which was quite effective in shock action and pursuit, but rather clumsy and dangerous in skirmishes. Some armies gave their cavalrymen a little training in dismounted combat—which had, indeed, been the original function of dragoons—but by the time of Waterloo this was rare.

The operational formation of the cavalry was the regiment, usually composed of several squadrons, each of two companies or troops.

Cavalry Regimental Organization				
Army & Type	Elite	Line (men per line)	Totals	Note
British				
Household		4 (76)	4 = 304	A
Regular		6 (76)	6 = 456	A
KGL		8 (88)	8 = 719	B
Brunswicker Hussars		8 (60)	8 = 730	C
Uhlans		2 (124)	2 = 249	C
Dutch-Belgian				
Regular A		8 (100)	8 = 818	D
Regular B		6 (100)	6 = 618	D
French				
Carabiniers	1 (62)	7 (62)	8 = 502	E
Chasseurs	1 (78)	7 (78)	8 = 650	E
Cuirassiers	1 (62)	7 (62)	8 = 502	E
Dragoons	1 (78)	7 (78)	8 = 650	E
Guard Heavy		8 (130)	8 = 1012	F
Guard Light		10 (130)	10 = 1300	F
Hussars	1 (78)	7 (78)	8 = 650	E
Lancers	1 (78)	7 (78)	8 = 650	E
Hanoverian		8 (64)	8 = 516	G
Prussian				
Landwehr A		8 (45)	8 = 380	H
Landwehr B		6 (45)	6 = 285	G
Landwehr A		8 (78)	8 = 650	G
Landwehr B		6 (78)	6 = 475	G

Regiments were grouped in brigades. The French and Dutch-Belgians then formed these into divisions and even corps, cadres which did not exist in the British or Prussian service.

The figures given in the table above are ideal ones and include only mounted combatants. In all armies, cavalry regiments included numbers of non-combatants such as blacksmiths. Some figures have been estimated. In practice, regiments were not usually at full strength due to the exigencies of war, recruiting difficulties and the effects of disease. The 164.5 French squadrons taking part in the Waterloo campaign average 130 men apiece, while the 118 Prussian ones ran some 140 men and the 106 British and Allied ones about 150. Letters in the right hand column refer to the following notes:

A. Due to the peculiarities of British military policy, Household Cavalry Regiments (1st & 2nd Life Guards and Royal Horse Guards) consisted of four troops, while all others comprised six. A squadron was composed of two troops, as in most armies.

B. Two companies made a squadron.

C. There were two companies to the squadron. Note that the Brunswick Uhlan squadron was almost as strong as most Prussian landwehr regiments.

D. Carabineer regiments had six companies, organized in three squadrons, while light dragoon and hussar regiments were variously of

six companies in three squadrons or eight companies in four squadrons.

E. Two companies made a squadron. In line regiments the 1st Company of the 1st Squadron in each regiment was an elite company, composed of particularly distinguished soldiers.

F. There were no elite companies in the cavalry of the *Garde*. One squadron in the *Chasseurs* was composed of Mamelukes, while the *Polish Lancers* comprised the 1st Squadron of the *Lancers*

G. Two companies made a squadron.

H. Regiments were variously of six or eight companies without regard for type, with two companies to the squadron.

Staffs. There were great differences in the number of officers assigned to staff duties in each of the armies.

Figures in the table below include the commanding officer, but exclude enlisted personnel, who were never particularly numerous, and, save in the case of the army headquarters themselves, aides-de-camp, usually young officers looking for a fast track to the top, but more likely to get killed quickly while carrying dispatches, and

Number of Staff Officers					
Contingent	Army	Corps	Division	Brigade	Regiment
British	73	6-8	3	2-4	
Brunswick			6		
Dutch-Belgian		9	5	3-4	2-3
French	85	6-8	2	2	5-9
Prussian	58	20		5	8-10

medical officers. Also not included are civilians, many senior officers having a civilian secretary to assist them or a civilian physician to look after them, while others sometimes brought curious friends and relatives along, who not infrequently became involved in staff duties. The French *Garde* had a headquarters of eight, while the regular corps made do with six and the cavalry corps got by with only two, a commander and a chief-of-staff. The notional corps commanded by Prince Frederick of Orange (the Dutch-Belgian 1st Division and the Netherland Indian Brigade) had a staff of 17, plus the prince!

In many ways the Prussian approach to headquarters staffing was the most efficient of all three armies, providing sufficient manpower at all levels to get the job done. Napoleon's headquarters staff as given here includes only officers whose duties were connected to the *Armee du Nord*, there were additional personnel responsible for assisting Napoleon in his roles as head of state and chief war lord of France. Wellington's staff was rather bloated by the need to have liaison officers for all the many foreign contingents with the army, plus official observers from Spain, Prussia, Russia, the Netherlands, Austria and the British government. Also included were Ms. Mary Sullivan, famous "girl" reporter for *The Times*, the naval hero Admiral Sir William Sydney Smith, who rode down from Brussels on the 18th, met Wellington at Mont St-Jean late in the battle, and rode back with him to Waterloo that evening, about which he later wrote "Thus, though I was not allowed to have any of the fun, I had the heartfelt gratification of being the first Englishman that was not in the battle who shook hands with him," and Baron Henri Jomini, the military historian and theoretician, who unfortunately missed the action entirely.

CHAPTER IV

Along the Sambre

1-16 June

By early June it had become apparent to all that Napoleon would strike in Flanders. Wellington and Blucher, commanding the Allied forces there, were well aware of this and laid their plans accordingly. In late May Blucher had sought to secure Wellington's consent to an offensive of their own in early June. The latter had demurred. The two commanders then went on to develop a plan which was predicated on the assumption that, given the dispersed nature of the enemy's forces, they would have about three days forenotice of a French offensive. On receipt of evidence of a French concentration, Wellington and Blucher would themselves begin to concentrate, the former at Gosselies and the latter at Sombreffe, before joining forces at Charleroi. This done, they would commence operations. Though the Allied forces would lack unity of command, cooperation between the two commanders was expected to be good. Their plan took into account Napoleon's considerable talents, and attempted to maximize the principal advantage which they possessed, numbers and time. Even Napoleon would have difficulties making headway against an army of 225,000 men with but 122,600 of his own, doughty fighters though they might all be, particu-

French troops on the march.

larly in view of the limited time he would have to secure a victory.

Napoleon was not unaware of the general intentions of his enemies. If they combined in the field, he was finished, able to do little more than conduct a fighting withdrawal. It was precisely with this possibility in mind that he had evolved his plans for an offensive making use of the strategy of the central position. It was a plan worthy of his greatest efforts. The existence of a permanent army corps enabled Napoleon to practice what may be termed "dispersed concentration" of his forces. As each corps was essentially a small army of all arms, it was capable of considerable operational independence. Thus, he masked his intentions by spreading his corps all over northern France. From the *I Corps*, at Lille, to the *IV Corps*, at Metz, the French army stretched along the frontier for about 275 kilometers, while Napoleon and some of his *Old Guard* were at Paris, about 230 kilometers to the rear. But though the army was dispersed, each corps was relatively compact, with all elements within a day's march of each other. Thus, when the order to march came, each corps could set out almost immediately, along a distinct and well-defined route of march, so that it could reach the concentration area, just south of the Sambre in the vicinity of Beaumont

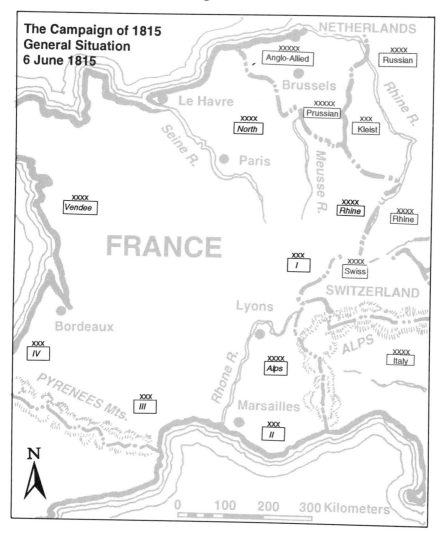

The Campaign of 1815
General Situation
6 June 1815

and Philippeville, within two or three days. This movement would be well covered by cavalry and local forces, to screen it from prying eyes. Once concentrated on the Sambre, Napoleon would take the offensive against an ill-prepared enemy.

Napoleon's estimate of the possibilities was a reasonable one. The Allied forces were widely dispersed, covering the French border on a front of over 300 kilometers. Unlike Napoleon's dispersal, many of Wellington's subordinate formations were themselves spread widely over the countryside, with elements of one of his divisions scattered in an area nearly 60 kilometers across. The Prussians were somewhat better concentrated, each of their army corps being able to concentrate within 12 hours, and their entire army within 36, but they were still spread rather thinly. By moving quickly Napoleon would catch the Allies off balance, with their concentration incomplete. To accomplish this the army would advance behind a screen of light cavalry, with some stiffening from heavier troopers, both to seek out the enemy and to deny him information. Boldly thrusting itself between Wellington and Blucher, the bulk of the army would locate the main forces of the latter, and advance to contact in order to bring about a decisive action. Meanwhile, a couple of corps would hold Wellington off until the main body had done its work. Since an army corps was sufficiently strong to sustain considerable pressure for at least a day, there was ample time for Napoleon to beat Blucher and then shift front and come up to the support of the troops confronting Wellington. Thus, in the space of a few days, two full scale battles would be possible, each against a force roughly the equivalent of Napoleon's own. It was a bold plan, but militarily workable. Napoleon put it into operation on 6 June.

The concentration of Napoleon's *Army of the North* was the last truly brilliant operation of his spectacular career. Beginning on 6 June 86,000 infantrymen, 22,000 cavalrymen, 9,000 artillerymen and 2,500 engineering, service and staff personnel with 366 pieces of artillery and tens of thousands of horses and vehicles were concentrated by rapid marches from an area of over 30,000 square kilometers into one of but 500 square kilometers in eight days, all without arousing the suspicions of the enemy, under whose collective noses the movement took place. A great many diversions and deceptions were practiced in order to achieve this remarkable degree of secrecy. Aware that enemy agents were keeping track of his movements, Napoleon remained in Paris until the last possible moment, not departing for the front until 0400 hours on 12 June. Meanwhile cavalry patrols and *National Guard* forces were active in petty raids and movements all along the frontier, and particularly in the area to the west of that in which Napoleon planned to undertake his offensive. These had the effect of attracting Wellington's attention to this stretch of frontier, about which the latter was most sensitive, since a French offensive emanating from that quarter would most directly threaten his line of retreat to Antwerp and the sea. By the morning of 14 June the bulk of the army was in position just south of the frontier, where Napoleon joined it later in the day. The mood of the troops was excellent. General of Division [*General de Division*] Maximilien Foy, commanding the *9th Division*, wrote in his diary, "The troops exhibit, not patriotism, not enthusiasm, but an actual *mania* for the Emperor and against his enemies. No one doubts that Victory will decide for France." But if the troops had confidence in their Emperor, they were far less confident of some of their officers, many of whom seemed of doubtful loyalty. Indeed, so suspicious were the troops of their superiors that at one point an old soldier broke ranks and approached Napoleon himself. The Emperor, who allowed his oldest "comrades" some degree of familiarity, gave the man leave to speak.

"Sire, do not trust Soult: he will betray you."

When Napoleon replied, "Do not be uneasy, I will answer for him," the man said, "Be it so" and returned to the ranks.

Though Soult's loyalty was not, in fact, an open question, that of other officers was. Nor were such suspicions confined to Napoleon's troops, for they were shared by Wellington. Some days earlier an acquaintance had asked, "Do you calculate upon any desertion in Bonaparte's army?"

To this the Duke replied, "Not a man, from the colonel to

the private....We may pick up a marshal or two, perhaps; but not worth a damn!" It was a prescient observation.

Napoleon's deception plan worked well, confusing the Allies as to his intentions. But it did suggest to them that he was up to something. They began pulling in some of their more widely scattered forces. By 14 June the Allied armies had reduced their dispersal by about half, being loosely concentrated in the area between Liege and Coutrai, about 150 kilometers across. It was the Prussians who were the first to receive firm word of Napoleon's new position. Early on 14 June pickets from their I Corps posted below Charleroi spotted numerous camp fires just across the frontier. Having counted on having at least three days' notice of a French offensive, Wellington and Blucher now had to cope with one on barely a day's notice. Napoleon had stolen a march on them! On 14 June, with some elements, the French army made final preparations for battle. That night the Prussians began pulling in their outposts.

The French army began to stir at about 0230 on 15 June. At dawn Napoleon issued a stirring proclamation to his troops, "Soldiers! Today is the anniversary of Marengo and Friedland. For all true Frenchmen, the moment has come to conquer or die!" Then, behind a screen formed by a dozen light cavalry regiments, the *Army of the North* moved out. The movement started well, but then the frictions of war set to work.

Over on Napoleon's left, the *II Corps*, under General de Division Honore de Reille, found itself impeded by the stout resistance of elements of the 2nd Brigade of the Prussian I Corps. There were hot little engagements at Thuin and particularly in some woods south of Marchienne-au-Pont. Casualties were light, for the Prussians had no intention of making a stand in such exposed positions and soon pulled out. Nevertheless, their resistance meant that *II Corps* was unable to get across the Sambre until 1000 hours. Meanwhile, the movement of the

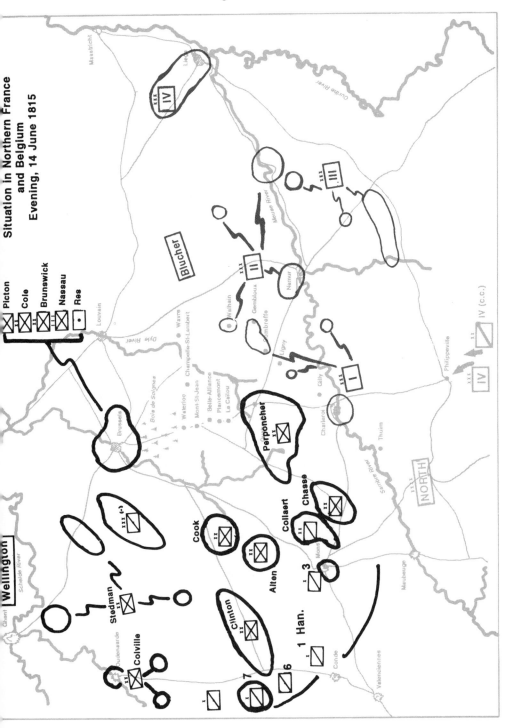

Situation in Northern France
and Belgium
Evening, 14 June 1815

main body of the army became hopelessly muddled when Napoleon's untested chief of staff, Marshal Nicolas Soult, entrusted his instructions for General de Division Dominique Vandamme, commanding *III Corps*, to but a single messenger, who managed to get lost, thus delaying delivery. When the courier finally arrived at *III Corps* headquarters, Vandamme was not present. A courier sent to find him also got lost, falling from his horse and breaking his leg in the bargain. As a result, the message was still further delayed and Vandamme's corps moved out very late and in a considerable muddle, with some elements getting entangled with those of General de Division Georges de Lobau's *VI Corps*, which was supposed to follow behind *III Corps*. Moreover, as *III Corps* was supposed to support *I Cavalry Corps* at Charleroi at 1000 hours, this delay left the cavalrymen unsupported against the 1st and 2nd Brigades of Generalleutnant Hans von Zeithen's Prussian I Corps. Not until 1100 hours was the town cleared, through the personal intervention of Napoleon, who committed the engineers and marines of the *Garde Imperial* to the support of the cavalrymen. Acting as infantry, the guardsmen and cavalrymen rushed across the Sambre bridge into Charleroi even as the Prussians abandoned it. By noon the town was in French hands, nearly two hours later than planned. The French troops began to spread out north of Charleroi.

Over on the French right the *IV Corps*, under General de Division Maurice Gerard, had originally been intended to cross the Sambre at Charleroi, but the delay there caused Napoleon to issue revised instructions. As a result, the corps detached itself from the main body in order to cross at Chatelet. There was some delay in implementing the revised plans. The situation was further complicated by the fact that at about 0500 on 15 June General de Division Louis Bourmont, of the *14th Division*, deserted to the enemy with his staff, and was shortly revealing Napoleon's plans to the enemy, though gallant—and crude—old

Blucher refused to meet with him, saying *"Hundsfott bleit hundsfott."* As a result of the ensuing confusion, only half the corps had crossed the Sambre by nightfall, against limited Prussian resistance.

Even as the French started to cross the Sambre, the Allied commanders began to act. Blucher ordered Zeithen's I Corps to pull back from the frontier and take up positions at Gosselies and Fleurus, to cover the arrival and concentration of the rest of the army at Sombreffe. This was a bold and dangerous move, for Blucher was implementing his original plans unchanged, despite having only a day's notice of the French movement. Given the situation he was concentrating his forces much too far forward; if they moved swiftly the French might easily overwhelm I Corps and then catch the balance of the army still forming up at Sombreffe. It was a serious error. Nevertheless, the movement was well conducted. Zeithen's 1st Brigade fell back along the Brussels-Charleroi road towards the crossroads of Quatre Bras, while his 2nd Brigade fell back on the village of Gilly. Pressed by cavalrymen from General de Division Claude Pajol's *I Cavalry Corps* and General de Division Remy Exelmans' *II Cavalry Corps*, the 2nd Brigade then fell back to Soleilmont, where it was joined by the 3rd and 4th Brigades. Napoleon acted swiftly. He brought up the *Young Guard* and Vandamme's *III Corps*, and deployed them for battle in front of Soleilmont, giving him some 20,000 men and over 50 guns against Zeithen's 18,000 infantry and 60 guns. Zeithen, however, refused to accept battle, falling back. As a result, the only fighting was a rearguard affair and I Corps escaped, retiring on Fleurus. Meanwhile, Zeithen's 1st Brigade had fallen back on Gosselies, along the road to Quatre Bras. All of this movement did little to alleviate the danger in which the Prussian army had been placed by Blucher's forward deployment. But Blucher wasn't the only Allied commander blundering on 15 June, for Wellington was committing a few of his own.

Jean Victory Constant-Rebecque

Jean Victory Constant-Rebecque, baron and major general (1773-1850), was of Swiss origins, a cousin of Benjamin Constant de Rebecque, the noted politician, orator and novelist. As a young man he enlisted in Louis XVI's *Gardes suisses*. When the Revolution came he went abroad, serving variously Switzerland, the Netherlands, Prussia, Britain and the Netherlands again as a staunch opponent of both the Republic and Empire. While in British service he was selected by the exiled House of Orange as the military tutor of Prince William of Orange, with whom he went to Spain in 1811 to serve under Wellington.

Upon the liberation of the Netherlands from French domination in 1813, Constant-Rebecque was appointed chief of staff to the new kingdom and set about building an army, a task in which he proved rather successful. Chief of staff to the Prince of Orange's I Corps during the Waterloo campaign, it was Constant-Rebecque's quick thinking and initiative which led him to disobey Wellington's original movement instructions, causing him to direct the deployment of his corps towards Quatre Bras, thereby enabling Wellington to inflict a reverse on the French on 16 June. On the field at Waterloo, Constant-Rebecque proved a valuable officer.

After the war Constant-Rebecque served in a variety of military posts. In late 1830 he was again named chief of staff of the Netherlands Army, but he was unable to effect reforms quickly enough to avert a Dutch reverse in the Belgian War for Independence. He was dismissed in 1837 and retired to an estate in Silesia.

A good staff officer, Constant-Rebecque's greatest services were in organizing the Dutch-Belgian forces which performed with some distinction during the Waterloo campaign and, above all, in his knowing when to disobey orders.

Wellington learned of the French movement to the Sambre very late, only on the afternoon of 15 June. However, the numerous skirmishes and combats there failed to convince him that this was Napoleon's main effort. The French raids and diversions further to the west had caught his attention and he had become convinced that Napoleon intended to strike at his lines of communication with the coast. Thus, at 1500 he issued instructions placing his troops on alert. At about 1700 the youthful Prince William of Orange came in with word that the Prussians were heavily engaged along the Sambre around Charleroi. Wellington decided to alert his troops. Conferring with several subordinates he ordered I Corps, under Prince William, and II Corps, under Lieutenant General Lord Hill, to concentrate to the west and southwest of Brussels behind a thick screen of cavalry, while retaining the Reserve under his own command in Brussels, and ordered reconnaissance in the direction of Mons. As a result, he was sending the bulk of his army in the wrong direction, thereby eliminating any possibility of early cooperation with Blucher and, in the bargain, exposing Brussels to a possible advance from the south. Meanwhile, the French were very definitely on the move. Thus, even as the French army was crossing the Sambre in strength, both Allied commanders had committed dangerous errors. Wellington's, however, proved the less serious. When Major General Jean de Constant-Rebecque, the Prince of Orange's chief of staff, received the Duke's instructions he was appalled, for it was becoming clear to him that the French were advancing directly on Brussels from the south. Acting contrary to his orders, he consulted with Lieutenant General H.G. de Perponcher-Sedlnitzky, who commanded the 2nd Dutch-Belgian Infantry Division. He instructed the latter to send Prince Bernard of Saxe-Weimar's brigade to probe southwards from the crossroads village of Quatre Bras, about 20 miles south of Brussels.

By about 1530 Napoleon issued new instructions to his forces. Marshal Michel Ney, the "bravest of the brave," was to command the left wing, comprising General de Division Jean-Baptiste d'Erlon's *I Corps*, Reille's *II Corps* and the *Guard Light Cavalry*, over 45,000 men with about 100 pieces of artillery, with orders to advance towards Brussels. Recently promoted to marshal, Emmanuel Grouchy, who had never commanded so much as a brigade in combat before, was given the right wing. His command included Vandamme's *III Corps* and Gerard's *IV Corps*, along with General de Division Claude Pajol's *I Cavalry Corps* and General de Division Remy Exelmans' *II Cavalry Corps*. All in all, Grouchy had some 45,000 men with about 100 pieces of artillery along with instructions to dislodge the Prussians from Fleurus. Napoleon himself retained control of the bulk of the *Imperial Guard*, Lobau's *VI Corps*, along with General de Division Francois Kellermann's *III Cavalry Corps* and General de Division Edouard Milhaud's *IV Cavalry Corps*, altogether about 30,000 men with over 150 pieces of artillery, as a central reserve. Many of these troops had not yet managed to cross the Sambre when Napoleon issued his instructions, but both Ney and Grouchy had about half their assigned forces available and immediately began their movements.

Ney, newly arrived from Paris, borrowed a horse and got off to a good start. He sent Baron Piré's *2nd Cavalry Division* and General de Division Charles Lefebvre-Desnouettes' *Guard Light Cavalry Division* north along the Charleroi-Brussels road. Ney's cavalrymen very soon located the Prussian 1st Brigade, still about Gosselies. Although Generalmajor von Steinmetz, commanding the brigade, was considerably stronger than Ney's cavalrymen, with some 7,500 men to 4,700, he wisely pulled back after a brief skirmish, realizing that to attempt a stand would expose him to the full weight of whatever was behind the French troopers. By 1730 the place was in French hands. This was a critical development, for Steinmetz had uncovered the road to Quatre Bras, a major crossroads little more than 20 kilometers south of Brussels. However, Ney now made two errors. First, he pursued Steinmetz in a rather leisurely fashion as the latter's brigade marched about 6.5 kilometers north, and then took the road eastward to Ligny, using only General de Division Jean-Baptiste Girard's *7th Division*. More seriously, rather than pressing on in the direction of Brussels, Ney paused to wait for d'Erlon's *I Corps*, sending only Piré and Lefebvre-Desnouettes northwards to reconnoiter. At about

1900 the troopers ran into trouble at Frasnes. The 2nd Battalion of the 2nd Nassau Regiment, supported by a battery, altogether no more than 950 men under Major Piet van Normann, were there in response to Baron Constant-Rebecque's technically illegal orders to Count Perponcher-Sedlnitzky. Piré and Lefebvre-Desnouettes could easily have overwhelmed the little detachment, had they been aware of its true size. But the Dutchmen were generating a lot of firepower from their eight pieces of artillery, creating the impression that they were far more numerous than was actually the case. The two French cavalrymen proceeded cautiously, passing the word back to Ney. Ney essayed a feeble probe with some infantry and the Nassauers fell back about three kilometers to the edge of Bossu Wood, where the balance of Prince Bernard of Saxe-Weimar's brigade lay, some 4,500 men. Ney smelled a rat. Fearing a trap, he called off the action at about 2000 and bedded his troops down for the night along the road all the way back to Marchienne-au-Pont. As Ney's troops went into bivouac, Constant-Rebecque ordered the balance of Perponcher's 2nd Dutch-Belgian Infantry Division to Quatre Bras, meanwhile pulling the Nassauers back another mile to that vital crossroads. Ney had just lost his best chance to seize the main road to Brussels without a fight.

Over on the French right, Grouchy was doing badly as well. He got off to a late start and was agonizingly slow in reaching Fleurus. Finally, at about 1730 an angry Napoleon browbeat him into action. Within a short time Grouchy's troops had cleared the outskirts of the town of Prussians, who were pulling back in any case. Then, although now in a position to press on against light resistance, Grouchy lapsed into lethargy once again. By 2000 his troops were going into bivouac all along the road from Fleurus back to Chatelet. Thus, although there yet remained nearly two hours of twilight during which maneuvers were perfectly possible, the French army would work no more this day.

Napoleon had returned to his headquarters at Charleroi

at about 2100, having spent about 15 hours in the saddle. He was rather satisfied with the day's activities. Despite the muddled crossing of the Sambre—nearly half his strength was still to the south of the river—the army had attained all of its objectives but two, Quatre Bras and Fleurus. His army was well concentrated and he had clearly secured the central position. On the morrow he would be able to bring about a decisive action with the Prussians, who had already gotten a foretaste of what he had in store for them.

At about the time Napoleon returned to Charleroi, Wellington was preparing to attend the Duchess of Richmond's ball, partially as a display of confidence and partially out of ignorance of the day's developments. Around 2200 Wellington received a critical message, this time from Generalleutnant Augustus von Gneisenau, Blucher's chief of staff, informing him that Blucher was concentrating on Sombreffe and inquiring as to Wellington's intentions. Wellington, in his shirt sleeves and slippers, told his Prussian liaison officer, Generalmajor Carl von Muffling, that he still believed the French activity at Charleroi was a ruse, and that the main blow would come through Mons, but that he would have an answer for Gneisenau as soon as he had more definite news. Despite his confidence, he issued orders modifying his earlier instructions and alerting the Reserve for a possible early movement. Muffling reluctantly went back to his quarters, while Wellington finished dressing. As he completed his preparations a dispatch arrived from Major General Wilhelm von Dornberg, an expatriate Westphalian commanding the British 3rd Cavalry Brigade. Earlier in the day Dornberg had refused to forward to Wellington a highly accurate report from the army's principal intelligence officer, the able Lieutenant Colonel Colquhoun Grant. But his own patrols in the direction of Mons had now convinced him that the French movement on Charleroi was not a feint. Wellington rapidly issued orders for the army to concentrate at Nivelles and Quatre Bras, south of Brussels. This done, he went off to the ball at about midnight, stopping on the way to inform Baron von Muffling of his new dispositions. While Wellington had erred, misjudging Napoleon's intentions and giving new orders which would require time to implement, Constant-Rebecque had not. Indeed, not only had he ordered Per-poncher-Sedlnitzky's division to Quatre Bras, but, in further disobedience to his orders, he had begun shifting troops eastward. Meanwhile, the Duke enjoyed the party, there meeting Lady Charlotte Greville, who was to be his companion for a midnight supper. After a few turns around the floor greeting some of the guests, the Duke led Lady Charlotte into the dining room shortly before 0100 on. the 16th. Even as they did so, a number of officers were already quietly drifting away from the party in response to the orders Wellington had issued earlier, going directly to the front, where many would fight and some die over the next few days still wearing their gala finery. In the dining room, even before the Duke and Lady Charlotte could take their seats, a mud-bespattered cavalryman interrupted, passing a message to the Prince of Orange. The Prince, just 23 years of age, handed it unopened to Wellington, who, in an extraordinary display of *sang-froid*, shoved it in his pocket and continued his conversation with Lady Charlotte. Like many others among the guests, Lady Charlotte noted that the Duke was preoccupied. A few minutes later Wellington stepped aside to read the message. The dispatch was for Orange, from Constant-Rebecque, informing him that the French were advancing on the crossroads at Quatre Bras, which was but lightly defended, and that only because of his insubordinate action in posting Saxe-Weimar there. Wellington took the news calmly. He conferred briefly with the Prince of Orange, affirming Constant-Rebecque's arrangements, issuing orders confirming the concentration at Quatre Bras. Then, ordering up a carriage, he turned to the Prince of Orange, saying, "I

Gebhard Leberecht von Blucher

Gebhard Leberecht von Blucher, Prince of Wahlstadt, generalfeldmarschall (1742-1819), was born to a noble family in Mecklenburg-Schwerin, one of the most conservative German principalities. Enlisting in the Swedish cavalry at the age of 14 at the onset of the Seven Years War (1756-1763), he shortly thereafter became a prisoner of the Prussians. Abandoning Swedish service, he enlisted in Frederick the Great's 8th Hussars, with which he served until the end of the war when he took his discharge and settled down to an estate in Silesia, where he remained for nearly a quarter-century. In 1786 Blucher returned to his regiment, rising to command it by 1793, and led it with great skill and elan during the Valmy campaign. The resulting reverse which Prussia suffered at the hands of the new French revolutionary armies led to a peace which was to last over a dozen years. Meanwhile Blucher was promoted generalmajor in 1794 and generalleutnant in 1801.

During the long peace Blucher rose to high rank. Among those who urged Prussia to prepare for renewed war with France, he was largely ignored. When war finally did come in 1806, Blucher was given a command in the Duke of Brunswick's army, which was crushed in a spectacular double-envelopment by the numerically very inferior army corps of French Marshal Louis Davout. This, coupled with Napoleon's simultaneous destruction of the balance of the Prussians at Jena, caused the Prussian Army to disintegrate. Blucher was responsible for the only creditable

think it best for you to miss supper, Your Royal Highness, and proceed at once to your troops in the field," and dispatched the young man to the front. Wellington remained at the ball for nearly another hour. Then he announced, "I think it is time for me to go to bed," and walked towards his room with his host, the Duke of Richmond, titular commander of the Reserve Corps, of whom he asked, "Do you have a map in this house?" As some aides lit candles, the Duke produced a map, and Wellington allowed himself a burst of temper, shouting, "Napoleon has humbugged me, by God! He has gained 24 hours' march on me."

Wellington looked at the map. It was familiar territory to

Prussian performance during the campaign: taking control of a portion of remnants of the army, he led the pursuing French on a merry chase which did not end until he was run to earth near Lubeck more than three weeks later, virtually the last Prussian troops to surrender. Captured, Blucher was inactive during the campaign of 1807, which saw Prussia's final hopes crushed along with the Russian Army at Friedland. Although Blucher was restored to duty after the Peace of Tilsit, French pressure kept him relatively inactive.

Virtually expelled from the army in 1812, when he urged the king to aid Russia against Napoleon, Blucher came into his own the following year when he was appointed commander of the Prussian Army in the field. Blucher led his troops with determination and some skill in the campaigns of 1813 and 1814,

playing a distinguished role in numerous battles. After Napoleon's first abdication Blucher, by then a field marshal, was preparing to retire but was recalled to duty for the Waterloo campaign, during which his determination to see the thing through was of vital importance in securing the Allied victory. After Waterloo Blucher urged draconian penalties against France but was largely ignored. Already ill, both physically and mentally, and loaded with honors, he quietly retired.

Blucher was a big crude man, of hearty appetites, little learning and no polish. Despite being overfond of gin, convinced that the earth was flat and, during the Waterloo campaign at least, suffering under the delusion that he was pregnant with an elephant by a grenadier of Napoleon's *Garde Imperial*, Blucher was a tough, able commander.

Generalfeldmarschall Gebhard von Blucher. By no means a cerebral soldier, and arguably deranged, Blucher was a tenacious, brave campaigner.

him. He had spent the preceding weeks profitably making staff rides all through the region between Brussels and the French frontier, and had marked out several possible lines of operations and battle sites. The Duke of Richmond asked, "What do you intend to do?"

Wellington toyed with a pencil. "I have ordered the army to concentrate at Quatre Bras," he said, underlining the name of the village on the map. He laid down the pencil and went on, saying "But we shall not stop him there, and if so, I must fight him *here*," and traced with his thumbnail a ridge line about a dozen miles south of Brussels, just below a place called Waterloo. A few minutes later he went out into the Rue de la Blanchisserie and into the predawn darkness of Brussels, which was already stirring with the mustering of troops, the blare of bugles and the rattle of drums and the skirl of bagpipes. Shortly the Duke was himself on his way south.

Blucher was also moving his men. The defection of Bourmont had placed Napoleon's plans in his hands and he had acted on them, urging his forces forward and passing the word to Wellington. Thus, as the French army slept, Prussian and Allied troops were on the march through the hot night.

As was its custom, the French army rose early on 16 June. Napoleon issued his orders. Having obtained a rough idea of the Prussian dispositions, he believed that Blucher would retreat rather than risk a general action in so exposed a position; even that impetuous old hussar could see how impossible was his situation. Napoleon's orders therefore reflected this contingency. Reinforced with Kellermann's *III Cavalry Corps* in place of the *Guard Light Cavalry*, Ney was to operate against "the English," seizing Quatre Bras in preparation for an advance on Brussels as soon as the reserve came up to his support, while Grouchy was to advance on Sombreffe and Gembloux so as to keep the Prussians entertained, while holding himself in readiness to assist Ney should the latter require such. Napoleon had thus reversed his initial plan to destroy Blucher before taking on Wellington. Not until about 0800 did the true situation begin to become clear. Then, even as the final orders for the day's operations were being dispatched, word came from Grouchy that his reconnaissance had spotted strong Prussian forces advancing on Sombreffe from the vicinity of Namur. Perhaps Blucher intended to stand and fight after all! But Napoleon retained some doubt as to this. Rather than immediately act on Grouchy's information, he decided to investigate.

Feeding the Fight

Because the campaign of 1815 was so short neither side had any particular problems supplying the food, fodder and ammunition needed by the armies. The French Revolution had taught armies to travel light and to minimize their supply needs. Prior to the Revolution, and for more than a century since the Thirty Years War (1618-1648), armies in Western Europe had supplied themselves by means of elaborate systems of fortified magazines. These spared civilians the depredations of foraging troops, but greatly slowed the pace of operations, since the armies were more or less tethered to their magazines by their lengthy—and vulnerable—supply trains. Moreover, supply by wagon train was not very effective beyond about 80 kilometers from the source of supplies.

There were some simple mathematical and physical reasons for this limitation. A wagon with a cargo capacity of one tonne required six horses and at least one driver. These themselves required 75 kilograms of food and fodder a day. If the wagon is required to haul supplies 80 kilometers from its base to an army operating in the field, a journey of about 5 days, the horses and driver need 10 days' worth of rations for the round trip. This comes to 750 kilograms, or about 75 percent of the wagon's "lift" capacity. So operations in the pre-Revolutionary period tended to be somewhat leisurely: an army would advance to invest an enemy

fortification and lay siege to it. If the siege were successful, the fortress could then be used as the base of operations for the next year's campaign, since considerable time would be required to accumulate supplies. This was one reason armies liked to campaign along major rivers, since the use of river transport greatly facilitated supply.

The French Revolution wrought a major change in the way armies were supplied. Attention to administrative detail was not one of the strong points of the armies of Revolutionary France. They were poor and ill supplied and began to live off the land as a matter of course. Making a virtue of a necessity, the French soon organized this initially chaotic "system" of procuring supplies, appointing officers to take charge of local resources and distribute them as needed. The introduction of hardtack—euphemistically called "bread"—made the movement of armies even easier, as a soldier could readily carry several days' worth of "biscuit" in his knapsack. It was this improvisation which gave the French a major strategic advantage for much of the period of the Revolutionary and Napoleonic Wars, since their opponents long continued to operate on the magazine system. But the French practice of living off the land had its limitations. A given region could support an army roughly equal to its own population for a couple of weeks without major harm to its ability to sustain civilian life. So the system worked best in areas which were rather thickly populated, such as northern France, Belgium, southern Germany and the Po Valley in Italy, where the populace was quite dense. When the French tried this approach in more thinly settled areas, such as Spain, Poland and Russia, they found it didn't work very well. As a result, the French partially reverted to the use of supply trains, at a time when their opponents were partially adopting the French practice of living off the land.

A look at the supply needs of one of the armies involved in the Waterloo campaign will give some idea of the complexity of the problem. Calculations regarding supply are based on simple constants, the daily ration requirements of men and horses. The typical human ration for the period amounted to about 2.0 to 2.5 kilograms a day, including some packaging. This broke down to about .45 kg of meat, usually salt pork or fish, .45 kg of fresh bread or biscuit, .45 kg of potatoes or dried peas, .5 to 1.0 liters (i.e. kilograms) of wine or beer and about .07 to .1 kg of other consumables, including salt, sugar, coffee, tobacco, even candles. For a horse, the daily ration requirement was about 12 kilograms, 5.0 to 5.5 kg of feed and 6.0 to 6.5 kg of cut fodder: horses cannot eat grass very long and be expected to do work.

Napoleon's *Armee du Nord* had about 122,600 men and at least

47,000 horses (about 25,000 in the cavalry, 12,000 for the artillery and 10,000 for the infantry and supply columns). Daily human ration requirements were therefore about 275 tonnes, to which must be added the minimum daily horse ration requirement of about 270 tonnes, for a total of nearly 545 tonnes. An often overlooked aspect of the Waterloo campaign is that it was conducted just around harvest time; in fact, some actions were affected by the presence or absence of tall rye and other crops. One result of this was that even had the campaign gone on much longer than was the case, none of the armies would have been hard pressed for food.

Ammunition was another story. During periods of inactivity, the need to resupply ammunition would be negligible. But after a major battle, it could present a considerable problem. The total weight of the 40 rounds carried by each of the army's 88,000 or so infantrymen— presumed to be sufficient for one major battle—was only about 110 tonnes, all of it carried in the ammunition pouches of the troops, plus several additional issues carried in the company, battalion and army supply trains, for a total of perhaps 330 tonnes. The artillery would have required at least 520 tonnes for a complete resupply. Since ammunition could not be procured locally, this was yet another argument for relying heavily upon local resources for food and fodder.

General Confusion

There were a lot of generals involved in the Waterloo campaign, far more than would be the case for an equivalent combat force today. This is largely due to changes in the nature of war and the character of armies since 1815. While some technical problems with titles and staff positions make it difficult to determine the actual number of general officers involved, the accompanying table is approximately correct.

The Prussian figures in the table below are similar to those prevailing in most major armies during the Second World War. Those for the French suggest a contemporary Third World force rather than a highly successful army. This is an unfair comparison. While Napoleon did distribute rank lavishly, the French military system, which had grown out of the Revolution, called for generals to be right up front, with consequent heavy losses in their ranks. This had a marvelous effect on morale, encouraging the troops to greater efforts.

Higher military ranks in the period of the Waterloo campaign were rather confusing, as demonstrated by the accompanying table.

The French rank system was more complicated than may appear

Generals in the Waterloo Campaign		
Army	Number	Men per General
French	164	747
Anglo-Allied	46	2,435
Prussian	30	4,340

Comparitive General Officer Ranks, 1815			
British	French	Dutch Belgian	Prussian
Field Marshal	Marechal de l'Empire	Feldmarshaal	General-feldmarschall
General		Generaal	General
Lieutenant General	General de Division	Luitenant generaal	General-leutnant
Major General	General de Brigade or Marechal de camp	Gerneraal majoor	Generalmajor

from this table. To begin with, the highest actual rank in the army was *general de division*; *marechal* was technically a distinction, not a rank. A corps commander who was officially a *general de division* might by courtesy be designated a *general de corps d'armee*. However, a *general de division* might also sometimes be referred to as a *lieutenant general*, particularly if he was functioning in a staff position. Meanwhile, the chief of staff of the army was designated *major general*. In addition, an officer commanding a brigade was more likely to be designated a *marechal de camp* (literally, "field marshal") rather than a *general de brigade*, which was reserved for officers with special duties, such as the commanders of the regiments of the *Garde Imperial*. This complexity had developed as a result of the Revolution, which favored functional titles for military officers, *chef de bataillon* for example, rather than major. Unfortunately, staff personnel often required rank, so the old Royal hierarchical titles of rank survived alongside the functional Revolutionary ones.

Further complicating matters was the fact that in all armies an officer's social rank was often used rather than his military rank. Thus, although Wellington was a field marshal—in about five armies—he was usually referred to as "His Grace, the Duke" without his military rank. In Wellington's case this could become quite complicated, as he was a duke thrice over, the Portuguese and Spanish having dubbed him such even before the British, and he was also a prince of the Netherlands. As each of these gave him a different title, references to him in Portuguese, Spanish or Dutch works can easily become obscure: for example, the Portuguese know him as the Duque de Douro, and one Portuguese language history of the Peninsular War nowhere uses any other name for him. And then there is the problem of multiple ranks. Wellington was not the only officer to hold high rank in several armies; the Prince of Orange was a full general in the British Army, the Duke of Brunswick a British lieutenant general, and so forth.

Other Officers. Although the French had a far higher proportion of generals than did their foes, overall they actually had proportionally fewer officers. On paper, a British battalion had about 30 officers and a Prussian one about 24, while a French battalion had to get by with only about 20. Actually, the figures for the French and Prussians are inflated somewhat due to the presence of regimental staffs, which did not exist in the British Army. Excluding regimental staffs, the situation becomes even more favorable to the British than at first glance. Deducting regimental tactical and staff officers, 5 to 9 men in French regiments and 8 to 10 in Prussian, reduces the number of officers in the French battalion to about 17 to 18 and the Prussian battalion to about 21 to 22. With the higher proportion of officers, 30, in each of their battalions the British were able to supervise the troops much more closely, which was an important reason for their steadiness in action.

CHAPTER V

The Battle of Ligny

16 June

*I*t was at about 1100 on 16 June that Napoleon reached Vandamme's *III Corps*, drawn up near the village of St. Amand-le-Chateau. From there he could see elements of Zeithen's I Corps. Concluding that the Prussian force was a screen to cover the concentration of the main body further to the rear, he decided to attack at once, intending to push through Zeithen in order to bring the Prussian main body to battle or force it to retire still further. Napoleon thus reverted to his original plan, to take on Blucher before Wellington. But the attack could not take place immediately. Fresh orders had to be issued. Although Vandamme's *III Corps* was at hand, Gerard's *IV Corps* was yet some distance away, and the bulk of the reserve was even further back; though the *Imperial Guard* had been on the march since 0400, Lobau's *VI Corps* had not yet even been ordered to move up. At least three precious hours had been lost.

Had Napoleon been in a position to attack soon after he arrived on the field, he would have been confronted only by about 30,000 men of Zeithen's I Corps, with perhaps 80 pieces of artillery. Shortly after noon, Prussian strength was more than doubled by II Corps under Generalmajor Georg von Pirch. And around 1400 Generalleutnant Jo-

Dominique Joseph Rene Vandamme

Dominique Joseph Rene Vandamme, Count of Unsebourg and general of division (1770-1830), entered the Royal Army as a teenager, serving as a volunteer in the West Indies. During the Revolution he raised an independent company of chasseurs and commanded it with skill in the Low Countries. Made a general of brigade in September of 1793 and of division in 1799, Vandamme performed his duties skillfully and aggressively in numerous actions but, aside from being made a count in 1808, was never again promoted, being frequently insubordinate, foul tempered, a grafter and a looter. Made a prisoner during the 1813 campaign, Vandamme managed to survive insulting Tsar Alexander and was released in 1814 but was exiled from France by Louis XVIII.

Vandamme returned to France when Napoleon resumed the throne in March of 1815 and was given command of the *III Corps*, which he led with considerable success at Ligny. With Gerard, one of the officers who urged Grouchy to go to Napoleon's support on the 18th, Vandamme fought well at Wavre and led the rear guard during the retreat of the *Armee du Nord*. After Napoleon's second abdication he lived in the United States for several years, returning to France as a private citizen in 1819. Granted a pension as a retired officer in 1825, Vandamme was the only one of Napoleon's 1815 corps commanders who did not eventually secure a marshal's baton.

A good commander, utterly loyal to Napoleon, Vandamme's temper and tongue certainly held back his career. Yet it is difficult to fault his lack of patience with Grouchy on the morning of 18 June.

hann von Thielmann's III Corps began to come up, bringing a further 24,000 men and 48 pieces of artillery. Thus, by mid-afternoon Blucher had about 84,000 men available, including 8,000 cavalry, with about 208 guns and howitzers. Blucher disposed his troops before Sombreffe, along a front of about 11 kilometers, with his left sheltering behind Ligny Creek, a small but useful obstacle. Several little villages were incorporated in the Prussian lines, notably on their right. Zeithen's I Corps held the right of the line, with the 1st and 3rd Brigades holding the three St. Amands, while his 4th held Ligny, so that the corps had a

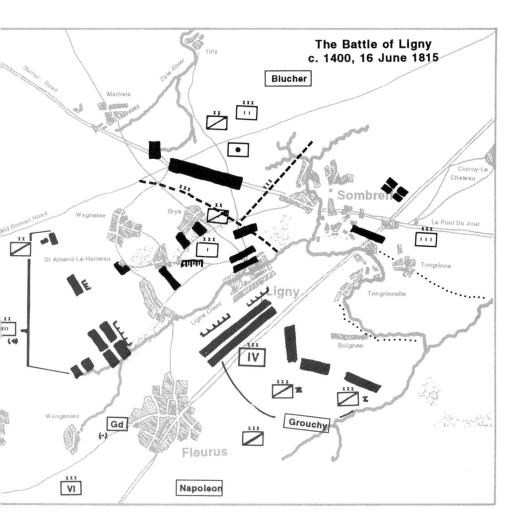

The Battle of Ligny
c. 1400, 16 June 1815

90 degree angle in its front; his 2nd Brigade was in reserve a little to the rear. Thielmann's III Corps was stretched out on the left, to give security to that flank and cover the arrival of General der Infanterie Friedrich Wilhelm von Bulow and the IV Corps. Pirch's II Corps was positioned as a general reserve directly behind Zeithen, able to support either flank. The position was not the best, for it was overly long given the number of troops, and it had a peculiar "S" shape, curving around with a prominent salient in the center, which was Ligny village. Zeithen's 4th Brigade held Ligny, facing southeast. Some 800 meters to its right was the 3rd Brigade, holding St. Amand-le-Chateau and facing southwest, with the 1st Brigade to its immediate right in front of St. Amand-la-Haye and the 2nd Brigade in reserve. Moreover, while many of the front line troops were often well situated, sheltering behind hedgerows and rough barricades, many others were deployed along exposed forward slopes, as were virtually all of the reserves. Nevertheless, Blucher believed it could be held, particularly since von Bulow's IV Corps, some 30,000 men with 88 pieces of artillery, was marching hard to his support. Meanwhile, at 1300 Wellington rode the eight kilometers from Quatre Bras to confer with him.

The two field marshals met at a mill, Wellington in his customary plain blue overcoat and Blucher in his equally customary martial splendor. As the two surveyed the field from the upper story, they spotted a party of French officers off in the distance, one of whom was clearly Napoleon, prompting Zeithen's chief of staff, a Lieutenant Colonel von Reiche, to remark that at that instant, "Perhaps the eyes of the three greatest military commanders of the age were directed at one another." Wellington asked a few questions about the Prussian dispositions and plans. He politely expressed reservations about the fact that many of the troops—even those held in reserve—were exposed to artillery fire, suggesting that the men might be better posted on reverse slopes. The Prussian explained that they believed it important for the troops to see their foes. Wellington retained serious doubts about the Prussian ability to hold in their chosen position, confiding to Lieutenant Colonel Henry Hardinge, his liaison officer at Blucher's headquarters, "If they fight here they will be damnably mauled."

Nevertheless, after a bit more conversation, the Duke said, "Well, I will come; provided I am not attacked myself." A few minutes later he took his leave.

By about 1400 Napoleon had available fewer men than did Blucher, roughly 65,000, with nearly 200 guns. On the right he gave Grouchy Pajol's *I Cavalry Corps* and Exelmans' *II Cavalry Corps* with instructions to pin down Blucher's left flank which consisted of Thielmann's corps. In the center, at right angles to the right flank, was the bulk of *IV Corps*, about 15,000 men, directly confronting Zeithen's men across Ligny Creek, while Napoleon's left, comprising Vandamme's *III Corps* reinforced with a division from *II Corps*, was to engage Blucher's center and right. In immediate reserve, ready to crush the enemy's center at the right moment, were the *Imperial Guard* and *IV Cavalry Corps*. To turn the action into a smashing victory, Napoleon had Soult issue orders for Ney to fall on the Prussian right flank at about 1800, after driving the "English" out of Quatre Bras. Curiously, the 10,000-strong *VI Corps*, available near Charleroi, had not been instructed to move up. Then, with all apparently in readiness, he attacked.

The fighting was intense from the start. It began with a massive cannonade, shot and shell battering the Prussian lines and tearing great gaps in the reserves posted on exposed forward slopes in the rear. On the right, Grouchy led his cavalrymen forward to hold Thielmann in place, preventing him from supporting the Prussian center and right. On Napoleon's left Vandamme attacked the St. Amand villages. He deployed his troops in line so that, with gaps between divisions, his front was some three

Standing at the foot of a windmill at Fleurus, Napoleon is seen issuing orders for the attack on the St. Amand villages to the northeast, out of the picture to the right. Note that the artist has exaggerated the height of the hills in the distance.

kilometers wide. The *7th Division*, from *II Corps*, was on Vandamme's left, with his own *11th* and *8th Divisions* in the center, and the *10th* in echelon on the right, initially held back from the fighting. The troops moved out well, Vandamme's men smashing into Steinmetz' brigade at St. Amand-le-Haye. Resistance was very determined and the Prussians, fighting well behind available cover, inflicted considerable casualties on the French. Gradually, however, the French made headway, pressing the Prussians back. By 1600 the *8th Division*, supported by a brigade from the *11th*, had smashed its way into St. Amand-le-Chateau, despite the fact that much of II Corps came to support the Prussian defenders. Vandamme sent the *11th Division* into St. Amand-le-Hameau. Under the direction of their commander, General de Division Baron Berthezene, the troops deployed in open order behind available cover and withheld their fire until the enemy were quite close—about 100 meters—before opening up with devastating effect. The attack collapsed. Meanwhile, Vandamme sent the *7th Division* in against St. Amand-la-Haye. The struggle for this village was unusually intense. The division stormed into the village, threatening to turn Steinmetz' right. Steinmetz juggled his forces and counterattacked, driving the French back. But General de Division Jean-Baptiste Baron Girard led his men back into the village. Blucher committed the 2nd Brigade to Steinmetz' support and the French were thrown out again. Once more Baron Girard went forward, though the odds had lengthened. Finally, shortly after 1800, Blucher himself led six battalions from the 5th Brigade plus some cavalry into a counterattack, and once again the Prussians drove the French back. This time the Prussians held: it had required nearly two hours and odds of about five-to-one for them to do so. Casualties had been heavy on both sides, the *7th Division* losing some 50 percent of its manpower in killed and wounded, including Baron Girard and both brigade commanders. On the *IV Corps* front the struggle was equally severe.

The attack of *IV Corps* on Ligny commenced somewhat later than that by *II Corps* on the St. Amand complex. The delay was caused by Comte Gerard's desire to make a personal observation of the Prussian lines. This reconnaissance enabled him to deploy his attacking forces to the best advantage, using a denser formation than Vandamme had employed. Comte Gerard put the *13th Division* on his left and the *12th* to its immediate right, some 8,500 men on a front of only about a kilometer. In addition, his reconnaissance had convinced him that his right and rear were at risk should Grouchy's cavalry fail to keep Thielmann's III Corps in check, so he posted his *14th Divison* to his right rear to support the troopers in case of need. Only then did he order the soldiers forward. The attack met fierce resistance from Generalmajor von Jagow's 3rd Brigade, posted

Another view of Napoleon and his staff at Fleurus, surrounded by the **Garde.** *In the distance can be seen the St. Amand complex of villages.*

in the village and its environs on both sides of Ligny Creek. The *12th Division* went forward directly against Ligny four times, only to be driven back each time by stout Prussian counterattacks. But the pressure on the Prussians was severe and the 3rd Brigade had to be reinforced with the 4th in order to hold the line. Casualties were heavy: in the *12th Division* alone the *30th of the Line* lost about 700 men out of some 1,200 with which it began the fight, including its commander, 2 out of 3 battalion commanders, 5 captains and 11 other officers killed, with most of the remaining ones wounded. Nevertheless, the remainder carried on. On the fifth try, with General de Brigade Francois Rome in the lead, the regiment was more successful. The Prussians fell back, leaving the south side of the burning village in French hands. But the attack then stalled, as the troops attempted to press on, for they had to fight their way across a few narrow bridges and fords over the creek which ran right through the center of the village.

Even as the struggle opened, Napoleon issued fresh orders for Ney. At about 1513 the chief of staff, Marshal Soult, instructed Ney, "...do not hesitate even for a moment

Nicolas Jean de Dieu Soult

Nicolas Jean de Dieu Soult, Duke of Dalmatia, Marshal of the Empire (1769-1851) was the son of a notary from the south of France. He enlisted in 1785 and rose to sergeant in the early days of the Revolution. Passing to the volunteers as an instructor officer in 1792, Soult began a rapid rise. By 1794 he was general of brigade. Taking part in the Rhine, Swiss and Italian campaigns, by 1799 he had risen to general of division. Created a marshal in 1804, he commanded various corps during the campaigns of 1805-1807 before being spent to Spain, where he began a long duel with Wellington broken only by a brief tour in Central Europe in 1813. Although Wellington was generally successful in this protracted struggle, Soult gave him a good run for his money, almost winning the last battle of the war at Toulouse in early 1814.

With Napoleon's first abdication, Soult entered Bourbon service as minister of war. Although initially inclined to oppose Napoleon upon his return, for fear of civil war he soon rallied to the Emperor, who made him his chief of staff, since he had once understudied the great Berthier, (then dead). Soult did not perform impressively in this role, being too inexperienced at staff work, and would almost certainly have proven more valuable in the field in command of a wing of the army.

After Napoleon's second abdication Soult went into exile for a time. Returning in 1819, he was restored to duty. After the liberal monarchy was established in 1830, as war minister he reorganized the army, for which he was created Marshal-General of France, only the fourth man in history to have received this dignity.

Soult was short, bowlegged and, by some accounts, had a slightly clubbed foot. As a commander he was cool and resourceful tactically, an excellent administrator, but a poor strategist, albeit that he could conduct a retreat better than most officers. Wellington considered him a dangerous, wily foe, which is perhaps the best testimony to his abilities.

---

to carry out the maneuver ordered by the Emperor," to which Napoleon added a brief verbal message, telling the courier to order Ney to take Quatre Bras without delay. But hardly had the courier, Colonel Forbin de Janson, ridden off with this message, when word came that Ney had become enmeshed with sizeable enemy forces at Quatre Bras, thus making it highly unlikely that he would be able

A modern view of Napoleon's windmill at Fleurus. Captain Coignet, whose memoir of the campaign is quite valuable, says that Napoleon observed the Prussians through "a hole in the wall," but the Engineers of the Garde also built a wooden observation platform for the Emperor. Note the monument dedicated to France's three victories on the site, the last being that which is usually called "Ligny." Photo by Ed Wimble.

to fall on Blucher's right flank. Thus, at 1520 Napoleon penciled a note instructing Ney to send only d'Erlon's *I Corps*, retaining the balance of his forces for the action to his front. This message was entrusted to General de Brigade Charles de la Bedoyere, erstwhile commander of the *7th of the Line* at Grenoble, who rode off to deliver it. In addition, realizing that Lobau's *VI Corps* had not yet been issued orders, Napoleon belatedly called it forward. Meanwhile the action at the front raged on with great bloodshed. Despite heavy casualties, the persistent French pressure began to pay off. Zeithen's corps took a severe beating and Blucher was forced to commit virtually all of Pirch's corps to its support, while Napoleon still had perhaps 10,000 troops uncommitted and yet another 10,000 near at hand. In effect, Napoleon was beating Blucher's

84,000 men with but 60,000 of his own. The time was ripe for a decisive blow.

At 1700—while the struggles for St. Amand-la-Haye and Ligny were at their most intense—Napoleon ordered up the *Imperial Guard*. The artillery got into action quickly, deploying in such a way as to enfilade either wing of the Prussian army or fire upon their reserve at need. However, it required nearly an hour to get the veteran guardsmen into position for the final blow. By 1800 all was in readiness and Napoleon was about to send them into action when Vandamme rode up. A force of perhaps 20,000 troops had been spotted approaching his rear, explained the tough, blunt-spoken Vandamme, and his scouts had reported "they are enemies." His troops were becoming nervous, engaged in the front with the Prussians and threatened from the rear. Napoleon at once suspended the intended attack, ordered the 4,800-strong *Young Guard* under General de Division Philibert Duhesme to Vandamme's support, and sent a number of staff officers to reconnoiter the situation.

Napoleon's virtual suspension of the fighting came as a welcome respite for Blucher. The old marshal realized that the battle was lost, for neither Bulow nor Wellington would be able to come to his aid this day, but he intended to salvage something from the disaster. If he could hold long enough, nightfall would bring an end to the ordeal. While Napoleon pondered the possible threat to his rear, Blucher attempted to reform his battered lines and gather some troops for a counterattack to relieve some of the pressure.

At about 1830 some of Napoleon's staff officers returned with word that the approaching column was in fact d'Erlon's *I Corps*. In riding for Ney's headquarters, de la Bedoyere had come upon d'Erlon's column marching north on the road to Quatre Bras. Aware of the contents of Napoleon's order to Ney, he wisely passed it on to d'Erlon's leading division commander, General de Division

A modern view of the front gate of the **Ferme d'En Haut,** *which covered the Prussian position at Ligny church, and was so fiercely contested during the battle that afterwards it was so littered with corpses that one French general found his horse unwilling to budge for fear it would tread on a body. Photo by Ed Wimble.*

Pierre Durutte. Unfortunately, de la Bedoyere misunderstood the direction which Napoleon wished d'Erlon to take, and thus the corps commander moved southeastward, placing him in Napoleon's rear, rather than northeastward, which would have put him on Blucher's extreme right. Napoleon immediately sent d'Erlon instructions to march to the left, in order to place himself in position for a decisive blow against the Prussians. Then he calmly resumed preparations for his grand attack. Within a short time his messenger had returned with word that d'Erlon had turned back towards the west after dropping off the *4th Infantry Division,* under Durutte, and the *1st Cavalry Division,* under General de Division Baron Jacquinot, to cover the Prussian right. Thus, rather than some 20,000 fresh troops ready to fall on the enemy's flank, Napoleon had but 6,000, barely sufficient for a screen. It was an incredible failure of command and control. As there was nothing which could be done at the moment, Napoleon returned to the situation at hand.

Conditions at the front had deteriorated. The morale of the men of *III Corps*, shaken by the fierceness of the fight and d'Erlon's sudden appearance in their rear, had received a further blow when Blucher delivered a counterattack shortly after 1800. The resolute Prussians managed to throw back the French, permitting them to retake part of St. Amand-le-Chateau. But Blucher could not follow up his success, for there were no fresh troops available. The French rallied. Duhesme's *Young Guard* went in and rapidly cleared the village once more and the lines were quickly restored. Napoleon was now determined to have done with Blucher. He resumed preparations for a final blow. All was soon in readiness.

At 1930 the *Guard* went into action. Altogether five regiments took part, in two columns, one on each side of Ligny village, attacking with Gerard's *IV Corps* between them, supported by the fire of 60 guns and backed up by the *Guard Heavy Cavalry* on the left and Milhaud's *IV Cavalry Corps* on the right. Attacking on a relatively narrow front in columns of double companies, the guardsmen swept forward in a driving rain. At about 2000 they hit the Prussian defenders, briefly grappled with them, and then drove them back with the bayonet. Having secured the far side of the creek, the guardsmen advanced into the relatively open ground beyond it and deployed into line. The Prussian 6th Brigade, deployed with some other units on heights about 500 meters beyond the creek, brought them under fire and some II Corps cavalry attempted an attack. Some of the *Old Guard* battalions formed square, beating off the attack. Then the French threw back the 6th Brigade with a series of attacks in column, pushing it on to the open ground before Brye. Sensing an opportunity to save something from the wreck, Blucher placed himself at the head of all 32 squadrons of the I Corps' cavalry and charged. The guardsmen rapidly

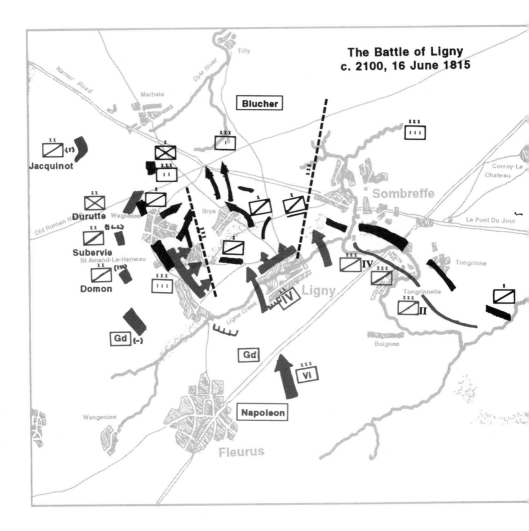

The Battle of Ligny
c. 2100, 16 June 1815

formed square. The Prussian horse swept down on the squares, only to be beaten back by sustained volleys pouring from the disciplined ranks. By now Milhaud's cavalrymen had passed through the burning village, and were deployed on a broad front. They came to the support of the *Guard*, sweeping back the Prussian troopers. There was a sharp clash near the mill of Bussy, and then the Prussian squadrons were driven off. By about 2100 the action was over, the battle at an end, as the leaderless Prussians streamed for the rear, for Blucher himself had become a casualty.

During the cavalry action Blucher's mount had been shot. The old marshal was badly dazed as he hit the ground and was pinned beneath his horse. There, with only a topographical service officer, Lieutenant Colonel Count von Nostitz, by his side, the old man lay ignored in the midst of the battle. Nostitz threw a cloak over the bemedaled marshal so that he would not be recognized. Twice French squadrons passed him. Then some Prussian stragglers came by. Nostitz pressed them into service. They freed the semi-conscious, wisely unidentified officer, and carried him to the village of Mellery, placing him in a little house overflowing with casualties, among whom was the British liaison officer, Lieutenant Colonel Henry Hardinge, who had lost a hand at Ligny. There Blucher rested. Meanwhile, Gneisenau, his chief of staff, took control of the battered army. It had been a disastrous day for Prussian arms. Perhaps 16,000 men had been lost as well as 21 artillery pieces. The army was a shambles, and thousands were deserting the colors. But if the Prussians had lost, the French had not necessarily won. Certainly, they had not secured the overwhelming victory which Napoleon sought.

Napoleon had lost perhaps 13,700 men in the struggle for Ligny. Serious failings of command and staff had revealed themselves, and Napoleon himself was showing obvious signs of physical and mental strain. Although

Count Nostitz comes to Blucher's aid, after the old marshal is pinned beneath mount during the charge of the French 9th **Cuirassiers.**

most of the French Army was still relatively intact and in good condition, he failed to order a pursuit. Nevertheless, he appears to have been well satisfied with the day's events. Although the enemy had not been destroyed, he had been dealt a grievous blow. The two enemy armies had been kept apart; indeed, probably had been driven further apart by the day's events. As the French right wing bedded down on the field, it was time to consider the coming clash with Wellington, who had been tangling with Ney for most of the day.

Musketry

The musket was the principal military firearm of the Wars of the French Revolution and Napoleonic Wars. A smoothbore, muzzleloading piece, the musket had been introduced in the early part of the 16th century, but it did not attain perfection until the middle of the 18th, after of the development of the socket bayonet, the flintlock firing mechanism, and the iron ramrod, coupled with the discovery of cheaper sources of nitrates and more efficient processes for the production of gunpowder, which permitted greater reliance on fire power. Thereafter, the musket became the dominant battlefield arm, rendering excellent service until well into the 19th century. Nevertheless, the musket had severe limitations, for it was difficult to handle, had a poor rate of fire and was remarkably inaccurate.

Loading the long (from 95 to 150 cm) and heavy (from 4.5 to 7 kg) weapon was by no means a simple task. Under ideal circumstances a well-trained man could manage up to six rounds a minute. In combat one or two was more likely. The procedure may be summarized in far less time than it actually consumed.

Grounding his piece, the musketeer held it steady with one hand while taking one of the 50 to 60 heavy (from 30 to 40 grm) paper-wrapped cartridges from his ammunition pouch. Biting the ball end of the cartridge off and retaining it in his teeth, the man would prime his piece by pouring some powder into the pan. He would then pour the rest of the powder down the barrel, tapping the butt of his piece on the ground once or twice in the process. Then, spitting the ball into the barrel and jamming the paper wrapping in after it, he would take his ramrod and vigorously tap everything down. Replacing the ramrod in its slot under the barrel, he would lift the piece to his shoulder, cock the flintlock mechanism, aim after a fashion and fire.

This was a complicated process. In the British Army the drill for loading a musket involved 10 commands and a total of 20 separate motions, although in battle these were generally reduced to "Prime and load!" since the troops knew the drill. Even without the pressures and panic of battle, it was easy to make a mistake. One could spill the powder on the ground or forget to ram the charge home or, having done so, neglect to remove the ramrod from the tube. One's powder could be damp or flint worn. Misfires were common, and it was not unusual for a man to accidently double or even triple-load a piece in the heat of battle, only to have it blow up in his face. Even in the best of circumstances a piece would begin to foul after 10 or a dozen rounds, due partially to the uneven quality of gunpowder and also to the poor fit of ball to barrel.

Under the best conditions musketry was inaccurate. In battle it became even more so. As one contemporary officer put it, "...a soldier must be very unfortunate indeed who shall be wounded by a common musket at 150 yards, provided his antagonist aimed at him." In 1790 the Prussian Army conducted firing tests with its 1782 musket. The results were hardly impressive, given that the target, a wood and canvas construction supposed to represent the front of an infantry company (32 m by 1.8 m) actually offered roughly 42 percent more solid surface area than would have been occupied by the troops (30 sq m rather than 52 sq m). Moreover, the firing troops were performing under ideal conditions, with no one shooting back.

Prussian Musketry Trials of 1790	
Range	Hits
300m	20%
200m	25%
140m	40%
70m	70%

A later similar test, in which the target surface was actually painted with the figures of troops in ranks suggested that about 25 percent of the rounds would entirely miss the men. Even rounds hitting the painted figures were not necessarily injurious, since many would strike hats and coat tails. An analysis of combat statistics suggests that no more than 15 percent of the rounds fired seem to have hit anyone. And range was important to lethality: beyond 100 meters serious casualties were relatively few, at 50 meters the slaughter could be terrific. It was these basic facts which molded tactics. Firepower could be lethal only if delivered in great volume on a relatively narrow front. By forming troops up virtually shoulder to shoulder in two or three lines one could maximize their fire effectiveness. If a regiment in line massed 1,500 muskets that would mean 3,000 rounds a minute, which theoretically could be expected to inflict upwards of 450 wounds at ranges under 70 meters, though some analysts have suggested that as few as six rounds were likely to be lethal. Moreover, 70 meters could be covered by troops at a fast walk in about a minute.

None of this is by way of saying that the musket was ineffective. It was merely inefficient. Given that the tactics of the day attempted to maximize the effectiveness of the musket, by employing mass formations which could deliver a massive volume of fire, musketry could be quite deadly. It was not unusual for units to be seriously battered in action. At Ligny, the French *82nd Regiment of the Line*, two battalions totalling perhaps 1,100 men, was nearly wiped out in two hours of fierce fighting for the village of St. Amand-la-Haye, an action which saw the French *7th Division* suffer about 50 percent killed and wounded, including the commander and both brigade commanders. It would be difficult to sort out the casualties due to musketry from those caused by artillery, but in any case such enormous losses were not unusual in sustained fire fights.

Far more accurate than the musket was the rifle. At the start of the wars all armies made some use of rifle, particularly for their light infantry. The rifle could be deadly at far greater ranges than the musket. But although considerably lighter than the contemporary musket, the rifle was even more difficult to use and maintain, with a considerably lower rate of fire, due to difficulties in loading properly to attain the necessary tight fit between barrel and bullet: in some models one had to force the bullet down the barrel with a mallet! The British made the most extensive use of rifles, equipping entire battalions with them for service as skirmishers, but they had a particularly fine rifle, the Baker, one of the first machined and mass produced firearms in history. The French abandoned use of the rifle in 1807 by order of Napoleon himself, who thought them unnecessarily expensive. Most other armies, however, continued to maintain some rifle-armed troops for special duties.

There were several interesting aspects to the entire question of infantry firepower in the period. French powder, for example, was 75 percent saltpetre, 9.5 percent sulfur, and 15.5 percent charcoal, while English powder was 75 percent, 10 percent, 15 percent, a better blend, indeed almost of "sporting grade," since the relatively smaller proportion of charcoal made fouling somewhat less of a problem. The English also tended to issue better quality flints and to change worn flints more often: before one battle in the Peninsula Wellington explicitly ordered his troops to use fresh flints. The English also relied heavily on meticulously trained manpower, which combined with their better powder and flints, enabled them to develop and sustain a volume of fire upwards of 50 percent greater

Muskets and Rifles of the Waterloo Campaign					
Army	Piece	Cal	Wt	RPM	Range
Br	"Brown Bess Musket" (1695)	18.7	5.0	3/6	70/140
Br	Baker Rifle (1800)	16.2	4.3	1/2	140/275
Fr	Charleroi Musket (1777)	17.2	4.8	2/4	70/140
Fr	Imperial Musket (1805)	17.2	4.8	2/4	70/140
Pr	Potsdam Musket (1782)	19.5	5.7	2/4	70/140
Pr	Silesian Rifle (??)	15.0	3.6	5/1	140/275

than anyone else. On the other hand, although French muskets fouled more frequently than British ones, they were easier to repair if seriously damaged, having a detachable barrel. All armies, of course, relied on the bayonet for close combat, though it appears to have been far more important and effective psychologically than in terms of actual casualty causation.

Key to the table on the previous page: Army: Br,. Britain; Fr., France; Pr., Prussia. Piece: the customary name of the weapon, with the year of introduction where available: The Brown Bess, officially the "Tower Musket, Mark III" or "Land Pattern Musket," was actually a somewhat modified version of the weapon introduced in 1695, various new versions being introduced from time to time. Cal., is the caliber of the weapon in millimeters, albeit that manufacturing standards being what they were at the time, most weapons varied considerably. Wt., is the weight of the piece in kilograms, without bayonet, which would add an additional .5 to .8 kg, depending upon the army in question. RPM, is the number of rounds per minute the piece could fire given a reasonably well-trained soldier, with the sustainable given before the maximum: note that the rate of fire of the Baker Rifle is for patched bullets; with unpatched ones the rate of fire doubled but the effective range was halved. Range is given in meters, with the normal effective range given before the maximum effective. The weapons given here represent more than 90 percent of the pieces carried at Waterloo, the Dutch and other Allied forces being largely equipped with French muskets. Cavalrymen were normally equipped a carbine, technically not very different from the musket, albeit with a shorter barrel. Dragoons often carried a weapon intermediate between the carbine and the musket, in deference to their occasional role as infantry. Carbines and dragoon muskets were even less accurate and had even less range than did the standard musket.

The basic ammunition load of a French infantryman was 50 rounds, that for a Briton 60, unless he was a rifleman, in which case it was 80. Ammunition supply in other armies was within the same range. This was regarded as sufficient to permit the man to take part in a major battle, maintaining a steady fire for two or three hours. Note that this implied a rate of fire much lower than that which was possible given the weapons in question. Additional ammunition were held in battalion, regimental and other supply wagons.

CHAPTER VI

The Battle of Quatre Bras

16 June

On the night of 15 June, Marshal Ney had conferred with Napoleon over supper. At this meeting Napoleon appears to have informed Ney of his plan of operations only in a very general way. In brief, Ney's primary objective was to move in the direction of Quatre Bras and Genappe. In addition, he was to assist the Emperor at Ligny if called upon to do so, and to prepare for a general advance on Brussels as soon as Napoleon could come to his support with the bulk of the main body. Napoleon's carelessness in this regard was serious, for the Marshal had not been privy to the planning of the campaign, the Emperor having virtually excluded him from his counsels for weeks. Thus, Ney was apparently not fully aware that he was supposed to move aggressively on the morrow. As a result, when he returned to his headquarters at Gosselies in the small hours of 16 June, he issued no orders before retiring. It is possible that he expected written orders in confirmation of the oral instructions which the Emperor had given him, as had been the practice in the past. Nevertheless, in the absence of such Ney ought to have acted on his own initiative. He failed to do so, and as a result the entire left wing of the *Army of the North*, perhaps 45,000 men, remained inactive throughout the morning. It was not

Hendrik-George Perponcher-Sedlnitzky

Hendrik-George Perponcher-Sedlnitzky, baron and luitenant generaal (1771-1856) was a member of the minor Dutch nobility. He entered military service at a young age, and by 1793 was an adjutant to Prince Frederick of the Netherlands. Accompanying the House of Orange into exile in Britain, Perponcher entered British service in 1800.

Shortly after the reestablishment of the Netherlands Perponcher was promoted luitenant generaal. During the Waterloo campaign he commanded the Dutch-Belgian 2nd Division. On the eve of the campaign he concurred with Constant-Rebecque's decision to redirect the deployment of his division towards Quatre Bras. He commanded his division with some distinction at both Quatre Bras and Waterloo, where it was virtually annihilated.

After the wars Perponcher was appointed the Dutch ambassador to Prussia, a post which he held from 1815 to 1842, when he retired.

until 1100 that Ney received written instructions from Napoleon, written at about 0830, and issued his own orders for the day and it was nearly noon before his troops began to move. Precious time had been lost, time which was put to good use by the enemy.

Prince Bernard of Saxe-Weimar's 4,500 Dutchmen had clung to the Quatre Bras area through the night of 15-16 June. Aside from the brief skirmishing in the area between Frasnes and the Bossu Wood, the night had passed quietly. The Dutch troops were thinly spread on a broad front of about three kilometers, giving the impression of strength. Early that morning, the balance of Perponcher's 2nd Dutch-Belgian Division came up, bringing the total of allied troops to about 8,000, with 16 pieces of artillery. However, French forces in the immediate vicinity numbered some 18,000 men with 38 guns. Had they advanced immediately, the Allied situation would have been desperate indeed. To be sure, given time, more Allied troops would become available, but time was a commodity of which there was not expected to be a surplus. Yet remarkably, that is precisely what happened. As the morning turned to midday, and then midday into the early afternoon, the French remained inactive. Nevertheless, when Wellington rode up on his famous chestnut charger Copenhagen at about 1500, the situation was becoming desperate, for the Prince of Orange had entirely lost touch with the course of events. When the Duke questioned the Prince about some blue-coated troops he espied in the woods, the latter replied "They are Belgians," still wearing their French-style uniforms. In fact the troops were French, slowly skirmishing their way through the woods. If they had moved in strength, the best Wellington could have hoped to accomplish would have been to delay them for an hour or so. However, the French remained relatively inactive. There are several possible explanations for Ney's idleness. He may have assumed that his mission was not to move aggressively against the enemy to his front, or he may have been unfortunately lethargic. However, it may also have been the result of his experiences in the Peninsula, where Wellington's reverse slope tactics had proven devastatingly effective, a matter which would have dictated caution. Meanwhile things began to brighten for the Allied position at Quatre Bras. At 1420 a large dust cloud could be seen along the road from Brussels. It was the British 5th Division, the best in Wellington's army, some 8,000 men—more than half British or King's German Legion veterans—with a dozen pieces of artillery, marching hard behind their commander, Lieutenant General Sir Thomas Picton, a tough Peninsular veteran. Given a bit more time, Wellington would find his position secure. But time had finally run out.

At about 1430, the cry of *"Vive l'Empereur!"* arose from the French lines. Hearing this, Wellington, riding back from his conference with Blucher, observed, "That must be Ney going down the line. I know what that means. We will be attacked in five minutes." As he spoke 14 French guns opened up and the French infantry began moving forward.

Reille deployed his main force in four columns, each a brigade strong. In the fields off to the right of the Brussels road he positioned the two brigades of Baron Bachelu's *5th Division*, some 4,300 men altogether, while on the road itself and to its left were the brigades of Comte Foy's *9th Division*, 5,000 strong, so that the bulk of his forces were on and to the east of the road. Reille held Prince Jerome Bonaparte's *6th Division*, the strongest in the army with some 8,000 men, further back to advance in echelon on the left of the other divisions. Some 3,000 troopers of Keller-mann's *III Cavalry Corps* covered his exposed left flank, while 2,300 more in the *2nd Cavalry Division* under Baron Piré helped screen the advance and served as the reserve. The deployment of the troops was initially concealed by tall rye. The men moved cautiously, partially out of regard for the excellent defensive qualities of the Allied position with its numerous farm buildings and thickly growing fields; like Ney, but unlike the Emperor, Reille had considerable respect for Wellington, whom he too had encountered in Spain.

Perponcher had disposed his troops as effectively as possible given the circumstances. He placed Saxe-Weimar's brigade, some 4,500 mostly green troops, in the Bossu Wood, on his right. Dutch Major General Wilhelm van Bijlandt's 3,400 man brigade, which was mostly composed of militia, he placed in front of Quatre Bras, with the 5th Militia Battalion, some 480 men, blocking the road to Brussels from the farm of Gemioncourt. Finally, he took Bijlandt's 27th Jagers, an excellent light infantry battalion 800 men strong, and spread it in a thin line stretching for a mile across his entire front. Perponcher's defenses were mostly on the western side of the Brussels road and angled from it somewhat to the southwest.

By a fortuitous accident, Reille's attack formation was well suited to cope with Perponcher's defensive dispositions. As Bachelu and Foy advanced, their troops encountered light resistance, for there were few troops to their

The farm at Gemioncourt, heroically defended by the Dutch-Belgian 5th Militia Battalion against an entire brigade of Count Foy's 9th Division. A fairly typical example of a Brabant farm, Gemioncourt was a stoutly constructed enclosure of brick and stone, making an ideal improvised fort. Photo by Ed Wimble.

front, Perponcher having deployed his men more to the west. The 27th Jagers did what they could but were forced back after losses approaching a third of their strength. Bachelu's division seized the farm of Piraumont and threatened to move off to the northwest, severing Wellington's links with Blucher. Meanwhile, one of Foy's brigades became entangled at Gemioncourt with the Dutch-Belgian 5th Militia Battalion, who, although green troops, gave a good account of themselves before being ejected, losing in the process nearly two-thirds of their number. As this was taking place, Foy's left-hand brigade had attempted to seize Pierrepont Farm on the flank of the Bossu Wood. Saxe-Weimar's brigade gave them a rough time and it required the arrival of Prince Jerome's division to secure this strongpoint. These troops then pressed on to clear the Dutchmen out of the woods proper. Aided by the thick

Sir Thomas Picton

Sir Thomas Picton, lieutenant general (1758-1815) and son of a country squire, had joined the army as a young man. His service was considerable and varied, including service during the French siege of Gibraltar in the American Revolution. He later served as a civil governor in the West Indies, during which a Spanish governor put a price on his head, to which he responded with a polite letter telling the man to "come and take it." Charged with abusing his powers as an officer, he was dismissed from the army in 1803. After refuting the charges, he was restored to duty and sent to serve under Wellington in Spain and Portugal, where he greatly distinguished himself. Given the 5th Division in 1815, Picton fought at Quatre Bras, where he was injured but managed to conceal the fact, and Waterloo, where he was killed.

A big, hearty man, Picton was, like Wellington, a careless dresser, going into battle with a civilian coat and top hat. A fine commander, he cared not one whit about the dress of his troops, "so long as they mind their fighting," and they greatly loved him.

With their commander in their midst, the 79th Highlanders lead Picton's British 5th Division into action.

undergrowth, Saxe-Weimar yielded ground slowly, falling back in good order. By about 1500 Perponcher's lines were being stretched to the limit, under pressure from some 25,000 troops supported by dozens of guns. However, some 4,300 infantry and 900 cavalry of the Brunswick Corps were just then arriving down the Brussels road, following their somber Duke. This was a welcome addition to Perponcher's strength, for not only did he desperately need manpower in general but, aside from 50 stray troopers of the Prussian 2nd Silesian Hussars, he had no cavalry whatsoever. Two companies of jagers, among the best the Duke had, went in to support the struggle for the Bossu Wood, while the 2nd Light Infantry Battalion was sent to cover the Allied left, and the balance helped bolster Perponcher's sagging lines. It was at about this time that Wellington himself finally returned from his meeting with Blucher to take direct control of the situation. But perhaps more importantly, given the critical shortage of manpower, reinforcements began to arrive.

Major General J.B. van Merlen's Dutch-Belgian 2nd Cavalry Brigade, some 1,100 light horse, rode in along the road from Nivelles, a small but heartening reinforcement. Soon after, Picton's British 5th Division arrived and began forming a second line of defense behind Perponcher's weakening left. This gave Wellington, who arrived on the scene about this time, some 22,000 men with which to confront Reille's 25,000, a more sporting proposition than had hitherto prevailed. The youthful Prince of Orange, technically in command of the Allied troops at Quatre Bras, now took a hand in the action. At about 1530 he threw Merlen's brigade into a counterattack. The French recovered rapidly, and Piré's troopers pressed the attack in turn. Merlen's men were driven back with heavy losses. The thin skirmish line of the 27th Jager Battalion disintegrated, several hundred men and six pieces of artillery being taken by the enemy. The French infantry renewed the attack, only to be repulsed by Picton's men, who, led by the 79th

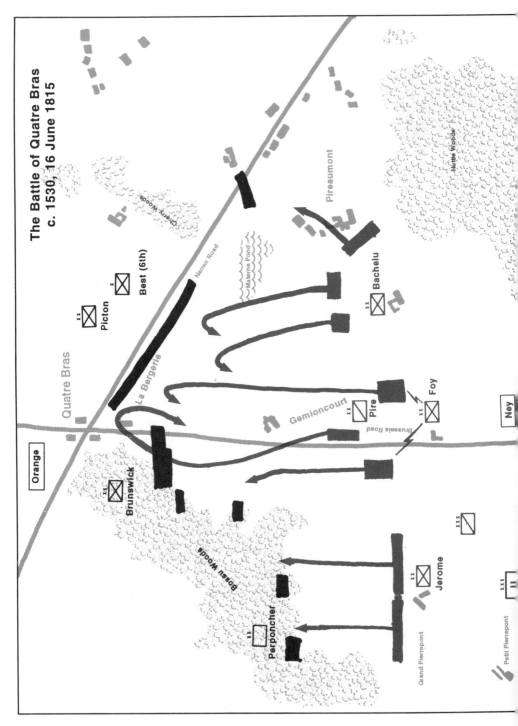

The Battle of Quatre Bras
c. 1530, 16 June 1815

Best (6th)

Picton

Quatre Bras

Orange

Brunswick

La Bergerie

Namur Road

Materne Pond

Cherry Woods

Pireaumont

Hutte Woods

Bachelu

Gemioncourt

Pire

Brussels Road

Foy

Ney

Bossu Woods

Perponcher

Jerome

Grand Pierrepont

Petit Pierrepont

Highlanders, drove back the French in some disorder, the *2nd Light Infantry* actually breaking to flee to the rear. By 1600 the front had stabilized once more, due largely to Wellington's near parity in numbers with Reille, about 22,000 men against about 25,000, though the French had about twice as many guns as the 38 Allied pieces at hand. The race against time had been won. If Quatre Bras fell to the French now, it would not be by default.

Ney's conduct of the day's fighting had so far been uninspired, lacking the dash and aggressiveness which had earned him his marshal's baton. He had completely failed to understand Napoleon's instructions and as a result had been dilatory in carrying them out. Not until shortly before 1530 did he begin to realize the full import of his orders, primarily because Soult's dispatches of 1400—instructing him to fall on the Prussian flank at 1800—finally reached him. And yet again he misunderstood his instructions! Rather than seeing that these new orders essentially canceled his prior instructions to seize Quatre Bras, he assumed that he had first to accomplish that task and then take the Prussians in the flank. Now he acted with commendable speed, sending an aide off to urge d'Erlon to bring his *I Corps* up to Quatre Bras as quickly as possible, while once more throwing Reille's tired troops against the Anglo-Allied lines. The renewed attack had mixed results. On Ney's left, Jerome pressed Perponcher back to the northeastern corner of the Bossu Wood before he could hold, while some of his men and some of Foy's battered the Brunswickers in front of the western side of Quatre Bras. Seeing his men waver, Duke Frederick Wilhelm of Brunswick put himself at the head of his Uhlans, some 240 men, and attempted a charge with the intention of easing the pressure on his infantry. The attack met with no success, as the French quickly formed square. Returning to his lines near the farmhouse of La Bergerie, the Duke attempted to steady his men, only to be struck in the side by a musket ball. Although the wound

Friederich Wilhelm von Brunswick

Friederich Wilhlem von Brunswick, Duke of Brunswick-Oels (1771-1815), was the son of the Duke of Brunswick who commanded the Prussian Army in their defeats by the French at Valmy (1792) and Jena-Auerstadt (1806), actions in which the younger Brunswick took part as a staff officer. Titular duke after his father's death at Jena, Brunswick was in fact a sovereign without a state, since Brunswick was incorporated into various appanages of the French Empire upon the Peace of Tilsit in 1807. The Duke went into exile in Britain. When Napoleon went to war with Austria in 1809, the Duke raised a free corps in Bohemia and took it on a raid into central Germany, intending to spark a general insurrection against the French. When this failed, he raided across north Germany to the coast, where the Royal Navy took him and his small army to safety.

Entering the British Army, the Duke and his troops fought under Wellington in Portugal and Spain, where he rose to a lieutenant generalcy. When Napoleon escaped from Elba, the Duke proceeded to join Wellington with his newly raised army, which fought with some distinction at Quatre Bras, where he was killed.

A dour, somber man, who dressed entirely in black in perpetual mourning for his father, the Duke was the brother of Charlotte of Brunswick, the unfortunate wife of the Prince Regent of England (the future George IV), who later involved her in a spectacular divorce.

was not instantly fatal, no surgeon could be found to stanch the bleeding and the Duke died within minutes, leaving the troops even more shaken than before. Wellington juggled units in the front lines to bolster the battered Brunswickers, who rallied surprisingly well in the circumstance. Soon after, Foy's and Bachelu's troops were hit by Picton's redcoats, who, aided by some of the Brunswickers, drove back the French in some disorder. At about 1530, Piré's *2nd Cavalry Division* went in. Supported by the *1st* and *6th Chasseurs*, the *5th* and *6th Lancers* charged against Major General Sir Denis Pack's British 9th Brigade, part of Picton's division, drawn up in line directly in front of Quatre Bras. The British formed square. Caught in the open with some chasseurs close on his heels, Wellington rode up to the square of the 92nd Gordon Highlanders. Shouting "Ninety-Second, lie down!" an instant later he leaped Copenhagen over the heads of his troops, with his aide Fitzroy Somerset close behind. The square reformed as the chasseurs came up. With the Duke calmly ordering volley after volley to be fired into the swirling cavalrymen, the attack was beaten off. But two regiments, the 42nd Highlanders and the 44th, took a severe drubbing. Having mistaken them for the Brunswick uhlans, they allowed the French lancers to get too close before attempting to form square. Suddenly the French executed a wheel to the right and then thrusted for the rear of the two regiments. Lieutenant Colonel Robert Macara, of the 42nd, saw the danger and ordered his men into square. Just as they were completing the square, however, some of the lancers became trapped inside. A wild and bloody melee ensued until the last of the cavalrymen was slain, though not before Macara was killed by a lance thrust, the first of three successive commanders of the regiment to succumb to the lance on this day. Lieutenant Colonel John M. Hamerton, of the 44th, chose a different way to extricate his battalion from disaster. He ordered his rear rank to turn about face and had it deliver a crushing volley into the already disordered ranks of the lancers, then formed square. In the melee, the regimental standard bearer, Ensign Christie was struck in the eye by a French lance. Despite his agony, Christie was able to save the colors. Meanwhile, one of Hamerton's junior officers, Lieutenant Alexander Reddock commanding the Light Company, found himself and his men isolated from the battalion's square. Surrounded by French lancers, Reddock ordered his men, who were virtually out of ammunition, to form a column of fours and then charged right through the enemy troopers. The determined little band reached the square. Since the 44th could not "open" to admit them lest the French also enter, Reddock had the presence of mind to order his men to lie

The Horse at War

The *Armee du Nord* had at least 47,000 horses (c. 25,000 in the cavalry, 12,000 for the artillery, and 10,000 for the infantry and supply columns), or about one for every 2.6 men. Since the Anglo-Allied and Prussian armies probably had a smaller proportion of horses than Napoleon's army, and since they had much smaller artillery contingents, it is probable that the total number of horses "engaged" during the Waterloo campaign was something around 140,000. This was a lot of horseflesh, and procuring horses for both riding and traction was a major headache in all armies. Napoleon's repeated disasters from 1812 onward had virtually denuded France of horses by the end of the wars. Were it not for the fact that the year between Napoleon's first abdication and his return from Elba had permitted a lot of importation of new horses, often from France's former enemies, Napoleon would not have been able to field so well balanced an army as he did for the Waterloo campaign.

For cavalry, most armies preferred animals of about 15 hands 2 inches at the shoulder (c. 1.6 meters) and of about 450-500 kilograms, although heavier mounts (up to 550 kg) were useful for cuirassiers. In 1812-1814, Napoleon had experimented to some good effect with shorter (14 hands/1.4 meters) and lighter (c. 400 kg), due to the terrible drain on horseflesh that he suffered, but such lighter mounts were suitable only for scouting and raiding, like the Cossacks on whom they were modelled. Horses for cavalry service were best procured at about five years of age, and were good for 10 or 12 years of service. For hauling artillery pieces and supply wagons, big, sturdy "cold blooded" horses like Percherons were preferred. Usually, only mares or geldings were used by armies, as stallions easily became uncontrollable around mares in season.

Active service was even more punishing to horses than to men. This was partially because horses are relatively more delicate than

---

down under the bayonets of their comrades. In a few moments the storm had passed, as Piré's men streamed back to their own lines, having lost many men killed and wounded, including the commander of the *6th Lancers*, a Colonel Galbois, who, despite a wound in the chest remained in command. Ney's attack had strained the Allied line, dangerously in some places. But it had held. The new front ran parallel to the Nivelles-Namur road—the princi-

men. For example, after a day's march (of about eight hours, broken in two segments, for a total of 16 miles), their hooves and shoes had to be carefully examined, and cleaned and repaired as necessary. In addition, their backs and throats were supposed to be examined for galls and sores, and their necks and legs carefully wiped down. If the weather was wet (as it was on the nights of 16-17 and 17-18 June), every effort had to be made to provide dry footing, lest their hooves become water logged. These were all things which were likely to be difficult, if not impossible to do even during a short campaign, such as that of Waterloo, which saw the armies marching and fighting for five full days. As a result, losses of 30-40 percent during a campaign were not uncommon, and they could easily be worse, particularly if it was a protracted campaign in the winter.

The most famous horses were the chargers which generals rode into battle. Actually, "charger" was a misnomer, since what a general needed was a steady, brave mount, that would do what he wanted, rather than a spirited war horse. Battle was tough on chargers: Marshal Ney lost seven during the campaign (two at Quatre Bras and five at Waterloo), by no means a record. During the Waterloo campaign Wellington rode Copenhagen, a chestnut, 15 hands at the shoulder. Foaled in 1808, Copenhagen was about five when he was bought by Wellington during the Peninsular campaign. Sure footed and calm, but with enough spirit when needed, Copenhagen bore Wellington through most of the famous battles in the latter part of the Peninsular campaign, most notably at Vittoria, the Pyrennes and Toulouse. Copenhagen died in 1836, at the relatively advanced age of 28. Napoleon, his health being poor, spent a great deal of the campaign in his travelling coach. Although he did ride on several occasions during the campaign, it is not clear what horse—or horses—he used, as is also the case with Blucher.

---

pal Allied lateral link—about 800 meters to its south. Ney began to worry, anxiously awaiting d'Erlon's arrival so that he could renew the attack. But d'Erlon did not come.

Despite the sound of heavy combat emanating from the direction of Quatre Bras, not 10 kilometers to the north, d'Erlon's I Corps had spent virtually all of 16 June in the vicinity of Gosselies. Sometime in the early afternoon he had ordered his troops northwards and then gone on himself to personally survey the situation at the front. Shortly before 1600 de la Bedoyere, who was carrying the message which Napoleon had scrawled in pencil around 1520 at Ligny, rode up to d'Erlon's leading division, that of General de Division Pierre Durutte. De la Bedoyere peremptorily ordered Durutte to change his direction and march northeastward. Unfortunately, either through a misunderstanding on his part or the illegibility of the Imperial handwriting, he directed Durutte to the French flank before St. Amand rather than the Prussian flank at Wagnelee. Having thus unwittingly set in train the series of events which would inspire temporary panic in Vandamme's *III Corps* before the St. Amand village complex and cause Napoleon to delay the final blow of the battle of Ligny for an hour, de la Bedoyere then rode off to find d'Erlon. When he finally delivered his message to d'Erlon, the latter rather reluctantly concurred with the dispatch of Durutte's division, ordered the balance of his corps to follow and passed the purport of the message on to Ney.

Thus it was that at about 1610 Ney learned that nearly half his army was marching off in the wrong direction, news which he greeted with a burst of his famous rage. Then, within minutes, aggravating both the marshal's temper and the tactical situation, who should ride up but Colonel Forbin de Janson, with the full text of Napoleon's earlier orders of 1513. Ney appears to have completely lost control of his temper and vented his rage on the unsuspecting courier, who became so flustered that he forgot to turn over the actual dispatch. Ney then sent the unfortunate officer back to Napoleon, telling him, "I am opposed by the whole of Wellington's army. I will hold on where I am; but as d'Erlon has not arrived I cannot promise any more." Since he did not read the actual text of Napoleon's message, Ney remained ignorant of the Emperor's intention to shift the center of gravity of the day's operations from his own left wing to the right. Thus, he continued to believe that it was his wing which was to make the principal effort of the day, which was no longer the case. Mulling the situation over in this light, Ney legitimately decided that he desperately needed support and therefore had to countermand Napoleon's orders. He dispatched a message recalling d'Erlon.

Though hardly "opposed by the whole of Wellington's army," the situation confronting Ney was becoming critical. Wellington had by now been reinforced by the leading elements of yet another fresh division, Lieutenant General Charles Alten's 3rd, which would ultimately number 8,400 Britons and Hanoverians, many of them seasoned troops, along with a dozen guns, thus giving Wellington something of a numerical advantage, with about 26,000 men against 25,000, though he was still inferior in artillery, with around 42 pieces to about 64. Even as Alten's leading brigade, some 2000 British infantrymen under Major General Colin Halkett, began entering the lines the fighting

Michel Ney, **Duc de Elchingen, Prince de la Moskova, Marechal de l'Empire.**

William, Prince of Orange

William, Prince of Orange (1792-1849) was a scion of one of the most distinguished noble houses in Europe. The stadtholders of the Dutch Republic since 1579, the Princes of Orange were ousted when the Netherlands were occupied by France in 1795. Prince William's father was installed as King of the Netherlands by the victorious Allies in 1814 and was himself proclaimed heir. Although young at the time of Waterloo, only 23, he had already been long at war, having gone to Spain to serve in British uniform on Wellington's staff in 1811. The long association with the Duke did little to enhance his limited native skills as a soldier, but when Napoleon escaped from Elba it proved politically necessary to give the young prince, who ranked as a full general in the British Army, command of the I Corps; his even younger and more inept brother Frederick of Orange (1797-1881), received a notional "corps" in the Reserve of the Anglo-Allied Army.

The Prince was not particularly popular with his troops, who called him "Slender Billy." During the Waterloo campaign his performance was at best mixed, his "best" decisions being those made by his chief of staff Jean-Victor Constant-Rebecque. After the war the Prince served in a variety of military and government posts until the abdication of his father brought him to the Dutch throne as Wilhelm II in 1840.

"Slender Billy," the Prince of Orange, the youthful and inept commander of Wellington's I Corps, leads Dutch-Belgian troops into action shortly after the repulse of the French cavalry attacks.

was becoming more confused. The impatient Ney, whose temper had barely cooled, threw caution and good judgment to the winds. Turning to Kellermann he said, "General, a supreme effort is necessary. That mass of hostile infantry must be overthrown. The fate of France is in your hands. Take your cavalry and ride them down. I will support you with all the cavalry I have." Kellermann, who had but one brigade at hand, was stunned, for the orders were suicidal. He asked the marshal to repeat his instructions, but an angry Ney replied, "Go! Go at once!" Kellermann had no choice but to obey.

Kellermann launched Baron Guiton's brigade of cuirassiers from the *11th Cavalry Division* against the British line at about 1700. Abandoning normal cavalry tactics, which called for a somewhat protracted approach at ever increasing speeds, he formed the men into a tight mass and threw them in at full tilt from the start, so that their momentum would enhance their courage. Perceiving that the attack would strike against Halkett's newly arrived brigade in front of Quatre Bras, Picton ordered the four British regiments to form square, but then rode off eastward to investigate the situation on his left. Just as the 69th had completed its square, the Prince of Orange rode up. Speaking to Lieutenant Colonel Charles Morice, he asked why the men were in square. Morice replied, "Your Royal Highness, I have just been ordered to do so by General Picton, who left not more than a few minutes ago." Orange, who was technically in command but had not been consulted by Picton on the deployment of Halkett's troops, and had frequently been ignored by Wellington in the course of the battle, said, "Colonel, there is really no chance of cavalry coming on. Reform column immediately and then get back into line." Having thus reasserted his authority, Orange, a juvenile incompetent of the bluest blood, rode off to issue similar instructions to the brigade's three other battalions. Moments later the French struck. Although Morice attempted to reform square, one com-

General de Division Francois Etienne Kellermann, commanding Napoleon's **III Cavalry Corps,** *is rescued by two of his cuirassiers after leading the attack of Baron Guiton's brigade, much against his better judgment.*

pany failed to comply. Captain Henry Lindsay of the Grenadier Company disobeyed Morice's orders and put his men in line, hoping to beat off the French with fire. The company was ridden down and the French then rode through the ranks of the 69th, dispersing the troops in all directions and seizing its colors in triumph. The French rode on, smashing into the 33rd, which had been Wellington's first command, as a new lieutenant colonel back in 1793. The battalion was still drawn up in line behind the 69th. Ineptly commanded by Lieutenant Colonel William W. K. Elphinstone, quite possibly the worst battalion commander in any of the armies during the campaign, the 33rd melted away. As its men fled with the French in hot pursuit, they infected the 73rd with panic, and the troops of both regiments fled to the refuge of the nearby Bossu Wood, where the latter quickly rallied. Although the 30th held, elated cuirassiers swept around it and within minutes were virtually in possession of the vital crossroads after which Quatre Bras was named. But, however admirable their skill and courage, cavalrymen cannot hold ground unsupported. Ney had committed little cavalry and no infantry to Kellermann's assistance. The Allies struck back. A concealed battery of the King's German Legion opened up, while the 30th and the rallied 73rd poured in a deadly fire from the fringes of the Bossu Wood. In but a minute or two the French triumph dissolved into disaster. Men and horses went down, panic spread, the cuirassiers fled, Kellermann himself, his mount having been killed, escaped only by clinging "to the bits of two of his cuirassiers' horses."

As his troopers streamed for the rear, Ney made another attempt. His artillerymen redoubled their efforts, while he threw in Piré's tired troopers once more. Although they attacked against the already battered 42nd and 44th regiments, Piré's lancers accomplished little, as they rode around the steady British squares. As the lancers fell back under sustained musket and artillery fire, Ney made still another attack, this time throwing in the *Guard Light Cavalry* under General de Division Charles Lefebvre-Desnouettes. Rather than renew the assault against Wellington's center, which had three times now proven unbreakable, Lefebvre-Desnouettes threw in half his division, 900 veterans of the elite *Lancers of the Guard*. With the Polish squadron in the lead, the lancers hit the British line eastward of Quatre Bras, while French skirmishers and artillerymen kept the entire Allied front under a sustained fire. Picton's regiments formed mutually supporting squares while Wellington brought up a battalion of Hanoverians from the newly arrived 4th Hanoverian Brigade. The French attempted to strike the 1st and 28th Regiments, which stood like islands in a sea of enemy cavalrymen. Three waves descended upon the 28th. Picton's strong voice rang out over the din, "Twenty-Eighth,

Remember Egypt!" recalling an heroic action in the regiment's recent past. The battalion held. During this action Picton sustained an injury, having several ribs broken, which he managed to successfully conceal from all save his orderly. The Hanoverians—green men all, but game—attempted to support their beleaguered allies. Caught in line as they advanced from the Namur road, they were smashed by the French cavalry and fled the field. But the attack had failed, galled by British artillery and musket fire. Lefebvre-Desnouettes had no choice but to fall back. To support this attack, Ney had ordered a brigade of Bachelu's division to fall on Wellington's far left. Bachelu's troops did well, pushing two battalions of riflemen from the British 95th Regiment back. Though the 800-odd riflemen, outnumbered by perhaps as much as 5-1, gave ground stubbornly, the village of Thyle fell and Bachelu's men got across the Nivelles-Namur road, thus severing Allied lateral communications. Wellington sent the raw Brunswick 2nd Light Battalion to the aid of the 95th. The Brunswickers, mistaking the green-clad riflemen of the 95th for the enemy, attacked them with commendable elan; fortunately, the error was discovered before disaster resulted. The arrival of the Brunswickers enabled the 95th to stabilize the front. By about 1800 things had grown relatively quiet. Despite the danger to his left, and the proximity of the French lines in the Bossu Wood to Quatre Bras, Wellington's line had weathered yet another storm.

By now the Anglo-Allied Army numbered some 36,000 men with 70 pieces of artillery, the balance of Alten's division having arrived, along with the stout British guardsmen of Major General George Cooke's 1st Division, and the 4th Hanoverian Brigade from the 6th Division, plus three more battalions of Brunswickers with 16 guns, and a few other smaller detachments. Wellington thus now outnumbered Ney, who, with his 25,000 men and 64 guns, was still awaiting d'Erlon. Ney's message recalling *I Corps* had been dispatched at about 1620. It had reached d'Erlon at about 1800 just as *I Corps* was within sight of the Ligny battlefield, sparking panic in the ranks of Vandamme's *III Corps*. D'Erlon promptly reversed his march, though not before ordering Durutte and the *1st Cavalry Division* to remain behind and support the Emperor. Thus, at about the time that Ney's last cavalry attack was failing, *I Corps* was still at least five kilometers off, a good two hours' march in the circumstances. In effect, *I Corps* was out of the game and Ney would have to make do with what he had.

Wellington was now in a position to make a few attacks of his own. Some few hours earlier, the situation on his left might well have proven disastrous, but he now had troops to spare. Alten's last arriving unit, Major General Count Kielmansegge's 1st Hanoverian Brigade, a largely green outfit albeit well seasoned with veterans of the King's German Legion, was on hand. Wellington rushed it to his left. Meanwhile, he sent Cooke's guardsmen into the Bossu Wood, rushing them into action in column of route. On both flanks the tide began to turn in Wellington's favor. On the left, aided by the 95th, the Brunswick 2nd Light Infantry and Kielmansegge's Hanoverians began pushing Bachelu's tired troops back, while on the right Cooke's guardsmen, fighting from tree to tree, slowly drove Jerome's men through the Bossu Wood, though taking heavy losses. By about 1830 the situation on both of Wellington's flanks had improved greatly and Wellington began to think about a general counterattack.

Ney, meanwhile, was stubbornly refusing to recognize what his experience ought to have told him was happening, defeat. At about 1830, as he was attempting to reorganize for yet another blow against Wellington's center, he finally received Napoleon's message of 1513, that which Forbin de Janson had failed to deliver at about 1610, due to the marshal's ire. Ney abandoned himself to rage. He personally rushed to the front at La Bergerie, little more than a hundred meters below Quatre Bras, to which a small body of French stubbornly clung. Gathering this handful,

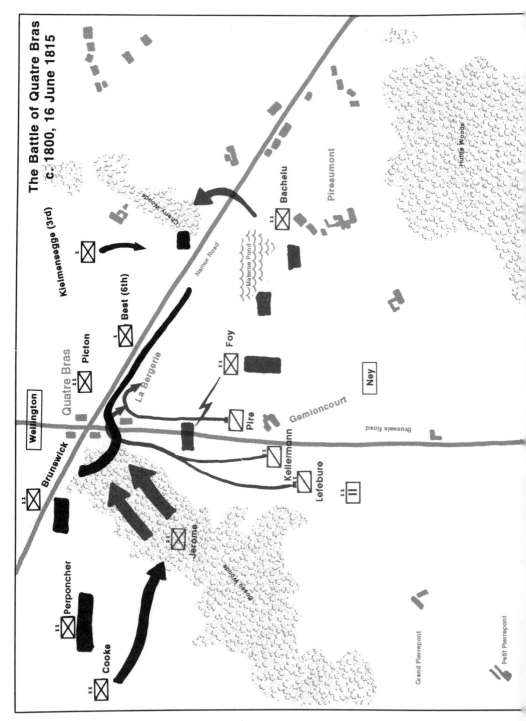

The Battle of Quatre Bras
c. 1800, 16 June 1815

Kielmensegge (3rd)

Best (6th)

Picton

Quatre Bras

Wellington

Brunswick

Perponcher

Cooke

Jerome

Bossu Woods

La Bergerie

Foy

Pire

Kellermann

Lefebure

Gemioncourt

Ney

Namur Road

Quarry Woods

Materne Pond

Bachelu

Pireaumont

Hutte Woods

Brussels Road

Grand Pierrepont

Petit Pierrepont

Ney led them forward in a feeble attack against Pack's battered brigade in front of Quatre Bras. The effort failed almost as soon as it began, with the troops barely coming to blows. But it lasted long enough for Ney to lose control of the situation entirely, just as Wellington decided to go over to the attack. Even as Ney wearily made his way back to the rear, Wellington threw the 92nd into action against La Bergerie. The Highlanders swept the tiny garrison out of the farm buildings in a few minutes. Heartened, Wellington ordered a general advance.

On Wellington's left, the Hanoverians, the Brunswick 2nd Light Infantry, and the 95th pressed Bachelu back, with Lieutenant General Sir James Kempt's 8th Brigade, of Picton's division, in support, driving on Piraumont. In the center, Halkett and Pack followed up the 92nd's success by attacking Foy's division in the direction of Gemioncourt. On the right, Cooke's guardsmen renewed their efforts against Jerome's tiring infantry. Everywhere the French fell back. By 1900 the Hanoverians had thrown Bachelu back south of the Nivelles-Namur road, while Cooke's guardsmen had ejected Jerome from the Bossu Wood, regaining the entire forest and only halting when an attack by the *Guard Light Cavalry* caught them in the open, with consequent heavy losses. Piraumont fell soon after, then Gemioncourt. The advance slowed, as much from fatigue as from French resistance. By 2100, as darkness began to gather, Ney broke off contact. Deploying a string of skirmishers between himself and Wellington, Ney drew his forces off southwards. Lacking cavalry, and with a largely exhausted army, Wellington decided not to pursue. The battle was over. Quatre Bras had been held. Wellington's tired troops rested on roughly the line which Perponcher's outnumbered men had held at the start of the battle, so many hours before, while Ney's went into bivouac about Frasnes.

Arguably, the battle had been a draw. The French had taken some 4,000 casualties against Anglo-Allied losses of

Michel Ney

Michel Ney, Duke of Elchingen, Prince of the Moskova, Marshal of the Empire (1769-1815), was the son of an Alsatian cooper and veteran of the Seven Years War. Enlisting in the French hussars at the age of 18, he was made an officer in the early days of the Revolution. He moved steadily, if unspectacularly, upwards through the ranks, campaigning in northern and eastern France. Ney first really distinguished himself at Hohenlinden in 1800, whereupon the hitherto unimpressive general of division began to rise more rapidly. Assigned the *Army of Switzerland* in 1802, he quickly brought the Swiss to their knees. Created a marshal in 1804, Ney's career was thereafter wholly intertwined with Napoleon's.

Ney commanded various army corps during the spectacular campaigns of 1805, 1806 and 1807, most often in the advance guard. In 1808 he went to Spain, where he did badly for three years, as did most French generals. Ney commanded *III Corps* with considerable distinction during the invasion of Russia, and proved an extraordinarily effective rear-guard commander during the disastrous retreat that followed, toting a musket with the infantrymen and by tradition being literally the last French soldier to march out of Russia. This was the acme of his military career, and his abilities and mental stability seem to have deteriorated rather rapidly thereafter. He performed erratically during the campaigns of 1813 and 1814, and served the Bourbons after Napoleon's first abdication.

Although Ney rallied to the Emperor after his escape from Elba, Na-

---

about 4,800, roughly half of whom were British. However, strategically Quatre Bras had been an Allied victory. By clinging to the place, Wellington had maintained his lateral communications with the Prussians. In addition, Allied resistance at Quatre Bras had prevented Ney from going to the support of Napoleon before Ligny, thus depriving him of the opportunity of totally smashing the Prussians. But perhaps most importantly, Quatre Bras had delayed Napoleon's timetable. The Emperor wanted Ney to take the place and be well beyond it by nightfall. Instead, Ney's outposts were in almost precisely the same positions as they had occupied on the previous night. He had gained nothing in return for the thousands of casual-

poleon treated him with considerable coolness during the period leading up to the Waterloo campaign, not summoning him to the army until virtually the last moment. Moreover, although Napoleon entrusted Ney with the left wing of the *Armee du Nord*, he appears not to have clearly explained his plan of campaign. As a result, Ney proved more energetic than skilled, more instinctive than cerebral. After the defeat at Waterloo, Ney was sentenced to death in an irregular proceeding: being a marshal, he could only be tried by other marshals, and when none were found willing to sit on the court he was tried as a peer.

The marshal met his death with considerable courage. As his titles were being read he remarked, "Why cannot you simply call me Michel Ney, now a French soldier, soon a heap of dust." Offered a blindfold, he spurned it, saying, "Are you ignorant of the fact that for 25 years I have been accustomed to face both ball and bullets?" Then he removed his hat, faced the firing squad, cried, "*Vive la France,*" and said, "Comrades, fire on me!"

A fairly tall (5'11"), large man with chestnut hair, a ruddy complexion, and a ferocious temper, Ney was at his best when commanding a moderate-sized force in the advance guard or the rear guard, his skills declining as the size of his command increased. A man of extraordinary courage, willing to get into the thickest of the fighting, he lost two horses shot from under him at Quatre Bras and five more at Waterloo, not to mention those lost in earlier campaigns. It was said that he had participated in 500 combats during his career. Napoleon dubbed him "The Bravest of the Brave."

---

ties and many hours which had been expended on 16 June. None of this was fore ordained. Indeed, Ney's chances on the morning of 16 June had been excellent, since he outnumbered the forces in front of him by at least three to one. However, he had never used his numbers properly, not once launching a full-scale grand attack on the Allied forces, but rather making numerous piecemeal efforts. Thus, as Wellington's troops increased in number, Ney's chances grew less as the day wore on. As a soldier the marshal had many strong points, but he had never performed well in independent command and it was clear to many that his mental stability had been deteriorating for some time. Thus, ultimately, the French lost the battle at

Augustus Wilhelm Gneisenau

Augustus Wilhelm Gneisenau, Count of Neithardt, generalleutnant (1760-1831), was the son of a Saxon officer. His early career included service with the Anspach-Bayreuth contingent in the British Army during the American Revolution and a tour in the Austrian Army. He joined the Prussian Army in 1786, in which he served in Poland during the Revolution of 1793-1794. His record was undistinguished until the collapse of Prussia at Jena-Auerstadt in 1806 when, as a major, he held Colberg against the French until after the Peace of Tilsit in 1807. Promoted and decorated, Gneisenau became a protege of the great Gerhard von Scharnhorst and involved in the reorganization and reform of the Prussian Army which turned it into one of the most effective forces fighting the French during the Befreiungskrieg (Liberation War) in 1813. By then he was chief of staff to Marshal Blucher. Ennobled after Leipzig, Gneisenau "made the pills that I am accustomed to administer," as Blucher put it, perhaps never doing so better than during the Waterloo campaign.

After Waterloo he served briefly as governor of Berlin and was promoted field marshal, but was essentially shelved due to his progressive ideas. In 1831 he was put in command of the Corps of Observation formed to ensure that the Polish insurrection against Russia did not spill over into Prussian territory. He died soon afterwards in the great cholera pandemic.

A brilliant staff officer with a liberal vision of the future, Gneisenau was used and then discarded by the reactionary Prussian state.

Quatre Bras because of Napoleon, who had placed the wrong man in command and failed to supervise him properly. As for Wellington, he had been lucky. Making no mistakes, he had employed his forces to their best advantage, making excellent use of ground and had been ever at the post of danger, thus able immediately to influence the course of the action. Now, with the battle done, it was time to prepare for another day.

Artillery of the Waterloo Campaign

Napoleon was a gunner and his battles reflected this. Among the first generals to see the possibilities of using artillery in mass, he believed that as the quality of his infantry declined the amount of firepower required to support it had to be increased to attain the same degree of success. Napoleon believed that the ideal ratio of guns to troops was five per thousand, a figure he never attained in practice. Nor did anyone else. It is worth noting the ratio of guns per thousand men in the armies which contended in Northern

The Waterloo Campaign			
Guns Per Thousand Men			
Army	Raw Totals Guns	Men	Ratio
French	364	122.6	3.0:1
Anglo Allied	203	112.0	1.8:1
Prussian	304	130.2	2.3:1

France and Belgium in June of 1815.

The figures in the above table are based on the totals for each army at the start of the campaign, and are greater than the numbers actually brought into action. If only infantry and cavalry are counted—on the theory that the gunners are part of the guns—the ratio of guns to troops is somewhat higher: French Army, 3.3 per thousand men; the Anglo-Allied Army, 1.9:1; the Prussian Army, 2.4:1.

The French artillery was the most proficient in Europe. It had gone into the Revolution with a totally new suite of pieces and a new doctrine. This system, designed by Jean-Baptiste Gribeauval, served well during the Republic and Consulate, but in 1803 Napoleon made a number of modifications including the reduction of the number of calibers from three types of guns plus one of howitzers to two types of gun and one of howitzers.

During the Waterloo campaign over 25 percent of Napoleon's artillery—was with the *Garde*, which formed his general reserve: each *Garde* infantry brigade had a 6-pounder foot battery attached and each cavalry brigade a 6-pounder horse battery and there were four batteries of 12-pounders—his "beautiful daughters"—attached to *Garde* headquarters. Each line infantry division had a 6-pounder foot battery and each cavalry division one of horse artillery. The army corps each had a battery 12 pounders.

Though the French were the masters when it came to artillery, the British were at least their technical equals. During the lengthy Revolutionary and Napoleonic Wars (1792-1815), they had greatly improved their expertise and equipment, reducing the number of calibers even further than the French, from three types of cannon and two of howitzers to a train of mostly 9-pounders and 5.5" howitzers, plus some 6-pounders for the horse artillery and Congreve Rockets. But British employment of artillery was hampered by an overall shortage of pieces, which prevented the use of massed firepower. However, since Wellington much preferred to fight defensive battles, this was not as serious a problem as it might have been. Indeed, arguably his persistent shortage of artillery forced him to develop superior tactics.

Wellington's British and King's German Legion batteries were virtually all composed of veteran troops. Each British division had two batteries attached, usually foot batteries but occasionally horsed ones. Dutch-Belgian batteries had a lot of veterans in them. Their divisions usually had a battery of foot artillery attached to each brigade, though some had horsed batteries. Unlike French practice, Wellington did not assign his horse artillery to the cavalry, but rather used it as principal artillery reserve, moving individual batteries into action as circumstances dictated. During the attack of the *Old Guard* he moved three batteries into exposed positions, two near Hougoumont, to enfilade the left flank of the French column, and the other near La Haye Sainte, to enfilade the French from their right flank.

The Prussian Army had been virtually destroyed in the disastrous campaign of 1806, leading to a radical reorganization. One result of this was a reduction in the number of artillery pieces to but four, 12-pounder and 6-pounder guns and 7-pounder and 10-pounder howitzers. This more or less brought Prussian practice into line with that of the other contemporary powers. In the period after Napoleon's catastrophic Russian campaign of 1812, the Prussian army expanded much too fast for it to maintain its technical skills. One result of this was that in 1815 its artillery was by no means as proficient as that of either France or Britain, though the guns were well and bravely served. The Prussians placed all of the eight or 10 batteries in each corps under a single artillery commander, who then parceled them out among the various brigades as needed. This was rather clumsy, for neither the brigade commanders nor the army commander had a pool of artillery resources available to them. Nevertheless, the system seems to have worked fairy well in practice.

It should be noted that all armies also had a small number of heavier guns for special uses, such as siege warfare. During the Waterloo campaign, the British actually brought some along, a dozen 18-pounders, while the Dutch had a 12-pounder battery, none of which saw any action, being left behind during the advance to the frontier, and the Prussians had some 10-pounder howitzers which did get into action.

Organization. Although all armies maintained battalions and regiments of artillery for administrative purposes, these never served in the field, the tactical unit was always the battery. There were two basic types of artillery, foot artillery, in which the gunners walked alongside the pieces or rode the limbers, and horse artillery, in which the men were all provided with mounts, even if only on the gun horses. Almost universally, both foot batteries and horse batteries fielded four to six guns and one or two howitzers. A battery was actually composed of two elements, the battery proper, which comprised the guns and between 90 and 150 artillerymen, and a separate train squadron, of 75 to 150 men, which transported the spare ammunition, repair facilities, and extra equipment. The use of half-batteries was quite common in all armies. Napoleon himself is said to have favored the permanent establishment of batteries at four guns and two howitzers, though he was unable carry this notion into practice due to the difficulty of securing sufficient numbers of properly trained artillerymen.

Serving the Guns. In action the actual working of the guns was in the hands of enlisted men, officers being responsible for tactical employment. Having arrived at a suitable position a seasoned crew could unhitch the gun teams, unlimber their piece, sight it, load and get off their first round in about a minute, and maintain that rate of fire or better for some time. An entire battery could manage the task in two or three minutes. Getting away required a few minutes longer. Each man in a gun crew had a specific task assigned, but was "cross-trained" so as to be able to serve in almost any capacity. The procedure was complex.

As the piece recoiled from its last round, the spongemen swabbed the tube to quench any live embers, while the ammunition handlers brought up a felt or serge-wrapped powder bag and the type of round indicated by the gunner. The loader inserted the powder charge into the tube and the spongeman shoved it home with the ram end of his swab, while the ventman placed his leathercased thumb over the vent as further insurance against premature explosion due to unextinguished embers. The loader then placed the projectile with its loosely attached wooden wad into the tube. As the spongeman shoved this down, the ventman jabbed a "pricker" through the vent into the powder bag to tear it, and then shoved a light metal or goose quill primer filled with high quality powder into the tear. The gunner then relaid the piece, adjusting elevation and deflection by the use of wedges, screws or main force. When he was satisfied, a slow match was then applied to the primer—or, if a friction primer was available, the lanyard was pulled—and the piece discharged. This started the whole process over again.

The normal projectile for guns, which had relatively long barrels and could attain considerable range with a flat trajectory, was shot, or ball. This was a solid sphere of metal designed to smash into things. If fired properly, so that it struck relatively hard ground in front of a target, such as a mass of troops, ball could be particularly devastating, since the impact would throw rocks and gravel at the troops and, moreover, the ball would ricochet, or bounce. Ideally a shot could bounce along for some time, each leap covering slightly less than half the distance made by the former, until it came to a halt, unless, of course, it hit something. Shot could tear great gaps in the ranks, which was one reason for the popularity of line formations and for the British reverse-slope defensive tactics, which massed the troops out of the line of fire. Howitzers had a short barrel and were designed for high-angle fire. Their normal projectile was the shell, a hollow metal sphere filled with powder and provided with a fuse. Before inserting the shell in the tube the loader had to cut the fuse to a length suited to the range required and, usually, apply a match to it too, making his job considerably more hazardous than under normal circumstances. Howitzers were particularly useful for getting at places behind obstacles, such as villages, forests, and hills thereby making them the best weapon for dealing with normal British defensive tactics. Howitzers could also be used to drop shells into the midst of large masses of troops. Both guns and howitzers were also provided with case shot, sometimes called grapeshot, for situations where the enemy was literally at point-blank range. Grapeshot was aptly named, for it was essentially a package which released numerous small lead balls upon leaving the barrel. A "taste of grape" discharged into the head of a charging column could cause horrendous damage and quite possible result in the failure of the attack. The British had two versions of case shot, a "heavy" round with 85 balls

to the canister and a "light" one with 27. During the wars the British introduced shrapnel, which was a combination of shell and canister, and proved particularly effective against massed bodies of troops.

Tactics. The French favored the aggressive use of artillery. Even a Grand Battery could be expected to limber up and advance upon command. Most other armies dispersed their artillery. Since Napoleon was usually on the offensive, his predilection for massed batteries and aggressive handling is understandable. His opponents, who usually fought defensively, favored greater dispersal of their batteries and more autonomy for them in action.

Offensively, Napoleon used his artillery to batter the enemy's infantry, pounding them with shot and shell until they were sufficiently softened up so that he could send in his own infantry or cavalry. Since the guns were mostly direct fire pieces of relatively limited range, their use in support of attacks was a delicate task, since they were usually unable to fire over the heads of friendly troops. At Waterloo the French were fortunate in that the contour of the battlefield permitted some firing of this nature in support of attacking infantry. Ideally, guns were supposed to accompany any attack, to help the troops overcome any obstacles for which sheer courage and dash were insufficient.

Artillery could be highly effective in defense. Counterbattery fire, that is, firing upon the enemy's artillery, was not usually considered profitable. However, at Waterloo,

Wellington ordered Captain Cavilie Mercer's battery of the Royal Horse Artillery into action against some guns which were supporting Prince Jerome's attack on Hougoumont, perhaps not so much with the intention of injuring the French artillery as harassing them so as to take some pressure off the beleaguered troops holding the farm. Standard defensive tactics, such as those used by Wellington at Waterloo, called for keeping one's guns relatively uncommitted until the enemy put in his infantry and cavalry. When these were within 1,000 to 1,200 meters range, one opened up, concentrating solid shot immediately in front of the advancing troops to attain maximum ricochet effect whilst showering them with shells. At about 300 or 400 meters one went over to direct fire using case shot for both guns and howitzers, double-loading the last round or two for good measure. Some idea of the potency of such can be seen by considering the capacity of a single unsupported battery of six 8- or 9-pounders and two howitzers to resist a frontal attack at 1,200 meters, which can be covered by cavalry in three to five minutes and by infantry in seven to 10 minutes, depending upon the nature of the ground and condition of the troops.

Effectiveness. Artillery was most effective in the defense, but even when used offensively it could be relatively devastating. Thus, Napoleon's reliance upon artillery to pound his enemy into senselessness before committing his own infantry and cavalry becomes quite understandable. Certainly the few times

Volume of Fire Discharged by an Artillery Battery Against Troops Attacking at 1,200 Meters				
Number of Rounds Delivered				
Attacker	Ball	Shell	Case	Total
Cavalry	24-36	3-5	12-24	39-65
Infantry	48-60	8-10	36-48	92-118

he suffered tactical defeats, such as at Waterloo, were primarily the result of committing the troops before the artillery had done its work, so that enemy troops and—more importantly—guns were relatively unshaken.

In general, a gun could be expected to inflict 60-120 casualties on the enemy for every hour it was in action, assuming relatively close combat. In this period about a third of all casualties were caused by the artillery, a significant proportion considering that the gunners rarely amounted to so many as 10 percent of an army.

Theoretically, heavier guns were more effective than lighter ones. A single round from an 18-pounder was equal in destructive force to two rounds from a 12-pounder, three from a 9-pounder, or 10 from a 6-pounder. However, lighter pieces could be fired more often, compensating to a considerable extent for their reduced effectiveness, and were much more maneuverable than heavier ones, so armies were inclined to stick with medium and light guns, dragging along a few heavy ones for siege work.

Notes for the table on the following page: The Dutch-Belgian artillery was composed largely of British and French pieces, while the

Artillery of the Waterloo Campaign								
Piece	Wt	Ln	Proj	Chg	Rng	RPM	Crew	Team
Heavy								
Fr 12-Pdr	2.0	2.3	5.9	1.9	1.8	1	15	12
Pr 12-Pdr	2.0	2.0	5.1	1.7	1.8	1	14	12
Medium								
Br 90Pdr	1.5	1.8	4.1	1.3	1.4	2	12	6-8
Light								
Fr 6-Pdr	1.2	1.8	3.0	1.0	1.35	2-3	10	6
Br 6-Pdr	0.75	1.5	2.7	0.7	1.1	2-3	8	6
Pr 6-Pdr	0.77	1.6	2.6	0.9	1.4	2-3	7	6
Howitzers								
Fr 6"	1.2	0.7	10.9	1.4	1.2	1	13	8
Br 5.5"	0.7	0.6	7.2	0.5	1.2	1	10	6
Pr 10-Pdr	1.4	1.1	10.0	1.3	1.8	1	12	8
7-Pdr	0.8	0.9	7.0	0.5	1.5	1	10	6
Rocket								
Br 12-Pdr	0.02	9.7	5.5	1.8	2.3	-	-	-

Hanoverians used British pieces. All figures have been rounded and some have been estimated. Some countries had slightly different versions of each piece for use as either field or horse artillery. Piece, is the standard identification for the weapon. Wt is weight in metric tons; note that the British had two models of 5.5" howitzer, that being given is the lighter one used by the horse artillery. Ln is length of the barrel, or chase, in meters. Proj, projectile weight in kilograms, with shot for guns and shell for howitzers: note that the "poundage" ratings of the pieces are not useful guides to projectile weight, due to differences in the definition of the pound from country to country: the old French pound was 8.3 percent heavier than the English one and the Prussian about 6.9 percent lighter. Chg, normal powder charge in kilograms required to fire the projectile its effective battlefield range: this figure could vary if greater or lesser ranges were desired. Rng, maximum range in kilometers: shot and shell were effective at between half and two-thirds the indicated distance, but case shot was no more than a third of it. RPM, sustainable number of rounds per minute.

Crew, the normal number of men required to serve the piece, its animals, and ammunition wagons: a Congreve rocket section had about 20 men. Team, the number of horses required to draw the complete equipage efficiently, including extra caissons, with the two figures for the British 9-pounder represent the difference between use as foot or horse artillery: a Congreve rocket had about 25 horses. Ammunition: 12-pounders and 9-pounders were usually provided with 200 rounds of solid shot ("ball") and 30 of case shot between immediate and reserve supplies. For lighter pieces the supply of solid shot could reach 300 rounds, with upwards of 50 rounds of case shot. Heavy howitzers usually were provided with about 150 rounds of explosive shell plus about 50 of case shot, while light howitzers had between 175 and 250 rounds of shell and only a dozen or so of case shot. The single section of Congreve rockets which was with Whinyates' 2nd Rocket Battery of the Royal Horse Artillery (Wellington having ordered the battery to convert to guns) appears have had a total of about 150 rockets, of which 52 were expended during at Waterloo and a score or so at Quatre Bras. Some idea of ammunition consumption may be gained by noting that British and K.G.L. batteries fired about 10,400 rounds during the roughly eight hours of Waterloo, an average of 129 rounds per piece.

All of Napoleon's guns were manned by regular personnel. About 130 of Blucher's artillery pieces were manned by landwehr.

Only about 100 of Wellington's guns were British-manned, with an additional 18 belonging to the King's German Legion.

The Artillery Allocations in the Waterloo Campaign			
Guns	French	Anglo-Allied	Prussian
18-Pdr		12	
12-Pdr	54		48
9-Pdr		70	
6-Pdr	210	81	174
Howitzers			
10-Pdr			16
7-Pdr			66
6"	18		
5.5"	82	40	
Totals	364	203	304

Of course, many variations existed in practice, particularly in the British Army.

Notes to the Battery Organization table on the following page:

A. The British Army called foot batteries brigades and horse batteries troops. Several foot batteries had four guns and two howitzers, rather than the normal five and one. Foot batteries had 9-pdrs, horse batteries usually 6-pdrs, though several had 9-pdrs, with eight-horse teams rather than six. One troop (Bull's) was composed entirely of howitzers, while one (Whinyates') had a section of rockets attached in lieu of the howitzer. The three 18-pdr batteries had four guns each, with no howitzers. The artillery organization of the King's German Legion was on the same pattern.

Artillery Battery Organization During the Waterloo Campaign						
Army	Type		Men	Pieces		Note
				Guns	How.	
Br/KGL	Foot		230	5	1	A
Br/KGL	Horse		231	5	1	A
Bruns			230	6	2	B
Du-Belg	Foot		248	6	2	C
Du-Belg	Horse		249	6	2	C
Fr	Foot:	Line	192	6	2	D
Fr	Foot:	Guard	234	6	2	D
Fr	Horse:	Line	192	6	2	D
Fr	Horse:	Guard	214	6	2	D
Han	Line		220	4	2	E
Pr	Foot		230	6	2	F
Pr	Horse		180	6	2	F

B. All batteries had 6-pdrs.

C. Figures include the paper strength of the associated train company, 123 men. Both foot and horse batteries had 6-pdrs, the latter having larger teams of horses. There was also a 12-pdr battery, not included in the army, at Braine-le-Comte, which was not engaged.

D. Figures include men in the train company associated with each battery, comprising 100 men in line batteries and 117 in the Garde, at least on paper. Most batteries had 6-pdrs, with some having 12-pdrs.

E. All batteries had 9-pdrs.

F. Several Prussian batteries were composed entirely of howitzers. Otherwise most had 6-pdrs. Manpower figures include approximately 30 ammunition supply personnel attached to each battery.

To gain some idea of the "typical" battery, consider that a British battery with six pieces had a limbered ammunition wagon for each piece, plus three spare limbered ammunition wagons, plus a special carriage to haul spare wheels, a portable smithy, a supply wagon and a baggage wagon. In the horse artillery guns had eight horses and limbered wagons six, while in the foot artillery guns had six horses and limbered wagons four. All other wagons had four horses. There were, in addition, in the horse artillery 48 horses so that some of the gunners could ride. Add to this horses for officers, the surgeon, and certain non-commissioned officers and technicians and the total number of horses came to between about 160 and 200. A limbered gun required about 30 meters of road space, so an entire battery of six pieces took up about 550 meters.

CHAPTER VII

Retreat and Pursuit

16-17 June

Each of the three principal commanders reacted differently to the outcome of the twin battles at Ligny and Quatre Bras. It was a critical moment in the campaign, in some ways the decisive moment, for the decisions made in the hours immediately following the fighting on 16 June irrevocably shaped the events to come.

For Wellington 16 June had by no means turned out unsatisfactorily. Despite a desperate battle initially against overwhelming odds, his men had held on to Quatre Bras. At nightfall they were still in position, stronger than at the onset of the battle, while Ney's French had fallen back roughly to the line from which they had started. Wellington's position was a good one, and he thought it could be held, given the balance of his army. Through the night the Anglo-Allied forces rested in their lines. Additional forces moved up, gradually raising Wellington's strength to about 45,000 men and nearly 100 guns, with upwards of 30,000 more troops still on the march. The only thing that troubled Wellington was the fate of the Prussians. Throughout the day he had heard the sounds of battle drifting over from Ligny. If the Prussians had held, his position was secure, if they had been crushed he was in grave danger.

Napoleon, in his most characteristic pose, wearing his threadbare old gray coat and his oversized bicorn hat.

The Prussians had taken a severe pounding on the 16th, a battering so serious that a scant decade earlier it might have sufficed to force a peace. Nearly half of Blucher's army had evaporated—dead, wounded or fled, with the old marshal himself among them. Blucher's chief of staff, Generalleutnant Augustus von Gneisenau had assumed command. Gneisenau mistrusted the British and believed that they had let their side down by not intervening at Ligny. It now rested upon his shoulders to decide what direction the army should take in retreat. His initial reaction was to fall back towards Liege, but he hesitated to do so in the absence of his commanding officer. As time passed, the pressure to take action became great. Corps commanders and staff officers requested instructions, time was wasting, a dangerous extravagance with Napoleon nearby. Meanwhile patrols brought in information. It be-

The Weather During the Waterloo Campaign

The theater of operations of the campaign of 1815 lies in an area characterized by rather hot, humid summers. It was particularly so for most of the campaign. Although there are no careful records of the prevailing weather conditions overall, a resident of Charleroi, at the southern edge of the area of operations, did have the presence of mind to make periodic checks of the weather for several days.

The high humidity resulted in reduced visibility for most of the three days and in unusually dark nights, despite a partial moon; only on the night of 18 to 19 did moonlight make night movement practical.

Weather During the Waterloo Campaign

Friday, 16 June

1200:	clear, warm, humid
1800:	rain, becoming heavy
1930:	thunderstorms

Saturday, 17 June

1200:	hot, humid
1500:	hot, thunderstorms
1800:	hot, showers
2030:	hot, raining

Sunday, 18 June

0800:	hot, rain ended, cloudy
1030:	cooler, clearing, very muddy
1100:	clear, with a mist rising from the wet ground
2100:	clear, moderate

came clear that it would be impossible to retreat directly on Liege, for elements of the French army, though inactive, were already athwart the shortest route, through Sombreffe and eastward to Namur and on to Liege along the Meuse. Sitting in the moonlight near the village of Tilly, Gneisenau consulted his subordinates. They examined a map. Various options were considered. A retirement in the direction of Louvain was obviously the best, for from there the army could easily make for Liege. Possible routes were discussed. Various suggestions were made and objections heard. Some officers found it difficult to locate certain towns on the map in the poor light. Then someone mentioned Wavre. Everyone could find it easily. And there in the moonlight Gneisenau gave the order: "Retreat on Tilly and Wavre." He ordered the remnants of the battered I and II Corps, perhaps 30,000 men in all, to retire on Tilly, while the relatively intact III Corps, with perhaps 20,000 men, was to fall back on Gembloux. Meanwhile he instructed Generalleutnant Friedrich Wilhelm von Bulow and his fresh IV Corps—30,000 men with 88 pieces of artillery—to link up with the III Corps at the earliest possible moment. These preliminaries completed, all the corps were to march on Wavre.

Gneisenau then rode off towards army headquarters, which had by now been established at Mellery. Unbeknownst to anyone, Mellery was the very village in which Blucher lay recuperating. The old marshal was soon located and Gneisenau rushed to his side in the dismal little house. Blucher was still somewhat dazed, but as game as ever. Calling for his favorite medicine, a concoction of gin, rhubarb and garlic, he drank it down. Refreshed, he sat down to discuss the situation with Gneisenau. The latter explained his plan to retreat on Liege by way of Wavre and Louvain. The marshal objected, for this meant abandoning Wellington. It was better to defeat Napoleon now, then to come back for another round later. Moreover, honor was involved. Blucher and Wellington had pledged mutual support in the event of a reverse. If the Briton had failed to intervene at Ligny it was because he was himself hard pressed. The army would not retreat. Nevertheless, Blucher approved Gneisenau's movement orders, for from Wavre the army could as easily move westward in order to support Wellington as northeastward in order to retreat.

An erstwhile hussar affectionately dubbed "Marshal For-wards" by his troops, Blucher may have been 73 and was probably deranged, but there was nothing wrong with his courage. Though defeated he was still game and had no intention of abandoning the field. Thus, amid the wounded and the dying, was made the single most impor-tant strategic decision of the campaign. Now all that mattered was time and the possibility that Napoleon would do something spectacular.

Napoleon's reaction to the events of the 16th was posi-tive. He was pleased for he believed that he had crushed the Prussians. Unfortunately, the rapidly gathering dark-ness—and perhaps a certain degree of lassitude—pre-vented him from organizing an immediate pursuit of the Prussians, but he did commit the *I* and *II Cavalry Corps* to reconnoitering their probable line of retreat, with the former scouting towards Namur and the latter towards Gembloux, while a small force was dispatched to Tilly to see if the enemy had taken that route to the rear.

As dusk turned into night the French cavalry pressed forward rather leisurely, several times running into groups of Prussians. No serious skirmishes occurred, and though many stragglers were encountered, few organized units were detected and the patrols soon returned. This evidence confirmed Napoleon's belief that the Prussians were beaten and in full retreat. He laid his plans for the next day. Grouchy would be left with about 33,000 men and instruc-tions to keep pressing the Prussians back but to maintain his freedom of movement. One division would remain at St. Amand in order to police the battlefield. The balance of the right wing and the reserve he would take with him in the morning to support the left wing at Quatre Bras, where he believed Ney to be in possession. Everything seemed to be going according to the plan to operate with two wings, shifting the reserve between them in order to confront first one and then the other of the enemy armies. Having dealt Blucher a decisive blow, he was now to do likewise to

Wellington, while Grouchy harried the defeated Prussians off the field. Unfortunately, Napoleon's assessment of the situation was seriously flawed and suffered not a little from overconfidence on his part. So careless was he that he failed to dispatch aides to ascertain the true state of affairs on Ney's front and left no instructions for Grouchy to conduct any reconnaissance during the night. Thus, when he went to bed at about 2300, he had made his own plans for the morrow, but had made no arrangements to ascertain the situation which would confront him.

The armies passed the night of 16-17 June partially on the march and partially asleep. Aside from a few leisurely patrols, Napoleon's men rested in bivouac wherever they were. Those of Wellington's troops who were already at Quatre Bras snatched what rest they could among the houses and the farm buildings, while those on the march fell out alongside the roads. The Prussians marched for several hours, and then camped. Of the three commanders, Wellington alone was active through most of the night. He initially believed that the Prussians had repulsed the French. His view began to change sometime around 2200, as he reached his quarters at an inn in Genappe, some five kilometers north of Quatre Bras. There he encountered a young captain, the brother of Henry Hardinge, who at that moment lay in the same house in Mellery that sheltered Blucher. Young Hardinge had come looking for a surgeon to take back to his brother, with whom he had been serving as a liaison officer. When questioned, the young man said that he could not be certain, but believed that the Prussians had been defeated, and in any case had certainly "suffered severely." This news does not seem to have shaken Wellington's view on the outcome of the day's fighting, but, ever cautious, he ordered an aide, Colonel Alexander Gordon, to conduct a reconnaissance. Gordon was back by midnight to report that he could find no Prussians anywhere but that there were French videttes near Sombreffe. Wellington ordered his more advanced outposts pulled back. Then, confident that nothing could be done before morning, he went to sleep.

Wellington rose at about 0300 on 17 June, roughly an hour before dawn. He immediately dispatched Gordon to Ligny and soon after rode off to Quatre Bras, which he reached at about 0600. He patiently awaited Gordon's return, sitting in a little hut among the Highlanders of the 92nd Regiment. It was chilly and after a few minutes he said, "Ninety-second, I will be obliged to you for a little fire." The sturdy Scots had one going in a few minutes and Wellington thanked them with some enthusiasm. He passed the time conferring with various aides and staff officers. He wondered aloud as to why he had not yet heard from Blucher. If the old man was ready to try and settle matters with Napoleon, so was he and this would be a good day to do so. It was not until 0730 that Wellington learned of the outcome of Ligny.

Gordon rode up, his horse heavily lathered. He whispered his news into Wellington's ear. The Duke gave not a sign of disappointment. He issued some orders to Gordon and turned to an aide saying, "Old Blucher has had a damned good licking and gone back to Wavre, 18 miles. As he has gone back, we must go too." He paused, perhaps thinking of the political implications of a retreat, and then added, "I suppose in England they will say we have been licked. I can't help it; as they are gone back, we must go too." Within minutes he began issuing orders to prepare for a retreat. The Prussian liaison officer, Baron von Muffling, was sent for. Then he closeted himself with his staff to work out the details. Maps were produced. There were difficulties in locating Wavre, for everyone looked to find it fairly close to Ligny. Muffling came up, confirming the worst. "But it is much further," he exclaimed, in French, the enemy tongue but the only one most of the British and Prussian officers had in common. Wellington gave him a look suggesting that the Prussians had not kept him informed. There was a tense moment. Then Muffling

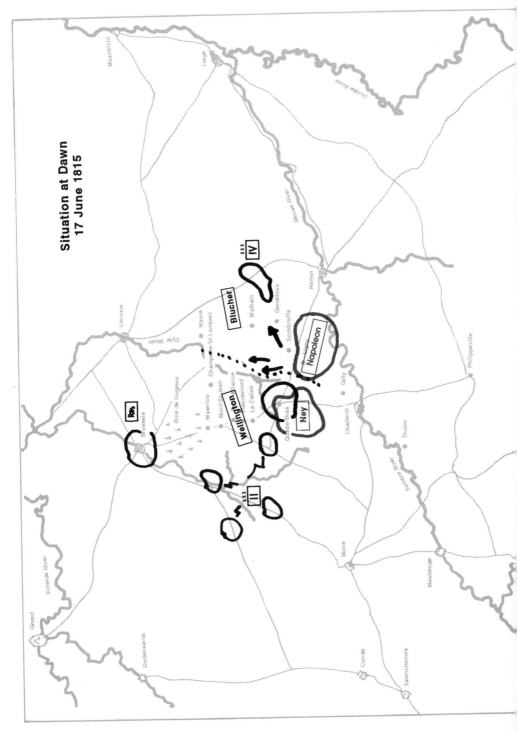

Situation at Dawn
17 June 1815

smoothed the matter over by suggesting that the courier had perhaps gone astray, though in fact the Duke was right, for Gneisenau had failed to inform his ally of the Prussian defeat. Nevertheless, the tension broke. It was agreed that the Allies still had the wherewithal to face Napoleon. The Prussian army was concentrating on Wavre, which was only some 11 kilometers east of the Brussels road, Wellington's own line of retreat. Muffling pointed out that the IV Corps, the strongest in the Prussian Army with over 30,000 men and 88 guns, had not been engaged at Ligny and was even now marching up to join the balance of the army, which, though battered, had gotten completely away from the French. It was agreed, then, that Wellington would retire about a dozen kilometers, to Mont-St. Jean, the point on the Brussels road closest to Wavre. Whether by design or coincidence, Mont-St. Jean was atop the very ridge line which, so many hours before, Wellington had indicated to the Duke of Richmond with his thumbnail, saying "I must fight him *here.*"

By this time Blucher was also astir, though somewhat hung over from repeated douses of his favorite medicine. He dispatched a courier to Wellington, informing him of his plans. Then he spoke with the wounded Hardinge, embracing him and calling him "Dear friend," all the while apologizing for his alcoholic aroma, "I'm a bit stinky." Then, bathing his bruises in brandy, he took a generous belt of hard liquor and rode off to rejoin his army. Advanced elements of the Prussian I Corps had reached Wavre. The II Corps was on the road again after passing the night near Tilly. The balance of I Corps and all of III Corps were resting near Gembloux, which they had reached at about 0600, after marching from Sombreffe at midnight. Meanwhile the unscathed IV Corps was getting ready to move out from its bivouac a few kilometers east of Gembloux, which it had reached at about midnight. Blucher still had about 80,000 troops at hand or nearby, almost 40 percent of them fresh men.

Wellington's staff conference broke at about 0800. As aides conveyed detailed orders for a retreat to the army, the Duke came out of the hut and began pacing back and forth in front of it, his left hand behind his back and a switch in his right to which he occasionally gave an absent minded bite. Shortly before 0900 Muffling joined him and the two sat on the grass. At about 0900 a courier arrived with Wellington's first direct communique from Blucher since their conference on the previous day. The message confirmed that the Prussians had fallen back, detailed their arrangements and inquired as to Wellington's intentions. Wellington's response was brief, but to the point. He intended to retreat on Mont-St. Jean and there to make a stand if Blucher would support him with two corps, or "even with one corps only."

The Allied retreat began at 1000. Aside from the wounded, who had been streaming north all through the night, the first man to go was the quartermaster general, Colonel Sir William H. DeLancey. A seasoned veteran, and an expatriate New York Tory, DeLancey's task was to mark out the positions which the troops would occupy as they came up to the new lines. Most of the officers, and virtually all of the troops, were unaware of the strategic situation and many objected to retiring from a victory. They grumbled, none so loudly as Thomas Picton, denouncing the idiocy of the Waterloo position while secretly nursing two broken ribs, but they marched. Wellington was careful not to alert the French of his activities. The front line was gradually thinned as division after division marched north. The cavalry, which had ridden up during the night, was deployed to cover the retreat with a strong contingent of artillery and a detachment of rocket troops. Several times during the retreat Wellington was seen to ride up to the front and, using his telescope, survey the roads to Frasnes and Namur, along which the French would have to advance. There was nothing to be seen, and he several times wondered if the French were not also retreating.

The French, concentrated in two great masses about Frasnes and Ligny, were by no means retreating. But neither were they advancing. Indeed, they were resting and continued to do so. They were permitted to do this by their Emperor, who was himself lethargic and inactive for much of the morning. He had passed the night at Fleurus, getting to bed at about 2300. He had stirred at about 0400—about dawn—and belatedly dispatched elements of Pajol's *I Cavalry Corps* to find out what the Prussians were doing. He had then gone back to sleep, rising at about 0600. He was having a leisurely breakfast at about 0700 when one of Pajol's officers rode up to inform him that a large body of Prussians had been observed moving towards Namur. This confirmed Napoleon's belief that Blucher was retreating. Shortly after this one of the imperial aides rode up from Ney's headquarters with the disturbing news that Quatre Bras was still in enemy hands. This was an unexpected and annoying bit of news but by no means devastating. After all, Ney still had a considerable force on hand, and the reserve was now available for use at Quatre Bras. Moreover, it seemed unreasonable that Wellington would attempt to continue to hold the place in view of the Prussian disaster. Napoleon dictated a confusing message to Ney, which gained nothing from passing through Soult's hands: "The Emperor is going to the mill of Brye, where the highway leading from Namur to Quatre Bras passes. This makes it impossible that the English army should act in front of you. In such an eventuality the Emperor would march directly upon it by the Quatre Bras road, while you would attack it from the front, and their army would be destroyed in an instant....His Majesty's wishes are that you should take up your position at Quatre Bras; should this prove impossible, report at once all details and the Emperor will act as I have told you. If, on the contrary, there is only a rear guard, attack it and seize the position. It is necessary to end this operation today...." This done, Napoleon completed his repast.

Around 0900 Napoleon rode off to visit the Ligny battlefield. He was in a good mood, and issued careful instructions for the care of the wounded. Then he visited with the troops for a while and spoke with Grouchy about trivial matters such as the impact the news of the victory over the Prussians would have in Paris. He made some remarks about the nature of war and peace. At one point he intervened to force a Belgian peasant to aid a wounded Prussian officer. This euphoric mood passed at about 1100, when he suddenly awoke to the demands of war. Turning to Grouchy, he told him to look after the Prussians. When the latter asked for orders, the Emperor said, "I will give orders when I judge it to be convenient," apparently intending to imply that Grouchy should use his judgment to act in support of the overall plan of operations. Soon after he rode off to Quatre Bras, where he would deal with the "English" while Grouchy took care of the defeated Prussians.

Napoleon reached Marbais, on the Ligny-Quatre Bras road, shortly after 1300. As he rode from Ligny he had become increasingly concerned about the lack of gunfire from Ney's front. And indeed, aside from some routine patrols, Ney's forces had been inactive all day. At Marbais, Napoleon found the troops sitting along the sides of the road, leisurely having their lunch, with Ney nowhere about. Almost as soon as he arrived a troop of French hussars appeared, with some English cavalry in pursuit, the two patrols having tangled briefly and the French having given way. He issued orders for an immediate advance, while dispatching a regiment of hussars to Frasnes to locate Ney. A woman camp follower of Wellington's army was brought in and questioned. Her information was stunning: Quatre Bras was virtually empty of enemy troops; Wellington had flown. An hour earlier it might have been possible to attain some major success against Wellington's rear guard, but now there was little that could be done. Ney came up with d'Erlon in tow. Pointedly

Henry William Paget

Henry William Paget, Marquis of Anglesey, Earl of Uxbridge of the Second Creation, lieutenant general (1768-1854) was of noble ancestry. He entered the British Army through purchase in 1793 and served in Flanders and Holland. Rising rapidly, by 1802 he was a major general commanding a cavalry brigade. He served under Sir John Moore during the latter's disastrous campaign in Spain in 1808. Soon after his return to England he eloped with the wife of Sir Arthur Wellesley's brother. Although this does not seem to have injured his personal relations with Wellesley, the ensuing scandal did little to enhance his career, and he did not serve again in a serious capacity until he was appointed to command Wellington's Cavalry Corps in 1815.

Uxbridge did well during the Waterloo campaign, losing a leg while at Wellington's side at the very moment of victory. He thereafter held a variety of important civil and military posts, including lord lieutenant of Ireland, in which capacity he helped convince the reluctant Wellington, by then prime minister, to support Catholic Emancipation, and he was subsequently master general of ordnance.

turning his back on Ney, the Emperor addressed d'Erlon, scolding him mildly for his peregrinations of the previous day and then saying, "France is lost! Go, my dear general, place yourself at the head of the cavalry and pursue their rear guard vigorously." But it was too late; not until 1400 was d'Erlon able to advance, making for Genappe.

While Napoleon had been frittering away the hours, Wellington's troops had been marching off. The Duke himself was among the last to go. He spent much of the morning sitting on the grass as his troops marched past him, but for a time snatched a few minutes sleep lying on his cloak, with a newspaper over his face. At about 1400, even as Napoleon finally got a pursuit going, the last of Wellington's infantry, the Guards Division, tramped off. As they marched, flashes of light could be seen glimmering in the distance on the road south. Wellington turned to

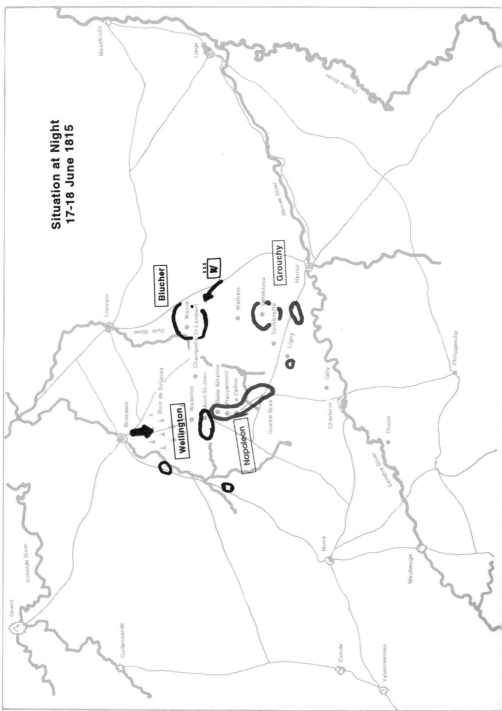

Situation at Night
17-18 June 1815

Lieutenant General Henry Paget, the Earl of Uxbridge, of the Cavalry Corps, commanding the rear guard, saying, "No use waiting. The sooner you get away the better. No time to be lost." Major General Sir Hussey Vivian, commanding the 6th Cavalry Brigade, handed Wellington a telescope. Far off to the south he could just make out the leading elements of the French cavalry, sunlight gleaming off their lanceheads. The Duke rode off. In a few minutes more and more of Napoleon's army came into view. Meanwhile, overhead the light began to fade as an enormous thundercloud engulfed the sun. The French drew nearer. The artillery of the British rear guard opened fire; under Napoleon's personal direction a battery of the *Imperial Guard* replied. The thunderous sounds of cannon fire were followed within seconds by an even greater blast as a violent thunderstorm burst upon the armies.

Even as the rains came down—reported by some as the heaviest they had ever seen—the Allied rear guard pulled out. The artillery fired a last round, limbered up and were away. The hussars of Vivian's 6th Cavalry Brigade were the last to go. The French came on as the troopers spurred their horses along the narrow paved highway, movement in the fields having almost instantly become impossible due to the rain. The narrow streets of Genappe slowed the retirement, permitting some of the French lancers to come to blows with some of the hussars. Just beyond the town Uxbridge had posted two batteries and several regiments. Now, as the French tangled with the hussars, he personally led the Life Guards in a charge. There was a bloody little mounted skirmish in the streets, then the lancers fell back, leaving their colonel dead. The British cavalrymen raced northwards from the town as their artillery got into action. Major Edward Whinyates' rocket detachment fired off scores of Congreve rockets, demolishing a French gun in the process. The French infantry began to come up, their movement hindered as much by the rains as by the Allied rear guard. Unable to advance on the road for fear of the

Waterloo Trivia

The French word *"bistro"* for cafe derives from the Russian *"Bystro,"* meaning "Quickly!" which was shouted at terrified French waiters by Russian troops participating in the Allied occupation of Paris after Waterloo.

The French government refused to take a formal part in the ceremonies marking the 150th anniversary of the battle of Waterloo (18 June 1965).

A 175th anniversary recreation of the battle of Waterloo (15-18 June 1990) involved some 3,000 re-enactors, including some 300 cavalrymen, from France, Britain, Canada, the U.S., Belgium, Italy, Switzerland, Czechoslovakia, both Germanys and the U.S.S.R, along with some 50,000 spectators.

There were two officers named Colquhoun Grant in Wellington's army during the Waterloo campaign: Lieutenant Colonel Colquhoun Grant, head of Welling-ton's intelligence service, and Major General Sir Colquhoun Grant, K.C.B., who commanded the 5th Cavalry Brigade. Both were veterans of the Peninsular campaign, during which the British distinguished between the two by referring to the first as "Grant of the Staff" and the second as "Grant of the Hussars." Eventually the nicknames used by the Spanish were adopted: since "Grant of the Staff" had a friendly disposition and was always doing good deeds (such as rescuing ladies in distress), he was known as "The Good Grant" in contrast to the cavalryman called "The Bad Grant," so known for his terrible temper.

After Waterloo the British 1st Guards were named the Grenadier Guards and permitted to wear bearskin caps, taken from the senior regiments of Napoleon's *Garde Imperial*, albeit the British 1st Guards never actually engaged the French *1st Grenadiers de la Garde* at the bat-

---

British artillery, they attempted to advance through the fields alongside it, only to become bogged down in what was rapidly becoming a quagmire. Despite this, they pressed on. By 1800 it was over. Although the rains had let up, the French could make little progress. Firing continued for a while longer, but neither side took or inflicted serious casualties. Almost all of Wellington's men were by then ensconced in the Mont-St. Jean position. At about this same time, Napoleon, his threadbare old gray coat soaked

tle, although they did rout the *3rd Chasseurs.*

Wellington's Spanish aide Lieutenant General Miguel de Alava is the only man known to have been present at both of Britain's decisive victories over Napoleon, the naval battle of Trafalgar (21 October 1805), when he was an observer with the Franco-Spanish fleet, and Waterloo.

Wellington's Russian aide Lieutenant General Count Carlo Pozzo de Borgo was actually a Corsican from a family at feud with the Bonapartes since the Revolution, when the former continued to support an independent Corsica while the latter threw in with France (in the early 1870s his son would build a villa in Corsica from the rubble of Napoleon's Tuileries Palace).

Napoleon's favorite remedy for virtually all ills was to douse himself liberally with *eau de cologne.*

On the morning of 19 June some British officers discovered the body of a "strikingly beautiful" young woman in the uniform of a French cuirassier officer about 100 meters south of Wellington's famous elm tree at the juncture of the Ohain and Brussels roads; the number of women who may have taken part in the battle in male guise is unknown.

A very popular dinner item among the Allied troops on the night after the battle of Waterloo was fried steak, courtesy of Napoleon, whose cuirassiers' breastplates supplied the frying pans and whose mounts the steaks.

All British soldiers who participated in the battle of Waterloo were awarded a campaign medal, the first such ever granted by the British Army, and were also credited with two years of extra time in the service.

Upon learning that Napoleon had regained the throne of France, Britain immediately appropriated £1,000,000 in subsidies for her Allies and another £2,000,000 for her own armed forces.

through and his cocked hat hanging limply on his head, reached the little roadside inn of La Belle-Alliance, about a kilometer south of Wellington's position.

Looking northwards through the gloom, Napoleon espied a long, low ridge. Suspecting that it was there that Wellington intended to make his stand, he ordered a probe. Milhaud's *IV Cavalry Corps* trotted up the road while several batteries of artillery fired in support. Within seconds 60 Allied guns opened up in reply. The French immediately fell back. The little exchange left Napoleon quite pleased, for it confirmed that he had indeed run Wellington to earth. It affected Wellington quite differently, leaving him furious, for, anticipating just such a probe, he had forbade a return of fire, which revealed his position. But the day was at an end.

It had been a day of hard marching rather than hard fighting. Both Blucher and Wellington had put their time to good use, but Napoleon had frittered away most of his, with possible fatal consequences for the morrow. Actual casualties were surprisingly small. The Anglo-Allied forces had lost perhaps a hundred men from all causes, the French a handful more. The Prussians had lost no one to enemy action, though perhaps as many as 10,000 men had deserted the colors. Nevertheless, like the French and their allies, they were ready for a renewal of the fighting.

CHAPTER VIII

With Marshal Grouchy

17-19 June

Napoleon entrusted Marshal Emmanuel Grouchy with the task of harrying the defeated Prussians from the field, to keep them from reinforcing Wellington's allied forces in the direction of Brussels. To this end he gave Grouchy the *III Corps*, *IV Corps*, *I Cavalry Corps* and *II Cavalry Corps*, some 33,000 troops, good men all, well seasoned and well commanded. But Napoleon had been rather casual in his final instructions to Grouchy, not really issuing any until about 1100 on 17 June, shortly before riding off to join the main body of the army before Quatre Bras. Grouchy, a newly minted marshal who had done well in subordinate commands in previous campaigns and performed creditably during the battle of Ligny the previous day, had already dispatched cavalry patrols seeking to locate the defeated foe.

Bulow's troops made contact with Thielmann's early on 17 June. Bulow immediately assumed command of III Corps and, on his own initiative, marched both formations towards Wavre. At 1020 Blucher, who had by then recovered his senses sufficiently to resume command of the army, confirmed Bulow's decision. It was perhaps one of the most critical decisions of the campaign, for by falling back on Wavre Blucher was abandoning his easiest line of

Emmanuel Grouchy

Emmanuel Grouchy, Marquis of Grouchy and Marshal of the Empire (1766-1847) was a member of the old nobility. Joining the Royal Army early, enrolling in the Strasbourg artillery school in 1780, he became a cavalry captain in 1784 and in 1786 an officer in the *Gardes Ecossais*, an element of the Royal Guard. Retired in 1787, Grouchy embraced the Revolution when it came two years later. He took part in the brutal suppression of a Royalist insurrection in the Vendee, helped crush an emigre landing at Quiberon Bay, took part in an abortive invasion of Ireland and eventually passed once more into the cavalry. Although he had some difficulties as a nobleman during the Terror, he returned to duty soon afterwards, rising to brigade and division command. He thereafter served with some distinction on numerous fields in command of both infantry and cavalry, to which arm he decisively returned in 1806. Sent to Spain in 1808, Grouchy was responsible for the brutal suppression of the Madrid insurrection of 2 May, which marked the onset of the "Spanish Ulcer" which would prove the graveyard of so many French soldiers over the next six years.

Grouchy commanded a cavalry corps during the invasion of Russia and led the *bataillon sacré*, a cavalry detachment composed entirely of of-

retreat, cutting himself off from his base at Liege and the most direct route back into Prussia. He was intent to render unto Wellington whatever aid he could. Of course, in order to do so he would have to avoid becoming enmeshed with the French right wing, a matter in which fate took a hand.

A combination of tired horses, poor staff work and bad luck caused Grouchy's cavalry patrols to lose contact with the Prussians early on 17 June. Heavy rains through much of the day frustrated his efforts to reestablish contact. By 1900 he gave up and bedded his troops down around Gembloux. In effect, the powerful right wing of the French army had frittered away an entire day, advancing barely eight kilometers in the 24 hours since the end of the fighting around Ligny. Grouchy immediately dispatched a message to Napoleon, informing him that the Prussians

ficers, during the retreat at the end of which his health was so precarious that he did not return to duty until 1814, when he commanded the reserve cavalry with some distinction. Although he served the Bourbons after Napoleon's first abdication, Grouchy immediately rejoined the Emperor upon his return from Elba. Napoleon made him a marshal and entrusted him with command of the right wing of the *Armee du Nord* during the Waterloo campaign despite the fact that he had never commanded a corps, with disastrous results.

Grouchy's performance during the campaign was very uneven. Personally brave, by one count he had been wounded 23 times during the wars, he was not an outstanding general. He bungled the pursuit on the 17th and showed a decided lack of initiative on the 18th, but did rather well thereafter, just a day too late. A man of considerable ability, he had been thrust into a situation for which he appears to have lacked confidence.

After Napoleon's second abdication, Grouchy fled to the United States, not returning to France until 1819. Readmitted to the army, albeit at a reduced rank, he rose again to marshal in 1831, with the installation of the liberal monarchy of Louis Philippe. He died in retirement.

Emmanuel, Marquis de Grouchy. A member of the old royal aristocracy who had sided with the Republic, Grouchy had never commanded more than a division when Napoleon jumped him to marshal. The Emperor entrusted him with half the army on a critical independent mission during the Hundred Days.

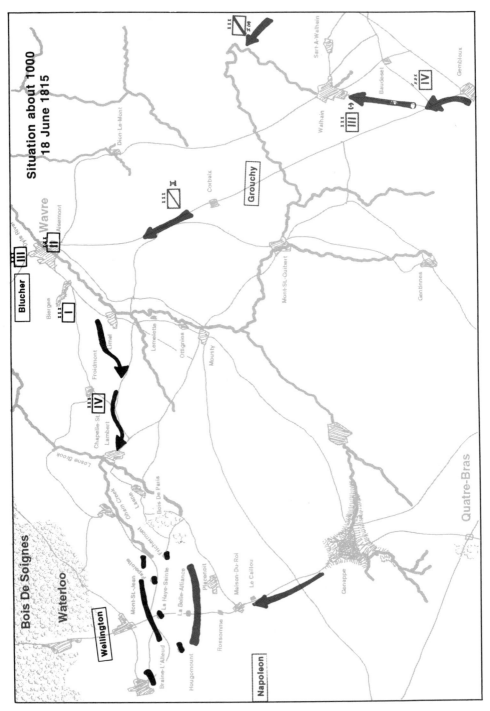

Situation about 1000
18 June 1815

Grouchy

Blucher

Wavre

Wellington

Bois De Soignes

Waterloo

Napoleon

Quatre-Bras

had broken into two columns, one falling back on Wavre and the other making for Liege. This was totally incorrect. The troops observed on the road to Liege comprised a mass of stragglers, perhaps 10,000 men in all. The main body of the Prussian Army, upwards of 50,000 strong, had taken the road to Wavre, while Bulow's 30,000 men were also on the march, moving up undetected from the north-west.

The bulk of the Prussian Army reached Wavre during the night of 17-18 June. Early on the morning of the 18th Blucher issued orders for the army to march to Wellington's assistance in the vicinity of Mont-St. Jean. As the army was in a considerable muddle, and I and II Corps particularly so, organizing the movement was unusually complicated and a massive traffic jam developed. Nevertheless, Bulow's IV Corps got off to a good start as the other corps began to sort themselves out.

Grouchy's troops were up early on 18 June. But they idled away precious hours. Grouchy issued his orders of the day late and it was not until 0730 that the troops began to move out, by which time Bulow's men had been long on the march. It is unclear as to whether Napoleon issued Grouchy any instructions on the morning of 18 June. By some accounts he did do so, instructing Grouchy to fall upon Wellington's flank. If this was the case, no documentation survives. Nevertheless, any analysis of Napoleon's basic strategy must inevitably lead to the assumption that the mission of the right wing at this stage in the campaign was to keep between the main body and the Prussians. By 0730 on 18 June Grouchy had already failed in his mission, for by then the Prussians were already closer to Napoleon than was Grouchy.

With II Cavalry Corps covering his front and I Cavalry Corps on his left, attempting to link up with Napoleon and the main body, Grouchy advanced on Wavre. Although Exelmans' troopers advanced aggressively, the rest of Grouchy's forces were somewhat lethargic in their move-

Maurice Etienne Gerard

Maurice Etienne Gerard, count and general of division (1773-1852), was the son of a royal huntsman. He entered military service as a private soldier in 1791 and served in all of the early campaigns of the revolutionary wars, meanwhile securing a commission and attaching himself to the staff of Jean-Baptiste Bernadotte, one of the most distinguished of the Republican commanders. By 1806 Gerard was a general of brigade, having served in Switzerland and at Austerlitz. He subsequently served in Denmark, was made a baron, fought at Wagram, Fuentes de Oñoro, Borodino and Maloyaroslavetz, meanwhile being promoted to general of division. He further distinguished himself during the retreat from Russia and in the campaigns of 1813 and 1814.

Gerard entered the service of the Bourbons upon Napoleon's first abdication but rallied to the Emperor upon his return from Elba, for which he was made a count. He commanded the *IV Corps* during the Waterloo campaign, serving with distinction at Ligny. Among the officers who urged Grouchy to "march to the sound of the guns" on the morning of 18 June, Gerard was wounded at Wavre that same afternoon. He fled into exile upon Napoleon's second abdication, not returning until 1817, whereupon he entered politics as a liberal. He helped rally the *National Guard* to the Revolution of 1830 and King Louis Philippe made him minister of war and a marshal. In 1832 Gerard commanded the French army which captured Antwerp during the war for Belgian independence. He thereafter served in various high military and civil posts and ended his days as a senator under Napoleon III.

Noted for his private charities, Gerard was one of the more active of Napoleon's corps commanders in 1815. An able officer, he had the misfortune to serve under a commander less capable than himself.

---

ments. At about 0930 elements of *II Cavalry Corps* ran into cavalry rear guards from the Prussian II Corps just south of Wavre. An inconclusive skirmish developed which lasted for about an hour. Casualties were few on both sides. However, the French did manage to take a few prisoners. When questioned, these men revealed that Blucher had ordered his army to march to the support of Wellington. Instantly aware of the consequences of this decision, Exelmans immediately passed the information back to Grouchy. At the very same time, Grouchy was just reaching Walhain, with *III Corps* and *IV Corps* following close behind. Sometime around 1100 Grouchy settled down for a leisurely lunch with his staff. By all accounts a rather sumptuous repast, the meal was disturbed at about 1130 by the sound of cannon fire coming from the north-west, roughly the direction of Mont-St. Jean, a dozen or so miles away.

The distant cannonade prompted General de Division Maurice Etienne Gerard, the commander of *IV Corps*, to urge Grouchy to march immediately to the sound of the guns, for they surely indicated that Napoleon was engaged in a major battle. Several other officers strongly supported this view. Had he followed this suggestion, Grouchy's leading elements would have reached Napoleon's right flank before Mont-St. Jean at about 1900. Grouchy demurred, observing that his instructions were to pursue the Prussians. An ugly scene developed, but Grouchy asserted his authority as a Marshal and resumed his lunch. As the leisurely meal went on, the Prussian Army put still more distance between itself and Grouchy. It was at 1230 that Exelmans' courier—dispatched at about 1030—finally reached Grouchy, having taken two hours to cover about six miles. Word that the Prussians were marching against Napoleon put an immediate end to Grouchy's leisurely repast.

Grouchy ordered his troops across the Dyle River. *III Corps* was to cross at Limale with *I Cavalry Corps*, while *IV Corps* was to advance to Wavre screened by *II Cavalry Corps*. Along the Dyle, Blucher had posted his III Corps under the Freiherr von Thielmann, whose chief of staff was one Carl von Clausewitz, later the author of the famous *On War*. Thielmann's corps, which numbered but 17,000 men, had been rather badly battered at Ligny and suffered from considerable straggling during the retreat. Moreover, one of its brigades had already marched off westward, though

Karl von Clausewitz

Karl von Clausewitz, colonel (1780-1831), was the son of a minor Prussian officer of dubious nobility. He enlisted as an officer-cadet at the age of 12 and went to war for the first time soon afterwards, being present at Valmy (1792), a defeat which caused Prussia to avoid entanglements with France for more than a dozen years. Clausewitz rose slowly through the ranks during the years of peace. At the time of the Prussian disaster at Jena-Auerstadt in 1806 he was a staff captain. Clausewitz greatly distinguished himself during the retreat, taking command of his battalion—the first and only time in his career that he would command troops—and leading it for nearly two weeks before being forced to surrender. His performance brought him to the attention of the Scharnhorst-Gneisenau ring, and he was soon brought into the work of reforming and reorganizing the Prussian Army.

Rather than serve France in 1812, when Napoleon demanded a Prussian contingent for the invasion of Russia, Clausewitz resigned from the service to enter that of Russia, becoming a general staff officer. Clausewitz helped negotiate the Convention of Tauroggen, which brought Napoleon's Prussian contingent over to Russia's side during the retreat from Moscow. Despite his excellent service, it took the personal intervention of the Tsar to get the King of Prussia to readmit Clausewitz—and several other former Prussian officers—to the Royal Army. Clausewitz performed staff duties during the campaigns of 1813-1814, and in 1815, as chief of staff of the Prussian III Corps, did a tremendous job of helping to pin Grouchy's attention at Wavre and Limale at the time that he was needed at Waterloo.

After the wars, Clausewitz remained on active duty, becoming a generalmajor and superintendent of the Kriegsakademie, during which he reformed the education of staff officers and found the time to indulge his taste for letters. Recalled to active duty as Gneisenau's chief of staff during the Polish Revolution of 1830-1831, Clausewitz perished with his commanding officer in the cholera pandemic.

As a soldier, Clausewitz' record was honorable but hardly impressive. But his experiences helped in the creation of his masterwork, *On War*.

---

it had been replaced by a stray brigade from I Corps, which Thielmann posted at Limale. Nevertheless, the Dyle position was a good one, with the troops posted on the high ground of the left bank, and with outposts scattered on the

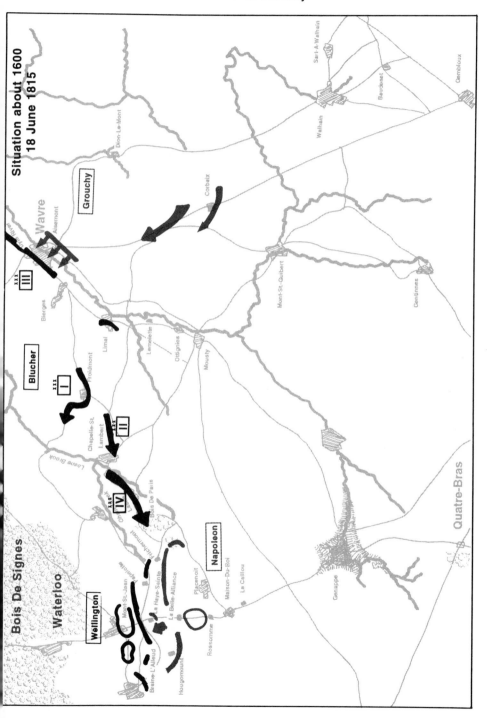

south side of the river. Serious fighting broke out in front of Wavre at about 1630.

When the fighting erupted along the Dyle, the main body of the Prussian Army, Bulow's IV Corps, was already nearly a dozen miles to the west, within about six kilometers of Mont-St. Jean. The sounds of artillery fire coming from Wavre, and soon afterwards from Limale as well, prompted several of Blucher's staff officers to attempt to convince him to turn the army about and march to the support of their embattled comrades. Blucher resisted the temptation, recognizing, unlike Grouchy, what his primary mission was: to march to the support of Wellington. Meanwhile, even as the Prussian main body marched somewhat reluctantly westward, the fighting along the Dyle grew heavier.

The French attack cleared the Prussian outposts from south of the Dyle River rather rapidly. However, as the French advanced closer to the Dyle they came under heavy and effective fire from the Prussian forces posted along the heights opposite. By 1700 fighting was fairly general along the length of the Dyle. Through a confusion in orders *IV Corps* arrived in front of Wavre, where it prepared to join fighting in support of *III Corps* and *II Cavalry Corps*. This left *I Cavalry Corps* unsupported against the Prussian brigade at Limale, with the result that, although supported by the *6th Cavalry Division* from *IV Corps* and the *21st Division* from *VI Corps*, it could make little headway. This situation might have become critical but for the fact that at 1700 Grouchy received new instructions. Napoleon ordered Grouchy to march immediately to his support in front of Waterloo. The marshal reacted with characteristic indecisiveness. He made one more attempt to drive the Prussians from Wavre. This failing, he instructed *III Corps* and *II Cavalry Corps* to keep up the pressure there, and marched off for Limale with *IV Corps*. Grouchy arrived at Limale just as *I Cavalry Corps* succeeded in clearing the village. The Prussians, soon reinforced by elements of their

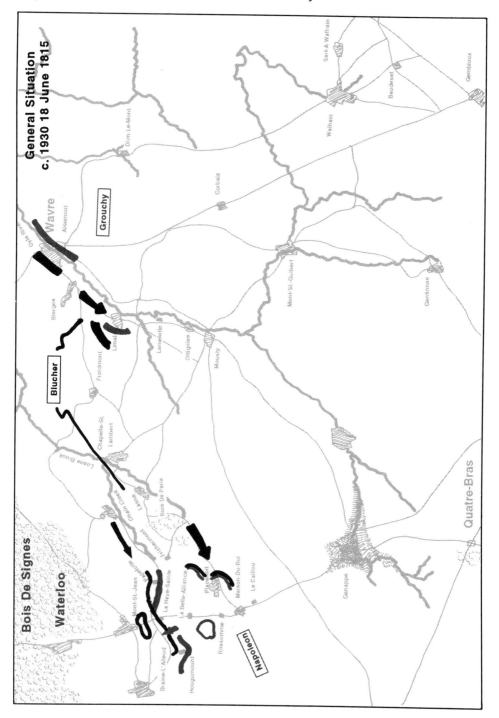

General Situation
c. 1930 18 June 1815

Wavre

Grouchy

Blucher

Napoleon

Waterloo

Bois De Signes

Quatre-Bras

III Corps, itself pulling westward, made a determined attempt to retake the place, but were repulsed by leading elements of *IV Corps*. The French troops then pressed on and secured a ridge some hundreds of meters west of the village at about 2300. Soon after, the fighting died down all along the Dyle.

Grouchy spent part of the night of 17-18 June profitably getting his troops into position to resume the fighting the next morning. As a result, the Prussians, who had spent much of the night further thinning out their lines and marching westward, were soundly thrashed at both Limale and Wavre. Grouchy was resting his troops after having secured the Dyle crossings when he received his first word of Napoleon's activities before Waterloo at 1030.

Joachim Murat and the Italian Campaign of 1815

The collapse of the Napoleonic Empire in 1813-1814 resulted in the dissolution of virtually all of the satellite states which Napoleon had imposed on Europe. The sole exception was the Kingdom of Naples, ruled by his dashing, inept brother-in-law Joachim Murat. Spurred on by his wife, Caroline Bonaparte, Murat had entered into negotiations with Allies even as he led the Emperor's cavalry against them. Open treachery soon followed and as a consequence Murat was permitted to retain his throne. However, Murat's tenure was precarious. While the Neapolitans liked him, their opinions mattered little. Austria and Bourbon France were distinctly hostile. Indeed, early in 1815 the Bourbons were laying plans for an expedition to unseat him, and a sizeable Austrian army remained in Northern Italy. Murat began assembling his forces. But, as a result of Napoleon's return from Elba, the expected invasion never came. Thus, Napoleon's return to power had an immediate beneficial effect on Murat's chances of survival on the throne of Naples. With the danger from France gone, he had only Austria with which to cope. Though Austria was immensely powerful in comparison with Naples, Murat believed that the chances for victory were good. Moreover, on 29 March, almost as soon as he was ensconced in Paris once again, Napoleon wrote to his errant brother-in-law, admonishing him to keep the peace for as long as possible, but to be ready "if we are forced to take up arms again." Not wishing to appear a stooge of Napoleon, he brushed aside his wife's pleas that, for maximum effectiveness, he should coordinate his moves with those of the Emperor. He chose instead to act independently, making a bid for power as champion of Italian independence, believing that he would secure massive support from the restive people of Italy.

Murat had a fairly strong, well-trained field army of about 50,000 men with 56 cannon, backed up by a further 10,000 garrison troops and some 30,000 militia. A substantial proportion of the troops were veterans, as were virtually all of the officers, many of whom served in Napoleon's old Royal Italian Army. Austrian forces were of approximately equal strength, but a number of their troops were Napoleonic veterans, whole battalions of the Royal Italian Army having been bodily incorporated into the Austrian forces in 1814. This was a potential source of weakness which Murat intended to exploit.

Based on the reasonable assumption the enemy would pull his forces northwards in order to concentrate for a decisive action in Po Valley, Murat developed a rather simple plan of campaign. He would concentrate his forces in two corps. The *Main Body* would be on the Adriatic coast with 36,000 infantry, 3,000 cavalry, and 46 pieces of artillery, while the *Royal Guard* was to operate on the west coast with 5,800 infantry, 2,400 cavalry, and 16 pieces of artillery. Each body was to advance northwards, pushing the enemy before them. When the *Royal Guard* reached Florence, it was to proceed over the Apennines to join the *Main Body* at Bologna. Then, the united army, by then presumably swollen with many thousands of volunteers and defectors from the enemy's ranks, would advance into the Po Valley for a showdown. His plans set, Murat moved with commendable speed.

The Austrians, of course, were by no means unaware of Murat's plans. Baron Vicenz Friedrich Bianchi commanded about 55,000 men grouped in three corps. His I Corps (20,600 men, including 2,500 cavalry, with 24 guns)—commanded by Count Adam Albrecht von Neipperg, the lover of Napoleon's estranged wife Maria Louise—was concentrated at Venice, his II Corps (14,800 men with 18 guns) at Mantua, and his III Corps (20,500 men, including 2,500 cavalry, with 22 pieces of artillery) scattered in Tuscany and the minor duchies to the north of Rome. As Murat had foreseen, Bianchi planned to let the Neapolitans advance northwards while he concentrated his own forces for a major clash in the Po Valley.

By 19 March—even as Napoleon approached Paris—Murat's forces were in position on the frontiers of the Papal States. On 22 March the Neapolitan army marched northwards. There was little resistance, for Papal forces were virtually non-existent and Austrian ones were held well back. Both columns made excellent progress. At Rimini on 30 March, evoking the historic glories of Italy, Murat issued a stirring call for all Italians to help in the task of liberation and unification. The response was poor. No more than 350 men came forward, mostly former Napoleonic officers. Despite this, Murat pressed on. His army made excellent progress as it marched northwestward along the historic Via Aemilia. On 2 April he reached Bologna with the *Main Body*. There he discovered that the advance of the *Royal Guard* had been delayed, partially as a result of his instructions that it avoid passing directly through the city of Rome in order not to offend the Pope, and partially by some effective rear-guard work by local forces in the Grand Duchy of Tuscany. Rather than await the arrival of the *Royal Guard*, Murat resumed the advance. The first serious encounter with the Austrians took place on 4 April.

About 12,000 men of the Austrian II Corps held the line of the Panaro, a small tributary of the Po. Murat committed about 8,000 men. Murat's troops successfully crossed the stream in the face of enemy resistance. The Austrians fell back, uncovering Modena. A number of small actions over the next few days completely cleared the Austrians from the south side of the Po. Then, on 7 April, Murat attempted to force his way across the Po itself. He committed about 7,500 men to the effort and succeeded in gaining a bridgehead at Occhiobello. But the Austrians, who numbered about

8,000, counterattacked, driving his forces back across the river with severe losses. The next day about 8,000 Austrians crossed the Po, and, marching nearly 30 kilometers southward, made a night attack upon a detachment of some 2,000 men whom Murat had posted at Carpi. Aided by a well-prepared position, the Neapolitans held into the morning of 9 April before being forced back. The Austrians were now in a position to threaten Murat's deep flank. Murat hesitated, then, on 10 April, taking counsel of his fears, he decided that the game was up, that the enemy was too strong. He ordered a retreat.

The army fell back in good order, closely followed by the Austrians, who made little effort to interfere. The pace of the retreat was leisurely, so that by 15 April Murat's army had fallen back no more than 50 kilometers from the Po, and was standing on the banks of the Reno, a small river a bit to the southwest of Modena. Here Murat decided to attempt a stand. He posted about 15,000 men with 35 guns along the banks of the stream and a further 2,200 with two guns at the village of Spilimberto, covering an important river crossing on his left flank. The Austrians committed over 20,000 men but had only 28 pieces of artillery. Along the Reno the Neapolitans did well, repeatedly beating off attacks by the bulk of the Austrian forces, who finally gave up. But the situation at Spilimberto turned out differently. Murat's detachment was surprised and destroyed by a considerably smaller enemy force. With the river line

breached and his flank uncovered, Murat chose to fall back once again. Over the next five days he retired about 100 kilometers, abandoning Bologna. On 20 April he halted on favorable ground on the Ronco, a small stream about 40 kilometers northwest of Rimini, on the Adriatic coast.

The Austrians had followed Murat's retreat closely. Bianchi, who now had both his I and II Corps at hand, surveyed Murat's position on the Ronco and decided to forgo a general attack. Instead, he sent II Corps southward into the Apennines with instructions to march south and then east, in order to outflank the enemy. He then used his I Corps to screen Murat's position. Murat was apprised of the Austrian flank march in relatively short order. Over the next few days there were several small, but sharp actions between the two armies, actions in which the Neapolitans generally came off well. Nevertheless, concerned over the threat to his flank, Murat resumed the retreat on 23 April. Rimini was given up as the army fell back southward and re-entered the Papal States. Rearguard actions were by now almost daily affairs, with particularly severe ones occurring at Macerata-Feltria on 29 April and Senigallia on 30 April. In these engagements the Neapolitans generally did well. But none of these actions was sufficiently decisive as to relieve the pressure on Murat's army. The retreat continued. On 1 May Murat re-entered his kingdom at near Ancona, just 42 days after marching north, having advanced some 500 kilometers, and then retreated the way he had come. At Ancona Murat finally linked-up with his *Royal Guard*.

The *Royal Guard* had advanced cautiously in the face of some skillful rear-guard fighting by the Austrian III Corps. By the time Florence had been secured, Murat had already fallen back from Bologna. Virtually isolated, the commander of the *Royal Guard* had chosen to fall back, retreating over the Apennines towards the Adriatic coast. It had been a difficult march, but the *Royal Guard* was relatively intact and rested by 1 May, for the Austrian III Corps had not pursued, but rather had advanced southward along the west coast, intending to strike directly at Naples.

Murat's situation was by growing desperate. Casualties, detachments, and desertion had reduced his forces to but 30,000 men. Though Bianchi had no more than half this number in his I Corps, which was pursuing him down the coast, he had an equal number in his II Corps, which was somewhere to the west, in the Apennines, in a position to take the Neapolitan army in the flank or fall on its lines of communications. And even as Murat contemplated his situation it grew worse.

On 1 May the Austrian II Corps, under Bianchi's personal direction, arrived on the coast at Tolentino, some 25 miles in Murat's rear, with 12,000 infantry and 24 pieces of artillery. Murat was now trapped between two enemy forces. Not lacking in courage, Murat decided on a desperate gamble. Leaving two divisions and some cavalry—about 12,000 men—to entertain the Austrian I Corps, he marched south with the *Royal Guard* and his two other divisions, perhaps 18,000 men in all.

Tolentino was actually the first general action of the entire campaign, for Bianchi had skillfully avoided committing his forces to a decisive action until he had the upper hand. At Tolentino he assumed a strong position on Monte Milone. Murat's leading elements came up late on 2 May and he immediately threw them into action. Attacking with considerable skill and elan they cleared the Austrians out of their position, though at considerable cost, a number of generals falling in the process. The Austrians fell back to a secondary position. Morale soared, not least of all that of Murat himself, for he saw the possibility of crushing Bianchi in a final action on the morrow. That evening he laid his plans. He would rest and reprovision his army during the morning of 3 May and then fall on the enemy in the late afternoon. Thus, early on 3 May many of his units dispersed themselves over the countryside in order to forage. If things had transpired as planned, the action might have turned out well. But the unexpected occurred.

Late on the morning of 3 May the *Royal Guard* suddenly advanced against the enemy without orders. Unable to recall them, Murat sent everything he had to their support. Rushing into the thick of the fighting, he personally led attack after attack. The Austrians held. One of the Neapolitan divisions broke. The

Austrians counter-attacked. Panic began to work its wiles upon Murat's troops. Murat ordered a retreat. Personally taking charge of the rear guard, he held back the Austrians, permitting much of his army to escape, though failing in his efforts to get himself gloriously killed in action. Once contact with the Austrians was broken, he eluded the trap, and led his troops on the road to Naples. On 18 May, after two weeks of constant retreat and rear-guard fighting, Murat re-entered his capital with but 8,000 men, the rest having melted away in the long trek over the mountains. At Naples, Murat made strenuous efforts to recreate an army, but could manage to raise no more than 4,000 additional troops. With Bianchi's II Corps close at hand, his I Corps mopping up the Adriatic fortresses, and his III Corps, after an initial reverse at Itri, just south of the frontier with the Papal States, now investing the great fortress of Gaeta, it was clear that the game was up. Telling his Queen "All is lost, Caroline, save my life, and that I have not been able to cast away," he fled to France.

Murat's Italian campaign was a failure. Whatever chance he had lay with in cooperation with Napoleon. An advance into northern Italy in the name of the Emperor might well have resulted in a general rising against Austria, and certainly, at the very least, in serious defections from the Austrian ranks. Such an advance, if carefully coordinated with Napoleon's operations, might have proven considerably more successful. But Murat, a dashing caval-ryman, among the finest of the age, was neither a politician nor a strategist. When he tried to play in those leagues he found himself outclassed and that they were more deadly than the battlefield. The result was a disaster. Game to the end, Murat made an abortive bid to return to his throne months after his doomed campaign. In the fatal conclusion to his career, he requested the firing squad to spare his face.

Murat took with him into northern Italy his first four divisions, the cavalry, the reserve, and the *Royal Guard*. The *5th Division* was in

The Italian Campaign of 1815				
Formation	Bns	Sqns	Bttys	*Men
NEAPOLITANS				
Royal Guard	9	8	2	8.2
1st Division	12		1	9.7
2nd Division	11		1	9.0
3rd Division	12		1	9.3
4th (Res) Division	9		1	8.4
5th Division	6			4.0
6th Division	3			1.5
Cav Division		11		3.0
Reserve	5	1	1	3.0
Gaeta Garrison	4		2	2.5
Total	71	20	9	58.6
AUSTRIANS				
I Corps	15	18	3	20.6
II Corps	15		4	14.8
III Corps	16	12	3	18.0
Tuscan Bde	3			2.5
Total	49	30	10	55.9

*in thousands

Calabria, where it had the mission of watching for a possible invasion from Sicily, still held by the deposed Neapolitan Bourbons. The *6th* was still in the process of formation in the Abruzzi. Each Austrian corps comprised an Advanced Guard and an infantry division. The Advanced Guard comprised three battalions of light infantry and a battery, while the infantry division consisted of two field brigades, each usually of six battalions and a battery, though one in II Corps with seven battalions. In addition, I and III Corps each had a cavalry brigade attached. The Tuscan Brigade was operationally attached to III Corps. Both sides had additional forces which have been omitted from this listing. The Austrians had strong garrisons in the famed Quadrilateral fortresses of Northeastern Italy, and could count on about 5,000 more troops of dubious quality from the Papal States and the minor duchies. Murat theoretically had 30,000 men available in the Neapolitan bourgeois militia, plus a small contingent of the *Royal Guard* which remained in Naples to protect Queen Caroline.

The Principal Engagements of the Italian Campaign of 1815				
Date	Action	Side	Strength	Losses
4 Apr	Panaro	*Neapolitans	8.0	0.8
		Austrians	7.0	1.0
7 Apr	Occhiobello	Neapolitans	7.5	1.2
		*Austrians	8.0	0.5
8-9 Apr	Carpi	Neapolitans	2.0	0.4
		*Austrians	5.0	0.5
15 Apr	Reno	*Neapolitans	15.0	0.5
		Austrians	20.0	1.5
15 Apr	Spilimberto	Neapolitans	2.2	2.2
		*Austrians	1.0	0.0
21 Apr	Ronco	*Neapolitans	1.4	0.0
		Austrians	4.0	0.2
23 Apr	Cesenatico	*Neapolitans	1.6	0.3
		Austrians	1.4	0.5
29 Apr	Macerata-Feltria	*Neapolitans	7.0	0.0
		Austrians	15.0	0.5
30 Apr	Senigallia	*Neapolitans	7.0	0.5
		Austrians	15.0	1.5
2-3 May	Tolentino	Neapolitans	15.0	4.0
		*Austrians	12.0	2.0

* Winner of the battle.

Tricks of the Trade

Seasoned commanders, Napoleon, Wellington and Blucher all understood and made use of many "tricks of the trade" which had been learned through centuries of military experience. Some of these were obvious, such as the rate at which armies march. But others were much less so, as can be seen from this sampler of the tricks of the trade.

Movement Rates. Each of the arms moves at a different rate, a matter which is of more importance tactically than strategically, since on longer marches it is the slowest moving arm, the infantry, which has the greatest endurance. Also, smaller formations will tend to march further in the same time than larger ones.

Rates for foot artillery are rather better than those for infantry, while those for horse artillery are not quite as good as those for cavalry.

However, siege artillery will move much slower than does infantry.

Detecting the Enemy. In daytime, the presence of concealed troops can sometimes be revealed by sunlight glinting off bayonets or lanceheads. Depending upon the angle of the sun, masses of troops can be detected at considerable distances by this method. While advancing in country in which the enemy might be encountered, wily commanders sometimes fired a few artillery rounds into seemingly peaceful woods to see if a sudden gleam of light resulted, a consequence of concealed troops reacting to the fire.

Dust clouds can be very useful, particularly if the enemy is engaged in a forced march. Cavalry raises a tall, relatively thin cloud, while that raised by infantry is lower and denser, and that of artillery and trains low, but denser yet. The

March Rates per Hour		
Pace	Infantry	Cavalry
Route Step	3 km	4 km
March	4 km	6 km
Forced March	5 km	10 km
Attack Rates Per Minute		
Pace	Infantry	Cavalry
Run	75 m	170 m
Charge	150 m	335 m

closer one gets, the more one can tell from what can be seen.

At night the presence of troops can sometimes be detected at some distance because large numbers of men, horses and equipment make noises which merge into a low, but steady hum, much as distant traffic noises merge into a hum in a modern city.

Visibility. Being able to judge distances was an obvious asset to a military commander, since it enabled him to assess march rates, ranges and so forth. How far one can see depends upon the weather, the time of day, the physical environment and the observer's own altitude. Church steeples, for example, are visible at up to 15 kilometers, while windmills, towers and other tall structures can be seen at about 10 km and the main features of houses at 4 km. Knowledge of these distances can help an offi-cer calculate the time necessary to get his troops from place to place. But visual clues can also be used to detect the presence of troops at considerable distances, and, as they get closer, other valuable information may be gained as well.

Napoleon made use of the first of these tricks when, at 1300 on 18 June, he noted that one of the hill-sides in the vicinity of Chapelle-St. Lambert, about eight kilometers away, was growing darker, and concluded that the Prussians were coming, a matter which was confirmed soon afterwards when a cavalry patrol brought in an enemy prisoner.

Numbers. By observing the physical dimensions of a unit, or its camp, it was often possible to determine the number of troops present. For example, in Napoleon's day, when on bivouac a reasonably well-disciplined army occupied about 10 acres of ground for every thousand

Distance Meters	Observable	Tip
8,000+	Troops massing	They darken hillsides.
1,500	Infantry in line	A solid black line can be seen.
	Cavalry in line	A notched black line can be seen.
1,200	Infantry formations	Suggests strength of the enemy, may suggest whether troops are seasoned or green by the "smartness" of the formations.
	Artillery pieces	Artillery strength of the enemy.
800	Individual movements	Suggests activities of troops.
600	Groupings of files	Confirms numbers and organization.
450	Individual figures	Identity of units may be possible based on headdress and colors.
300	Designs on flags	Identity of units is likely.

men (i.e., assuming a reasonable allotment of cavalry and artillery, plus supply wagons). Campfires can give a clue to enemy numbers, if one knows common practice (i.e., the "normal" number of men per fire), keeping always in mind that the enemy might light fewer fires than necessary—or more—as a deceptive measure.

One of the best clues to numbers is the length of a marching column:

Infantry in column of fours occupies about 270 meters per thousand men, with supply wagons additional.

Cavalry in column of fours occupies about 750 meters per thousand men, with supply wagons additional.

Artillery in file occupies approximately 550-750 meters per battery of six or eight pieces, including supply wagons.

Even the strength of an army corps can be estimated on this basis, a corps occupying about one kilometer per thousand men of all arms, so that, for example, a corps comprising 15,000 infantry in 3 divisions, 1,500 cavalry and 48 pieces of artillery, with 2,000 artillerymen, staffs, engineers and service troops would occupy about 24 kilometers if advancing on a single road.

Slopes. Since battlefields were rarely flat, it behooved an officer to understand the limitations which slopes put upon the capabilities of the troops. At a 10 percent slope infantry maneuver becomes difficult, cavalry may only charge uphill and artillery may be unable to maneuver. At 20 percent, infantry can only fight as skirmishers, cavalry may

walk uphill in some order, but cannot descend in any order, and artillery may find it impossible to move and will probably be unable to fire.

Battleline. An army corps deploying from the march required about two hours to get into action, depending upon strength, terrain and activity of the enemy.

Seasoning. In general, despite losses, infantry and artillery quality and performance will improve during sustained operations, while cavalry quality and performance will decline, as losses among horses are greater than those among men. In addition, guns are not lost as quickly as men, so the proportion of artillery in an army will tend to increase the longer the army is in the field, assuming no catastrophic reverses.

State or Intentions of the Enemy. There were a lot of little things which could tip off an observant commander as to the condition of the opposing army.

Campfires flickering: troops are astir when they ought to be sleeping (their comings and goings obscure the flames momentarily), a night movement is likely such as a surprise attack or withdrawal.

Batteries withdrawing from the line: retreat may be imminent.

Litter: if there is much discarded equipment and such along the enemy's line of march discipline is probably poor or the troops are green. If the enemy is retreating, morale is certainly low. Likewise, a lack of litter suggests that the troops are well in hand.

Deserters: their number is in general a good indication of the enemy's morale, and since they tend to increase before an attack, can help determine the enemy's intentions as well.

Small animals: large numbers of small animals, birds and insects suddenly emerging from a wooded area indicate something is scaring them in your direction, such as moving troops.

All of these examples seem rather straightforward, but in fact the tricks of the trade were not as simple as they look. One could acquire a knowledge of the tricks from handbooks, but learning to use them properly required considerable experience. Depending upon the distance, for example, a stand of young pines could easily be mistaken for infantrymen in line. Likewise, while pulling batteries out of the line of battle can indicate imminent retreat, it may also indicate that the batteries are being pulled back to reserve positions or that they are being replaced by fresh batteries from the reserve. So the tricks of the trade had to be applied with care.

The Conduct of Battle

Strategy is the movement of whole armies in theaters of operation so as to bring one's own forces against those of the enemy under the most favorable circumstances, so that battle can be joined. Grand Tactics is the maneuvering of large bodies of troops in battle against the enemy in order to inflict upon him the greatest injury with one's own firepower and mass. Tactics is the actual ways in which one's troops move and make use of their arms, the ground and the enemy's situation to defeat him.

Although there were many national styles to the conduct of war at the time of Waterloo, all were shaped by French practice. For some 20 years French arms had dominated the Continent, inflicting repeated defeats upon their foes. But each defeat helped Napoleon's enemies learn a little more, so that by 1815 they had adopted much of what was sound in French practice, or developed techniques of their own with which to counter the French.

Grand Tactics

Once his strategy had brought the enemy to the battlefield, Napoleon had but one purpose: destruction. He preferred to fight offensively under all circumstances, even when on the defensive, even when heavily outnumbered, as during the campaign of 1814. Normally he began to plan his battles even before the troops came into contact. He had only two basic battle plans, which might be the "Battle of Maneuver" and the "Battle of Attrition," shifting easily from one to the other as the circumstances dictated, even in the midst of combat itself.

The Battle of Maneuver. Napoleon's favorite grand tactical device, the battle of maneuver was characterized by movement supported by massive amounts of firepower. While the main body of the army held the enemy's attention to his front, strong forces supported by a "Grand Battery" of dozens of heavy cannon fell upon one of his flanks, crushing it, and then rolling up the rest of his line, and with cavalry thrown in to begin the pursuit. Napoleon occasionally used a variation of this technique, using a threatened flank attack to draw the enemy's reserves, and then smashing him frontally. Normally the development of this type of operation required some superiority in numbers, but at Auerstadt (14 October 1806) Marshal Davout managed to roll up both Prussian flanks although outnumbered by over 40 percent. The primary advantage of this type of battle was that it inflicted a major defeat on the enemy at minimal cost, such as Austerlitz (2 December 1805) or Friedland (14 June 1807). But things could go wrong. A quick movement of reserves in the enemy's rear could thicken up his threatened flank. An enemy deployed with strong natural or human supports on his flanks would be relatively immune to such a tactic. Moreover, such and action

required time to develop and a substantial superiority in numbers.

Napoleon attempted a battle of maneuver at Ligny, only to be frustrated by a combination of the failure of d'Erlon's corps to come up on the enemy's right, which both deprived him of his mass of maneuver and of the numerical superiority necessary to undertake a flanking movement, and by the dogged determination with which the Prussians resisted. He does not appear to have considered the possibility of trying maneuver at Waterloo, perhaps because of time and manpower constraints, and also possibly because of excessive confidence in his own prowess or contempt for that of his opponents: he had remarked "I say to you that Wellington is a bad general!" when Marshal Soult, with memories of repeated defeats at Wellington's hands during the Peninsular War, attempted to appraise him of the Briton's abilities.

The Battle of Attrition. The battle of attrition was a frontal slogging match in which firepower was poured into the enemy in enormous amounts until he appeared to be weakening, and then great masses of men would be thrown in to smash their way through his lines, the infantry going in first. Victory was secured by sheer weight of shot and shell and men. When the enemy crumbled, additional forces would be pushed forward, to complete and exploit the victory. Such a battle was costly, and not only to the loser. Indeed, the victor could easily come away as battered as the vanquished. But there were times when no other course was possible. Napoleon opted for the battle of attrition in about a third of his battles. Some were smashing victories such as Wagram (5-6 July 1809), others were marginal successes at best, such as Borodino (7 September 1812), and several were disastrous defeats, such as Waterloo (18 June 1815), where Wellington was so little impressed by Napoleon's skill that he called him a "pounder."

There was much that could go wrong in such a battle. The enemy might prove stronger, or more resilient than anticipated; the infantry and cavalry might be thrown in too soon; or the enemy might have a trick or two up his sleeve. Wellington's reverse slope defenses were a good antidote for the battle of attrition. The Duke put the bulk of his forces behind convenient hills and ridges, screening them from the brunt of the fire of a French "Grand Battery", so that he could commit them only when the French cavalry and infantry approached, as he did with remarkable skill at Waterloo.

Napoleon's two principal opponents in 1815 both had their grand tactics preferences. Marshal Blucher, quite aggressive despite his age, sought to crush his opponents offensively using masses of artillery and frontal attacks. The Duke of Wellington, in contrast, was a defensive fighter, indeed a counter-puncher. He held his troops under as much cover as possible, maintaining a very large reserve which he fed into action piece-meal, as local crises developed. Wellington was to let his enemy exhaust himself offensively before going over to the attack on a massive scale, with everything he had. This proved to be an extremely effective approach.

Tactics

Regardless of the type of battle he chose to fight, Napoleon made use of essentially the same set of tactics, inherited from the Republic, which had adopted and polished the final reforms under the Monarchy.

As in every period in history, tactics during the Napoleonic Wars were dictated by the nature of the arms available. The standard infantry arm was the musket, with its low rate of fire and poor accuracy. The evolution of tactics in the period had engendered considerable controversy. In the period before the French Revolution a remarkably flexible system of tactics had been worked out. These were the basis of the tremendous tactical superiority of the armies of Revolutionary and Imperial France. Reflecting the experience of the Seven Years War, all combined fire and movement in varying degrees. For a time the French infantry was undoubtedly the finest in the world. But its quality peaked by 1807. Thereafter, the lengthening casualty lists and the increased frequency of war made it increasingly difficult to maintain the quality of training which such excellence required. As a result, the French became less capable, while their foes, taking what was best in French practice, improved.

Earlier one of the most critically

important aspects of French tactics was the use of skirmishers. A portion of each regiment was supposed to be trained as light infantry, and a number of entire regiments were also assigned this role. At the onset of a battle, the light infantry were supposed to spread themselves thinly across the front of the army and, making use of available cover, maintain a harassing fire against the enemy. Occasionally, a third of the troops available were committed as skirmishers, while the balance of the troops were held back in anticipation of more serious combat. However, by 1815 French use of skirmish tactics had become rather perfunctory. Although none of the Allied armies had made such extensive use of skirmishers, by 1815 the British were much the better at the practice, as were some of their German allies and some Prussian units.

French tactical doctrine was extremely flexible, with several different methods of deploying the troops possible. Thus, the infantry could move from one deployment to another as circumstances changed. The Allies were by no means as flexible. However, by 1815 the declining quality of French infantry, coupled with the increased skills of their opponents made the two more or less an equal match.

Line. Line, or *order mince*, was the usual formation for protracted combat. The troops would be deployed on a broad front in usually in two lines, permitting each man to fire his musket at the enemy. Given a regiment of 1,500 men deployed in line some 3,000 rounds a minute could be sustained in combat on a front of about 700 meters, making the formation ideal for developing sustained fire power in great volume. But line was highly vulnerable to flank attacks, able to concentrate not more than eight to 12 rounds a minute on the flanks. Moreover, the line was ill-suited to rapid battlefield maneuvers, since it was difficult to maintain alignments while maneuvering. It was also quite useless for green troops, since it required considerable training and discipline to sustain in combat. The line was virtually the only tactical formation used by the British, who found it ideally suited to their preferred defensive posture in battle. The Prussians tended to prefer a thicker line, particularly for defensive fire, sometimes still using a four-man deep line.

Column. The column, or *order profond*, grouped the troops into a block to be used in shock action, as a battering ram to smash into the enemy. A column of three battalions could have each battalion formed with a front of 100-200 men and a depth of four or five, occupying an area of no more than 200 meters by five. The battalions would be one behind the other, so that the column would have, with intervals, a front of 200 meters and a depth of perhaps 25. Other possibilities were a "solid" column of 100 meters by 15, or a column of battalions in line, some 30 meters by five, and so forth. A column could move rapidly under virtually any conditions of ground or combat. It had the advantage of being useful for green troops, since the demands on training and discipline were minimal. The column was the ideal tool for smashing enemy formations rapidly after having softened them up with firepower. But it had severe disadvantages as well, for it was incapable of engaging in sustained fire combat, being able to deliver no more than 40 to 60 rounds a minute to its front, and perhaps 60 to 90 on the flank. Moreover it presented a considerable target, particularly to artillery, which could tear great swathes through the formation. Nevertheless, Napoleon's use of the column grew over the years, particularly because of the deteriorating quality of his infantry. At Waterloo, d'Erlon's *I Corps* undertook the first attack of the day in a series of very dense formations: one division deployed in two brigade columns, each comprising four battalions, one behind the other, presenting a division front with intervals of about 500 meters, and a depth of a dozen meters, for a density of about one for every 1.1 square meters. Two other divisions deployed on a single battalion front, about 200 meters, with all battalions in the division deployed one behind the other, for a depth of about 50 meters, for a density of about one man for every 2.4 square meters. In effect, these divisions represented a virtually solid mass of troops, with about one man per square meter, with little tactical flexibility and making a wonderful target. Only one division, the *4th* employed a looser, more flexible formation, "col-umns of battalions by divisions," in which each battalion deployed on a two company front—"by divisions"—with a width and depth of about 50 meters, giving a density per battalion of only about one man per five square meters. In addition, the battalions were deployed checkerboard fashion in two lines of four each, with about 100 meters between the battalions in each line and about 50 meters between the rows, so that the division had a front of nearly 600 meters and a depth of perhaps 150, for a density of about 22 square meters per man. Needless to say, such large formations invited high casualties. The Prussians used columns of companies or battalions in the attack. The British sometimes moved in column, but usually deployed into line for battle, although at Quatre Bras Lieutenant Reddock of the 44th did make an attack in column with his company. As some of Wellington's Allied troops had formerly been in French service, they apparently made use of the column regularly.

Mixed Order. Mixed order, or *ordre mixte*, was a combination of line and column, and the best French troops were capable of using it with considerable skill. Mixed order normally involved deploying one battalion of a regiment in line between two in column, like the Greek letter "pi," but occasionally with one in column between two in line, like the letter "T." The battalion in line developed the sustained firepower necessary to soften up the enemy, and the battalions in column prepared to attack with the bayonet at the opportune moment. In battle, a well trained regiment, such as Napoleon had in the period 1805-1807, could shift among the three orders quite handily. At Auerstadt Morand's division changed its deployment five times in the course of about as many hours, going from columns of march to a line of battalion columns to line proper to square and then back to a line of battalion columns. But by 1815 such capability was gone.

There was one other important difference between the British tactics, or rather Wellington's tactics, and those of the French, or indeed of the Prussians. Wellington liked to keep his troops under cover, using what are called "reverse slope tactics." This meant putting obstacles between the troops and the enemy, usually hills. The troops could be deployed on the reverse side of the hill, on the "military crest," which meant in such a way as to be able to see and fire over it without being particularly exposed. In contrast, the Prussians preferred to put their troops on frontal slopes, which exposed them to fire, but they believed that it was good for morale if the troops to saw the enemy.

As infantry was the queen of battle, the tactics of the other arms were essentially designed to support the infantry. **Artillery.** The principal functions of the artillery were to prepare for the attack of the infantry by battering the enemy's formations, and to assist in the defense of the infantry by smashing up the enemy's attacking forces. Although at times counter-battery fire was employed, it was usually not considered very profitable. The French, being most often on the offensive, preferred to mass their artillery in a "Grand Battery" in order to deliver tremendous firepower against the enemy. Wellington preferred to position his batteries across his front, to be used in local defense. Blucher tried to emulate Napoleon's practice at times, but was also willing to spread his guns around a bit.

Cavalry. The battlefield roles of the cavalry were rather restricted. It could be used in the charge, as a massed battering ram designed to smash through the enemy.

The charge was a carefully orchestrated undertaking, rather than a "hell for leather" flat out run at the enemy. As with the infantry, the cavalry had many different possible formations. It could deploy in line or in column, with varying depths and widths to the formation. De-

Advance Rates in the Charge				
	Cavalry		Infantry/Artillery	
Pace(kph)	Seconds	Meters	Seconds	Meters
Trot (10)	180-210	500-580	150-180	400-500
Gallop (18)	60-90	300-450	90-120	450-600
Charge (20)	10-15	60-100	10-15	60-100
Totals	4-5 min	860-1130	4-5 min	910-1200

ployment for the charge was best undertaken in a sheltered area as close to the objective as possible. The best ground over which to charge was that which had the fewest obstacles, offered the most direct route to the objective, thereby permitting momentum to be maintained, and was somewhat uphill, a slope of about 5 degrees being the maximum practical: downhill charges, so beloved of film makers, may look spectacular but were dangerous and relatively ineffective. The speed at which a charge was executed could vary, depending upon the terrain and the nature of the enemy.

The advance rate figures on the previous page are approximate, since local circumstances tended to dictate the actual rates and times involved. The idea was to get the horses to the enemy in fighting trim. They could actually run at much higher speeds, at least for short periods, but it was not a good idea to attempt higher rates of advance or maintain the charge for a longer time than suggested above. This would tend to break the horses' wind, leaving them "blown" and unfit for combat. In a properly

organized charge horse artillery accompanied the attack so that it could assist the cavalry in breaking enemy squares. And infantry was supposed to follow close behind, to secure the ground won by the cavalry, which was wholly incapable of doing so.

Cavalry's other battlefield roles, although less spectacular than the charge, were just as important. Defensively, cavalry could harass attacking enemy infantry by attacking it in the flanks as it advanced. It also had to protect the flanks of friendly infantry from enemy cavalry during attacks. And of course, cavalry was supposed to follow up the success of the infantry in breaking the enemy's line. Infantry caught by cavalry while on the march or in line without protected flanks was in serious trouble, but if they could form a square the cavalry was usually ineffective. When in square—the formation was sometimes actually rectangular or even oblong—the infantry presented a solid wall of muskets and bayonets, usually two to four men deep, bolstered by artillery. Though squares could break, particularly if attacked by artillery, it was rare for them to

Claims of Broken Squares During the Waterloo Campaign			
Action	Squares	Attacker	Note
Fleurus	Pr 26th, 27th, & 28th Rgts	Fr Gd Lt Cav	A
Quatre Bras	Br 42nd & 44th Ln	Fr 5th Lancers	B
	Br 69th Ln	Fr cuirassiers	C
Waterloo	Br KGL inf, 2 bns	Fr cavalry	D
	Pr inf, 2 bns	Fr dragoons	E

succumb to cavalry, though not un-heard of, as the accompanying table will demonstrate.

The table shown on the previous page should not be taken as defini-tive. Reliable evidence on the sub-ject of broken squares is highly elusive. Claims of broken squares were quite common, much more so than the event itself. At the same time, no one was inclined to admit that one of their squares had been broken. Given here are instances where some claim was made, albeit perhaps wrongfully, as explained in the accompanying notes, indicated by letters to the right of the table.

A. This report seems highly inac-curate. The Prussian 28th of the Line was engaged at Fleurus as part of the 2nd Brigade. In a rear-guard action, with the Prussians pulling out as Marshal Grouchy turned up with the advanced guard of his 45,000 man wing of the French Army, the regiment took a severe beating, losing about two-thirds of its strength, as did the its brigade-mate, the 3rd Battalion of the 2nd Westphalian Landwehr Infantry Regiment. However, it is not clear that these units were cut up by French cavalry, and in any case it could not have been the *Guard Light Cavalry*, which was at that time en-gaged with the Prussian 1st Brigade at Gosselies, some five miles to the west of Fleurus. The 26th and 27th were in the II and III Corps respec-tively, neither of which came into action on the 15th.

B. The 42nd Highlanders and the 44th appear to have mistaken the approaching French for the Bruns-wick Uhlans, which allowed the *5th Lancers* to get very close before the two regiments were ordered into square. As a result, the French took the squares in the rear as they were still forming.

C. When he saw the French cui-rassiers approaching, the division commander, Picton, ordered the 69th into square. This was done, but Picton then rode off and the Prince of Orange came up. He ordered the battalion to resume the line. When the Prince left, Lieutenant Colonel Charles Morice, ordered the battal-ion back into square, but one com-pany had not yet gotten into place when the French struck, breaking the square and scattering the regi-ment.

D. This report appears to be a highly muddled version of the expe-rience of the 5th and 8th Line battal-ions of the K.G.L. during Ney's assault of about 1800 hours, the only combined infantry/cavalry at-tack which the French made that day. Aware that there was a regi-ment of French cuirassiers in the vi-cinity, Baron Ompteda, commanding the 2nd K.G.L. Bri-gade, had protested an order from his division commander, Charles Al-ten, to attack the French *2nd Divi-sion* in the flank. The Prince of Orange intervened and Ompteda was forced to make the attack. As the brigade advanced, the French cuirassiers attacked, taking the 5th and 8th Line battalions in the right flank and cutting them to pieces. At no time were either of the two bat-talions in square.

E. This report seems highly dubious. The only Prussians engaged at Waterloo were those of Bulow's IV Corps at Placenoit and those of Zeithen's I Corps who struck d'Erlon's right flank near Papelotte and La Haye. There were only three regiments of French dragoons present on the field of Waterloo: *Dragons de la Emperatrice*, of the *Guard*, and the *2nd* and *7th Dragoons*, in the *III Cavalry Corps*, all of which had participated in the massive attack against Wellington's center at 1700 hours, and played very little part in the battle thereafter. They attempted to rally in a position more or less behind the left center of the French Waterloo front, about 2,000 meters northwest of Placenoit and about 3,000 meters from La Haye.

CHAPTER IX

Waterloo

Sunday, 18 June

*T*he field of Waterloo was quite small, little more than 5,500 meters wide. The principal terrain features were two low ridges stretching parallel to each other in an east to west direction across a shallow valley not 1,400 meters across, with the more northerly ridge less pronounced than that to the south. Neatly bisected by the road from Charleroi to Brussels, some 20 kilometers to the north, there were considerable wooded areas on either flank, and numerous small villages and farms scattered here and there about the field. The principal roads were old and "sunken," that is, lower than the surrounding countryside, due to centuries of use. The rains which had begun on the afternoon of the 17th continued intermittently throughout the night, not letting up until 0600 that morning, and turning the fields into a sticky mud, making life miserable for the troops, who had camped mostly in the open. As a result, the physical environment was not conducive to sweeping maneuvers and rapid marches, but rather favored defense. It was under these conditions that the climactic battle of Napoleon's spectacular career was played out, a battle which by its end would see upwards of 200,000 men and 500 guns crowded into this area of little more than eight square kilometers. Waterloo was not an elegant battle with great displays of tactical genius or operational brilliance. Rather, it was a slugging match in which the ability of the combatants to give and take hammer blows was of the greatest importance. In the end, the outcome was decided by the will and determination of two men, Wellington and Blucher, and by the failings of a third, Napoleon.

Morning: The Preliminaries

The men of Wellington's Anglo-Allied Army had taken up their positions on the afternoon and evening of 17 June. They spent a miserable night on the field; Sergeant William Lawrence of the 40th Foot later wrote, "the rain descended in torrents, mixed with fearful thunder and lightning." But as the troops got what rest they could, Wellington laid his plans. He knew the area well, having surveyed it the previous spring and he had spent the afternoon of 14 June riding there as well. It was very suited to his favorite defensive device, "reverse slope" tactics, in which the troops lined up behind various obstacles, such as hill crests. Thus posted, they were both out of sight and out of gun shot of the enemy, yet could deploy rapidly into position to receive an attack. Wellington had used this technique repeatedly and with great success while campaigning in Spain, Portugal and the south of France from 1808 through 1814.

Wellington personally sited virtually every battalion and every battery, each after a careful examination of the ground. The right flank was stronger than the left, partially for fear of a blow from that direction and partially in confidence that Blucher would eventually turn up on his left. This side was anchored on the considerable village of Braine l'Alleud by Lieutenant General David Henri Baron Chasse's Dutch-Belgian 3rd Division, with over 7,000 men and 16 guns. Chasse's men would form a bastion preventing any French attempt to turn Wellington's flank. About 1,800 meters to the east of Chasse's men, and linked to them by a thin screen of about 2,000 infantry and 800 cavalry, was Wellington's front line. This stretched for about 3,500 meters along the north side of the Ohain road, which ran in a depression along the crest of the ridge of Mont-St. Jean. On the right, closest to Chasse, were posted Cooke's British 1st Division, some 4,500 guardsmen, with some 8,000 men of Alten's British 3rd Division to their left, and, to its left just across the Brussels road, Picton's British 5th Division, reinforced to some 9,500 men by the attachment of the 4th Hanoverian Brigade from the British 6th Division. Perponcher's 2nd Dutch-Belgian Division had its two brigades in front of Picton's lines, with 3,700 Nassauers of Saxe-Weimar's 2nd Brigade on his left, and Bijlandt's 1st Brigade, some 3,400 men, on his right.

Several units were posted in advance of the main line. Over on the left some of Saxe-Weimar's men held the extensive farms of Papelotte, La Haie and Frischermont. In the center, about 120 meters south of where the Brussels road intersected the Ohain road, there was a sizeable sand pit, into which Wellington placed some companies of the 95th Rifles from Picton's division, while just across the Brussels road and about 100 meters further south, the 2nd Light Battalion of the King's German Legion, less than 500 men from Alten's division, held the farm of La Haie Sainte. The most important such outpost was about 1,200 meters south of Wellington's center right, the large estate of Hougoumont, a third of a square kilometer of farm buildings, orchards and fields surrounded by a hedge and containing at its heart a walled garden. This lay in the shallow valley between the two armies, closer, indeed, to the French than the Allied lines. In Allied hands, Hougoumont would permit the holders to enfilade any attack on Wellington's center, while in French hands it would form a bastion for the support of such attacks. In this exposed position were the 1st Battalion, 2nd Nassau Regiment, one of Saxe-Weimar's outfits reinforced with 100 Hanoverians from Major General Count Kielmansegge's brigade in the

The Time of the Times

Firsthand accounts of the battle often differ wildly in the times given for particular events, such as the onset of attacks. This is because there was no such thing as standard time in 1815. Since watches had to be set by solar time, this meant that it was rare for two watches to agree. For example, Wellington's official report of the battle has the French opening the ball at Hougoumont at about 1000, while Lord Hill reported it at about 1150, and an officer in the 52nd said noon! Had the armies been in the vicinity for some days the problem would not have been so acute, since eventually everyone would have more or less been on Waterloo area solar time. However, this had not been the case. For example, on 9 June, just six days before the first rounds were fired along the Sambre, the French *I Corps* had been at Lille, while the *IV Corps* was at Metz. Assuming an officer had set his watch at noon and then meticulously wound it twice a day but not reset it during the approach march, by the time the two corps reached the vicinity of Waterloo, the *I Corps* officer's watch would have read 12:40 p.m. at a time when the *IV Corps* officer's read 11:20 a.m., and it was noon at Waterloo. This is an extreme example, and unlikely to have actually been the case, but it demonstrates the problem quite well.

Dawn and dusk also present some difficulties. The terms were in common use, but are highly imprecise. In fact, sunrise and sunset are not as important militarily as nautical twilight. Nautical twilight is the period during which it is still possible to maneuver and discern objects, due to the lightening of the sky before the sun actually rises

---

3rd Division, perhaps 1,100 men in all. Completing Wellington's preparations, he deployed a thin screen of skirmishers about 100 meters in advance of his front.

Wellington was careful with his reserves. Behind Cooke's division, on his center left, he posted the entire British 2nd Division, some 8,200 men under Lieutenant General Sir Henry Clinton. In his center, close to the front behind Alten's division, to which they were subordinate, he posted three battalions of Nassauers, about 2,900 men, under Generalmajor A.H. von Kruse. Still further back, in a line stretching parallel with his front at about 450 meters from the Ohain road, Wellington posted six brigades of

over the horizon in the morning or after it descends below the horizon in the evening. Depending upon circumstances, nautical twilight lasts about two hours. Visibility, of course, would also be affected by weather. It was hot and humid during the Waterloo campaign, with a good deal of rain.

Figures in the table below are for the village of Waterloo, which lies at 50 40" North, 40 30" East. This is actually about two miles north of the approximate lines along which Wellington's army deployed and about three miles north of Napoleon's lines. This means that times cited above are about two minutes earlier than those on the Allied line and about three minutes earlier than those on the French line. Times at Quatre Bras are about 9 to 10 minutes later than at Waterloo, and at Ligny about 13 to 14 minutes later.

Sunrise and Sunset During the Waterloo Campaign				
Date (June)	Twilight (Begins)	Sunrise	Sunset	Twilight (Ends)
15	0153	0400	2036	2243
16	0153	0400	2037	2243
17	0153	0400	2037	2243
18	0153	0400	2020	2243

British cavalry, in position to serve both as an immediate reserve for counterattacks and also to provide inspiration for those in the front lines who might prove faint-hearted. Finally, held well back, were the 6,000 men of the Brunswick Corps—actually a division—burning with the desire to avenge their fallen duke, plus the 2,200 men of Major General Sir John Lambert's British 10th Brigade, part of the 6th Division, and the 3,500 troopers of Lieutenant General J.A. Baron de Collaert's Dutch-Belgian Cavalry Division.

Thus, excluding Chasse, but including the outposts forward of the Ohain road, there were about 30,000 men in Wellington's front line. In immediate reserve he had a further 21,000, approximately half of whom were cavalry-men, while further back still there were some 12,000 more men, about a quarter of them mounted troops. With Chasse, the artillery reserve, the engineers and sappers and various miscellaneous elements, Wellington had some 72,000 to 74,000 men on the field, supported by about 160 pieces of artillery and a rocket contingent. He could easily have had more, but still fearful of a sweeping movement against his rear he had left some 17,000 men and 30 guns at Hal, about 15 kilometers to his right, plus miscellaneous contingents elsewhere totaling perhaps 15,000 men with about 20 pieces of artillery. Though no more than 20 percent of these troops could be considered highly reliable, their absence from the field of Waterloo would be severely felt.

Wellington's deployment at Waterloo was a masterful example of his predilection for reverse slope tactics. Virtu-ally every battalion in the army was under cover. The only exceptions were Bijlandt's Dutch-Belgian brigade, which was, for some inexplicable reason, exposed on the for-ward—southern—side of the ridge of Mont-St. Jean, the crest of which runs only some 125 meters above sea level, though reaching 135 in places. Most of the brigades had their battalions posted in two lines, usually in checker-board fashion, with the forward ones close behind the crest of the ridge, so that they could see over the top yet not be seen. The rearward battalions were to be used to thicken the line or held in readiness to deliver quick counterat-tacks, by being posted further down the slope, which in most places averaged about 5 percent. Picton, however, had placed all of his battalions in the first line, leaving none available for immediate counterattacks. The front was liberally seasoned with artillery, so that, including Chasse's sector, there were about 80 pieces in the first line, with about the same number held in reserve, to be rushed into action where needed. Unlike Napoleon, who pre-ferred his batteries in mass, Wellington's were sited individually just forward of the infantry, with a considerable contingent of artillery, including all the horse artillery, held in reserve.

Wellington's dispositions for the battle clearly reveal his intent to fight defensively. Such a battle suited his temperament. Moreover, it suited his army. Many of his men were poorly trained, unseasoned and unreliable. Ways had to be found to use his less reliable troops to best advantage. For this reason, his front was held mostly by British and K.G.L. troops, interspersed to bolster the others. In addition, there was no place to run, for the expansive Forest of Soignies was just north of the battlefield. Normally one did not offer battle with such an obstacle to easy retreat in the rear, but in this case it might encourage the faint hearted. Thus, Wellington's decision to defend at Waterloo was a reasonable one. His plan was simple, to await Napoleon's pleasure, responding to his initiatives with vigorous counterstrokes until a decision could be reached. It was a simple plan, though perhaps not an obvious one. Indeed, that night Lord Uxbridge, who was to be Wellington's successor should the latter fall, decided he ought to inquire as to his commander's intentions. He tramped through the mud and rain from his quarters in the village of Waterloo, about three kilometers north of the main Allied line, to those of Wellington. There he put the question to the Duke. Wellington looked at him, saying, "Who shall attack first tomorrow, I or Bonaparte?"

"Bonaparte."

"Well," replied the Duke, "Bonaparte has not given me any idea of his projects: and as my plans will depend upon his, how can you expect me to tell you what mine are?" Then he stood up, placing his hand upon Uxbridge's shoulder, "There is one thing certain, Uxbridge, that is, that whatever happens, you and I will do our duty." Not long after, sometime between 2100 and midnight, the Duke retired.

At about the time that Wellington was getting to bed,

Blucher was conferring with Gneisenau. He had just received word from Muffling that the Duke was ready to give battle at Mont-St. Jean and had requested the support of a corps or two. The old marshal, still not fully recovered from his fall on the evening of the 16th, was enthusiastic about going to Wellington's support. Together with Gneisenau he penned his instructions for the day. Then he went over to the injured Hardinge, embraced him again, saying, "We are going to join the Duke!" and showed him the orders. They were fairly simple. Bulow's IV Corps was to march at dawn, followed by Zeithen's II, and by the balance of the army as soon as practical after that. A message explaining these arrangements was at once dispatched to Wellington.

The bulk of the Prussian Army had reached the vicinity of Wavre during the night of 17-18 June. Early on the morning of the 18th, Blucher issued orders for the army to march to Wellington's assistance in the vicinity of Mont-St. Jean. The army was in a considerable muddle, I and II Corps particularly so. Thus, organizing the movement required an excessive amount of time. Bulow's IV Corps, which was the first unit ordered to move out, was in fact the furthest from Wellington's lines, some five kilometers south of Wavre. Its columns crossed with those of the other corps as it marched, creating a massive traffic jam. Nevertheless, by 1000 the corps was well on its way, with its leading brigade within eight kilometers of Wellington's left flank, having covered some 15 kilometers since dawn. By this time Blucher had written Muffling to confirm that the movement had begun, adding, "Say in my name to the Duke of Wellington that, ill as I am, I will march at the head of my army to attack without delay the right flank of the enemy...." Not long after the old marshal rode out from Wavre. Reaching Bulow's troops, he put himself at their head, saying, "Lads, you will not let me break my word!" Curiously, no one on this determined march appears to have remarked upon the fact that there were as yet no sounds of heavy combat emanating from the northwest, despite the lateness of the hour.

Napoleon was awake for most of the night of 17-18 June. In the late evening he had dismissed a report from a cavalry patrol which had spotted Prussian troops near Wavre, putting the matter out of his mind. Part of the night he spent walking along the front lines, trying to estimate the strength of the Allied forces from the number of campfires which could be seen from time to time through the torrential downpour. Through much of the night he believed Wellington was planning to slip away. Some patrols brought back some useful information, as did a number of secret agents. Several Belgian deserters from Wellington's army were brought in as well. Upon interviewing these men he concluded that Wellington would probably make a stand where he was. In addition, Napoleon seems to have decided that the latter's Belgian troops might prove so unreliable that they would benefit him more than Wellington. Nevertheless, he still doubted that Wellington intended to fight in his present position, with so many unreliable troops in his ranks and the considerable Forest of Soignies in his rear, blocking easy retreat to Brussels. Some time after 0200, the gathering twilight revealed that the Allied army was still in place. He was greatly pleased by this. If Wellington, whom he considered a bad general, chose to fight he was more than happy to oblige. It was only at about dawn, around 0400, that he returned to his headquarters in the farm of Le Caillou, a bit more than three kilometers south of La Belle-Alliance, through which his front line ran. There he found a dispatch sent by Grouchy at 2000 on the previous evening. This had arrived two hours earlier, but no one had thought to send it on to the Emperor. Grouchy reported that, contrary to his earlier impressions, he believed it might be possible that the Prussians were falling back on Wavre. Should this prove correct, he went on, he would follow them in order to prevent their rendering support to Wellington. Although this confirmed the cavalry reports of the previous night, Napoleon did nothing about it for several hours. A dispatch issued at 0400 would have reached Grouchy in time for him by means of an oblique march to place himself in the path of the Prussian army east of Napoleon's position. Thus precious hours were lost, not for the first time in this campaign. Soon after this, Napoleon went to bed.

It is not clear just how much sleep the Duke of Wellington got on the night of 17-18 June. Some time after 0300 he was awakened, apparently to receive the message which Blucher had dispatched around midnight informing him that the Prussians were indeed coming. He had then spent some time writing a few letters and possibly getting a bit more sleep. Nevertheless, by 0600 he was astir. After a brief breakfast he rode with his staff the three kilometers from Waterloo, where he had made his headquarters, to his command post, a broad elm at the southwestern corner of the intersection of the Ohain and Brussels roads, almost precisely in the middle of his front at one of the highest points on the ridgeline which formed his principal position. The little cavalcade made an interesting sartorial display. There in the midst of a pomposity of officers in braid and feathers, gold and red and blue and green, and every other color, rode the Duke in his customary combat garb, an immaculate and natty but wholly unmilitary civilian ensemble comprised of a white shirt with white buckskin breeches and white cravat, over which he wore a civilian-style blue coat, finished off by a pair of black Hessian boots and a blue cloak. His cocked hat worn in fore-and-aft fashion rather than square, as was Napoleon's preference, bore the cockades of Britain, Portugal, Spain and the Netherlands, the armies in which he held field marshal's rank. As they rode to the front Wellington greeted the troops, who less loving than respecting him maintained a respectful silence, knowing how little he liked cheers. He paused at his command post for a time, taking tea with some riflemen. Then he made a tour of his lines. At about 1100 he chanced to visit Hougoumont. He decided that the 1,100 Nassauers and Hanoverians there were too few in number and perhaps too unreliable, and reinforced them with the light companies of the 2nd Battalion, Coldstream Guards and the 2nd Battalion, 3rd Scots Guards, raising the garrison to perhaps 1,300 men. He was still near Hougoumont when the shooting started.

Napoleon rose some time after 0600, not long after the rains had ceased. Over breakfast he conferred with his chief of staff Marshal Nicolas Soult. Soult was a veteran of the Peninsular War—as were also Reille and d'Erlon—and had tangled with Wellington often, giving him a run for his money several times and very nearly winning the final battle of the campaign at Toulouse on 10 April 1814. He urged caution, pointing out that Wellington was an excellent defensive fighter and that they had no firm notion of Blucher's whereabouts. In concluding, Soult suggested the immediate recall of Grouchy. Napoleon replied contemptuously, "I say to you that Wellington is a bad general, that the English are bad troops, and that this affair is only a *dejeuner!*" He similarly spurned Reille's advice. When his younger brother Jerome added his support to the arguments of the two veteran officers, pointing out that on the previous day his present innkeeper had overheard two British officers discussing Blucher's plans to join Wellington, the Emperor responded with "Nonsense," claiming that the Prussians would require at least two days to regroup. Clearly his mind had been made up, and there was little likelihood of his changing it. Nevertheless, he was not totally oblivious to reality. He had planned to begin the battle at 0900. However, General de Division Antoine Drouot, commander of the *Garde*, and d'Erlon both pointed out that the ground was far too muddy for artillery to maneuver easily or for ricochet fire to be employed with success. Napoleon concurred. The attack would have to be postponed for several hours to permit

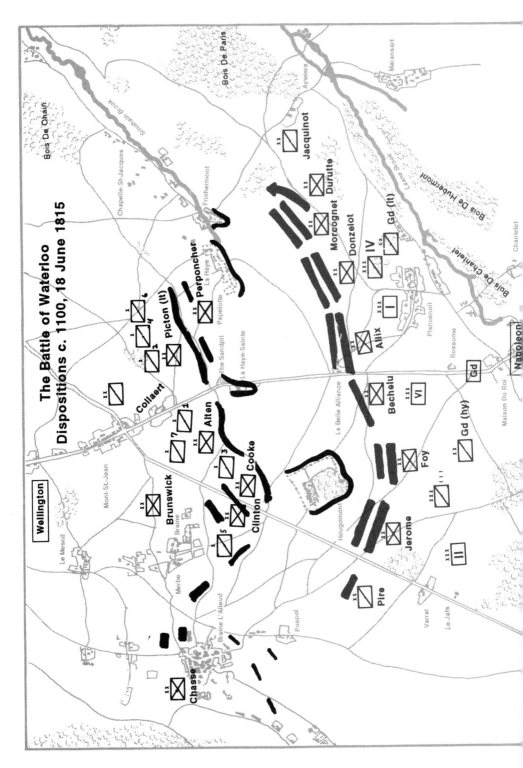

The Battle of Waterloo
Dispositions c. 1100, 18 June 1815

the ground to drain somewhat. At about 0800 a new plan was developed for an attack at 1300, with orders to this effect going out at about 0900. Soon after, Napoleon belatedly dictated a response to the message which he had received from Grouchy that morning. The reply was unclear and confusing, being neither a recall order nor a clear statement that Grouchy was to continue to operate independently: "His Majesty desires that you will head for Wavre in order to draw near to us, and to place yourself in touch with our operations, and to keep up your communications with us, pushing before you those portions of the Prussian army which have taken this direction and which have halted at Wavre; this place you ought to reach as soon as possible." Napoleon now did an unusual thing; he held a grand review of the army, in full view—though out of range—of the enemy, and was greeted with great enthusiasm by the troops. Why he did this has never been clear, for he had never done such a thing before. He may perhaps have intended to impress the Allied troops deployed across the valley, in which he somewhat succeeded, or perhaps he merely wanted to improve the morale of his own men, in which he also succeeded. Whatever the case, around 1100 he was back at his headquarters. Somewhere amid all this activity he appears to have snatched a nap for about an hour. Meanwhile the army got down to the serious business of preparing for battle.

The French were deployed on a front which at its broadest was about 5,500 meters. Covering the extreme right flank near Frischermont were the *7th Hussars*, reinforced to about 1,500 with cavalrymen from d'Erlon's *I Corps*. Baron Jean-Baptiste de Marbot observed afterwards: "...only my regiment, with three guns and a battalion of infantry, not nearly enough." Then came the four infantry divisions of the corps, altogether some 18,000 men supported by 40 pieces of artillery, stretching 2,000 meters westward to the Brussels road. To their left, extending 2,500 meters westward from La Belle-Alliance, were three divisions of Reille's *II Corps*, the *5th*, *6th* and *9th Divisions* of some 18,500 men with 32 guns, covered on their left by the 1,900 men and 6 guns of the *2nd Cavalry Division*. Most of the army was deployed to the rear. Behind d'Erlon was Milhaud's *IV Cavalry Corps* of 3,100 men and 12 guns. Behind the center just east of the Brussels road were some 2,300 men and 12 pieces of artillery in the *3rd* and *5th Cavalry Divisions*, operationally attached to Lobau's *VI Corps*, which had some 7,500 men and 30 guns posted on the west side of the Brussels road. Behind Reille was Kellermann's *III Cavalry Corps* with about 3,900 men and a dozen guns. The *Imperial Guard* was held still further back with the 2,400 men and 12 guns of the *Guard Light Cavalry* posted behind Milhaud's cavalry on the right, the 2,100 men and 12 guns of the *Guard Heavy Cavalry* behind Kellermann's troopers on the left, and the bulk of the 16,200 men and 80 guns initially posted behind Lobau's corps less than 1,500 meters from the front.

Napoleon's plan was simple. Noting that Ney would be in overall command of the attack, he went on to say that it would "...be delivered on Mont-St. Jean village in order to secure the crossroads at that place. To this end the 12-pounder batteries of the *II* and *VI Corps* will mass with those of the *I Corps*. These 24 guns will bombard the troops holding Mont-St. Jean, and Comte d'Erlon will begin the attack by first launching the left division, and, when necessary, supporting it by other divisions of the *I Corps*. The *II Corps* will also advance, keeping abreast of the *I Corps*." No drawn out preliminary skirmishing nor brilliant maneuvers, just a straightforward attack in the center with the intention of smashing into the Allied position. Napoleon himself had once remarked upon the frailty of plans in battle. This plan was like any other, and, regardless of its merits, it began to fall apart almost immediately.

1130: Hougoumont

At 1130 the French opened the ball with an attack on

Hougoumont by Prince Jerome's *6th Division*, the largest in the army with 8,000 of the finest troops available outside the ranks of the *Garde Imperial*. The attack was designed as a prelude to the main assault to be delivered at 1300. It had two goals, the first to draw Wellington's attention away from his center by suggesting that Napoleon intended striking his right and the second to protect the flank of *I Corps* during its advance. The attack began well. Under cover of artillery fire, Jerome's *1st Brigade* of 4,200 light infantrymen under General de Brigade Baron Bauduin advanced against the southwestern face of the estate on a broad front with skirmishers to the fore. They struggled across the encircling hedges and walls and plunged into the large wooded enclosure. Nearly an hour's heavy fighting was required to push back the Guardsmen, Hanoverians and Nassauers holding the orchards. These troops were all old friends, having fought it out in similar circumstances just two days before in the Bossu Wood before Quatre Bras. It had been an intense struggle then, and was even more so now. Bauduin fell, but his troops pressed on. Jerome committed some horse artillery against the park from the west and threw in his *2nd Brigade*, 3,500 men under General de Brigade Baron Soye. Thus reinforced, the French beat off a counterattack and pushed on. Wellington now intervened.

The Duke had been sitting on his chestnut charger Copenhagen calmly observing the fight from the lines of the Guards Division, about 500 meters away, in total disregard for the numerous stray rounds which fell about him. He sent in additional companies from the Coldstream and Scots Guards. Then he called upon Major Robert Bull's troop of the Royal Horse Artillery, unique in the army for being equipped entirely with howitzers. Saying, "I am about to do a delicate thing," Wellington ordered Bull to fire over the heads of the defenders. Bull's 5.5-inch howitzers were ideally suited to the task, hurling shells high over the garrison to fall among the attackers. But although

Jerome Napoleon Bonaparte

Jerome Napoleon Bonaparte, King of Westphalia, general of division (1784-1860), was the youngest brother of Napoleon. Benefiting from his brother's rapid rise, he had an excellent education and entered the French Navy as an officer in 1800. Jumping ship in Baltimore in 1803 he married a young beauty of the town, Ms. Elizabeth Patterson, and founded the American branch of the Bonaparte family which, numbering among its members Charles Francis Bonaparte, the founder of the F.B.I., endured until 1944. Napoleon refused to recognize the marriage and had it annulled before allowing Jerome back to France.

Prince Jerome was made a rear admiral and *Marechal de camp* in 1806. He commanded a Bavarian division and later a corps during the Jena-Auerstadt campaign, performing his duties without disgracing himself but with only marginal ability. The following year he was promoted general of division and proclaimed King of Westphalia, a state cobbled together from odd bits of Prussia and smaller German states, and married off to a German princess. In 1809 Jerome commanded a corps which included Westphalian and other German troops, again with some success. Given command of the right wing of the entire army during the Russian campaign, Jerome proved so inept as to incur his brother's wrath, to which he responded by abandoning the army and returning to his kingdom, which was overrun by Allied forces in 1813. Thereafter Jerome was unemployed until Napoleon's return from Elba.

During the Waterloo campaign Jerome commanded what was the largest and arguably the best division in Napoleon's army with considerable energy but little intelligence. He afterwards went into exile for many years, only returning to France in 1847. During the Second Empire (1852-1870) his nephew Napoleon III assigned him several notable honors and made him a marshal.

Like all of Napoleon's siblings, Jerome was not without ability, but the Emperor assigned him tasks for which he was unsuited. The present Bonapartist claimant to the throne of France descends from his son Prince Napoleon, nicknamed "Plon-Plon."

---

the shell fire slowed the French, it could not halt their advance. Soye's brigade managed to come around the western flank. A battery of horse artillery from Piré's cavalry division got into position to take Bull's howitzers

Jerome Napoleon Bonaparte, soi disant *King of Westphalia and general of division (here seen wearing his uniform as an admiral of the Empire), was brave enough to command a division, but not bright enough for the one his imperial brother gave him.*

under direct fire, forcing them to pull back. Shortly after noon, the bulk of the park was in French hands with the defenders confined to the farm house—grandiloquently termed a "chateau"—and its outbuildings. But the French could go no further. As they attempted to cross the 30 meters or so of open ground which separated the woods from the farm buildings, they came under intense musket fire from loopholes and windows. The attack faltered.

At this point Jerome's task was done. He had drawn Wellington's attention away from his center and neutralized any threat which might have been mounted from Hougoumont into the flank of the coming attack by *I Corps*. To be sure he had not taken Hougoumont, but then it had not been intended that he should do so. Napoleon certainly had not expected that the operation was to be more than a demonstration. Yet that is what it became.

Whether out of a desire for glory or because his blood was up, Jerome pressed the attack, ignoring the advice of

Waterloo, 18 June 1815: Hougoumont. The inner courtyard of the farm during its defense. Note the French prisoner in the right foreground.

A modern view of the walls enclosing much of the farm. As Gemioncourt, at Quatre Bras, Hougoumont was a stoutly built complex, well suited to serve as an improvised fortress. Note the loopholes made in 1815. Photo by Ed Wimble.

Sous-lieutenant Legros, nicknamed "L'Enfonceur — The Smasher," batters in a panel of the gates with a heavy sapper's axe, forcing them open. Legros led a determined assault party into the courtyard, where all but one of the assailants was killed in fierce hand-to-hand fighting with the Coldstream Guards.

A modern view of the gate through which Legros led his daring band of men from the 1st Light Infantry into the interior of the farm yard, which is little changed since 1815. Photo by Ed Wimble.

his staff. A number of attempts were made to storm the innermost position, each of which was beaten off by the defenders, firing through improvised loopholes, windows and doorways. Casualties began to mount. At about 1230 a detachment of the *1st Light Infantry*, the finest light regiment in the French army, stormed up to the north gate. Sous-lieutenant Legros, a huge man nicknamed *"L'Enfonceur*—the Smasher,"* battered in a panel with a heavy sapper's axe and forced open the doors in a determined assault into the courtyard. A wild hand-to-hand fight ensued with swords and bayonets, pistols and muskets. As the bloody melee went on behind them, five intrepid Coldstreamers—Colonel James Macdonell, three other officers and a sergeant—shoved the doors closed by main force against a mob of French troops trying to gain entry and braced them with a huge timber. Within minutes it was over with every one of the intruders slain save a forlorn drummer boy, who was taken prisoner. This was the closest the French came to taking Hougoumont. Rather than break off the action, for the chateau could easily have been destroyed by howitzer fire, Jerome dragged in nearly half of the 5,500 men in General de Division Maximilien Foy's *9th Division* for yet another try. Altogether four— possibly five—attempts were made to take the place by storm. Jerome's and Foy's men became bogged down in the struggle. Wellington too fed men into the fight, but in small numbers. Keeping his eye on the progress of the fight, he was able to dispatch additional troops as it seemed necessary, making use of a partially covered road which led back towards the Allied lines to effect the movements. In the end, he committed 13 companies from the Coldstreamers and Scots Guards, perhaps 1,500 men, plus Bull's howitzer battery to bolster the 1,100 Hanoverians and Nassauers originally posted there, though the latter were withdrawn after a time.

Hougoumont ran its bloody course more or less independently of the rest of the battle. Reille, Ney and Napo-

Elements of the **1st Light Infantry,** *pinned down in the orchard of the farm yard, where they died to the last man as the garrison— British guardsmen, Nassauers, and Hanoverians— strove to eject them.*

leon were all lax in permitting this combat to run on long after any useful purpose had been served. None seem to have taken any interest in the action, not even riding over to have a look, though at about 1445 Napoleon did order a bombardment with "carcasse," incendiary howitzer shells. Wellington, however, stayed close by. The little fight was one which he intended to keep going, not so much because Hougoumont had any great intrinsic or tactical value but because it was quite satisfactory in terms of the bloody mathematics of war. He was neutralizing over half an enemy army corps with only a brigade; little more than 2,500 Allied troops were tying down some 10,000 French. Wellington monitored the action at Hougoumont for over two hours. Then, shortly before 1300, he decided it was time to visit his command post at the broad elm near the center of the Allied line. It was clear that Napoleon's main effort was not going to be in the direction of Hougoumont.

Napoleon's inactivity through the entire morning was welcome, but could not be expected to continue. Now it was time for him to see what was going on elsewhere. And, indeed, Napoleon was at that moment preparing his attack.

The Emperor had spent the morning supervising the siting of a grand battery. Eighty-four guns—forty-four 12-pounders and forty 8-pounders—were lined up on a front of about 800 meters along a low ridge some 500 meters in advance of the French lines, all aimed directly at the center of the Allied line. This task was completed shortly before 1300. Since the firing of such a number of guns would soon fill the air with great clouds of smoke, Napoleon rode back about a kilometer from the front to the Rossomme farm, the highest place in the area at nearly 150 meters above sea level, in order to get a final look at everything through his telescope. All seemed satisfactory until he swept his glass across some hills about eight kilometers to the east. There, in the vicinity of Chapelle-St. Lambert, he noted that one of the distant hillsides was darkening. He was too experienced a soldier not to know that it indicated the presence of troops. In minutes the darkened area began to grow. Some officers speculated that they were Grouchy's men, but Napoleon apparently already suspected that it was indeed the Prussians come to succor their Allies. This suspicion was confirmed within minutes when the dashing Colonel Jean de Marbot came riding up. Marbot's *7th Hussars* had been sent out to reconnoiter at 1000. Scouting eastward in an effort to make contact with Grouchy, whom Napoleon still believed was about Wavre, the gallant Marbot—later the author of one of the finest memoirs of the wars—had instead come upon the entire Prussian IV Corps. Capturing a Prussian courier, he had hastened to bring the man back to the Emperor. Napoleon spoke with the prisoner, a non-commissioned officer of the 2nd Silesian Landwehr Cavalry, one of Bulow's regiments. The man was surprisingly well educated and spoke fluent French. He freely volunteered the information that 30,000 Prussian troops were on the march. "The troops you see are General von Bulow's vanguard." There could no longer be any question as to the identity of the men spotted beyond Chapelle-St. Lambert; they were Prussian.

Napoleon took the news with considerable calm, even as the first rounds of his bombardment began. He had no thought to call off the attack or change his plans. Turning to Soult, he said, "This morning we had ninety chances in our favor. Even now we have sixty chances, and only forty against us." Then he added a sentence or two to a message he was preparing for Grouchy, generally approving the latter's movements as reported in the dispatch he had read at 1000, adding that Bulow's corps seemed imminently likely to arrive on his flank, and adding, "So do not lose a moment in drawing near to us, and effecting a junction with us, in order to catch Bulow, whom you will catch in the very act of concentrating." It amounted to an order recalling Grouchy, but it was already hours too late. Then, as the grand battery fired round after round into the Allied lines, Napoleon calmly altered his dispositions to meet the anticipated attack on his right. All of Lobau's *VI Corps*, 7,500 infantrymen plus some 2,300 attached cavalrymen, were ordered to take up positions covering the army's deep right in the Paris Wood. Then he rode off to the front where *I Corps* was preparing to attack.

1300: The French Infantry Attacks

The grand battery which was to prepare the way for the attack by *I Corps* opened fire at 1300. The tremendous barrage was directed at Wellington's center and center-left, designed to smash the Allied units on either side of the crossroads and softening them up for an infantry assault. But the enormous amount of shot expended had less than a decisive effect. Napoleon's gunners were attempting to employ ricochet fire, aiming the cannon balls not directly at the enemy troops but rather at the ground in front of them. Ideally two things would result from such tactics: upon striking the ground the ball would throw large quantities of rocks and great clods of earth in the direction of the target thereby multiplying the number of potentially lethal projectiles, and then the balls would bounce through the target. A well-aimed ball might bounce several times if fired by this method, causing far more damage than if fired directly into a mass of troops. But ricochet tactics required relatively hard ground, and the soil in front of Wellington's line was still rather water logged, so that the balls often buried themselves rather than bounced, and more often hurled splashes of mud rather than rocks and clods at the enemy. In addition, Wellington's deployment minimized the exposure of his troops to artillery fire. Not only were most of the men posted on reverse slopes, but in virtually every battalion they were ordered to lie down when the firing began, thus reducing their exposure still more. Only one outfit suffered any great loss, Bijlandt's 1st Brigade of the 2nd Dutch-Belgian Division. Deployed forward of the ridge crest, the brigade took round after round. As the Allied troops endured the pounding, d'Erlon got his corps ready for the attack.

D'Erlon's divisions occupied in intervals a front of about 2,400 meters running from the Brussels road, on which rested the left flank General de Brigade Baron Quiot's *1st Division*, eastward to a position just below Frischermont confronted by General de Division Pierre Durutte's *4th*. For some unexplained reason, three of the divisions employed a rather clumsy tactical order massing in variations of "columns of divisions by battalions." Quiot's division advanced in two brigade columns, each comprising four battalions, one behind the other and presenting a front with intervals of about 500 meters with a depth of a dozen meters. General de Division Francois Donzelot's *2nd* and General de Division Baron Marcognet's *3rd Division* in the center each advanced on a single battalion front about 200

Jean Baptiste Drouet d'Erlon

Jean Baptiste Drouet, Comte d'Erlon, general of division (1765-1844), enlisted in the Royal Army in 1782 and passed easily into the service of the Republic, which made him an officer. By 1799 he had risen to general of brigade. Under the Consulate he fought in Switzerland and the Rhineland, rising to general of division by 1803. During the early empire he served as a division commander and staff officer to various corps commanders and was made a count. In 1809 he did well while in temporary command of a corps in Germany and in the following year was sent to Spain, where he served in various capacities until Napoleon's first abdication.

During the Restoration he served in the Royal Army with considerable friction and so easily went over to Napoleon upon his return from Elba. Given command of *I Corps* during the Waterloo campaign, d'Erlon was the victim of conflicting orders which kept him out of the fighting at both Quatre Bras and Ligny, which was where Napoleon wanted him on 16 June. Two days later he led the first French attack at Waterloo, sending his entire corps in against Wellington's left at about 1300 hours, an action which brought him little credit as he failed to issue clear orders or supervise it properly. His performance improved later, when, under Ney's direction, he conducted the attack which succeeded in capturing La Haie Sainte.

After Napoleon's second abdication d'Erlon was scheduled to be shot by the Bourbons, but managed to flee to Bavaria, where he was well regarded. Setting himself up as a brewer and cafe owner, d'Erlon remained in Bavaria until 1825, when he was allowed to return to France. Readmitted to the army, he was governor general of North Africa in 1834-1835 and ended his days as a marshal.

Drouet d'Erlon was typical of the many able subordinate commanders who made their reputations under the Republic and became the backbone of the *Imperial Army*.

---

meters, with all battalions in the division deployed one behind the other for a depth of about 50 meters. In effect these divisions represented a virtually solid mass of troops with about one man per square meter and little tactical flexibility, making a wonderful target. Only the *4th Division* employed a looser more flexible formation. Durutte put his men into "columns of battalions by divisions," in

which each battalion deployed on a two company front—
"by divisions"—with a width and depth of about 50 meters
and density per battalion of only about one man per five
square meters. In addition, the battalions were deployed
checkerboard fashion in two lines of four each, with about
100 meters between the battalions in each line and about
50 meters between the rows so that the division had a front
of nearly 600 meters and a depth of perhaps 150, for a
density of about 22 square meters per man. It has been
suggested that the clumsy deployment of most of the corps
was the result of an error in the transmission of orders, so
that instructions to deploy in "column of battalions by
divisions" came out reading "column of divisions by
battalions"—the sentence structure in French is identical
to that in English in this case—but this fails to explain why
Durutte employed a different formation. An additional
error was that very little cavalry was committed to support
the attack. While some light cavalry was assigned to cover
the flanks of the advancing infantry in order to protect
them from Allied cavalry, only the cuirassiers of General
de Brigade Baron Travers' brigade from Milhaud's *13th
Cavalry Division* were actually assigned to support the
attack. In an infantry attack of this nature, the cavalry
normally was needed to perform two tasks. In the final
moments of the attack they were expected to charge the
enemy infantry, forcing them to form square thus reducing
their fire while making them more vulnerable to fire and
shock. Should the attack tear open the enemy lines, the
troopers were to pour through and change local success
into smashing victory. There were thus several things
wrong with the way in which d'Erlon's attack was going to
be delivered. Yet no one, not even Napoleon, who by 1330
had moved up to La Belle-Alliance to observe the coming
attack, seems to have pointed out the flaws in the plan.
Whoever made these errors, whether Quiot, Donzelot and
Marcognet or d'Erlon as corps commander, or Ney, who
was in overall command, or Napoleon himself as supreme

commander, they were to be costly. By 1330 all seemed in readiness. Ney gave the command. Within minutes d'Erlon's corps was on the move.

With drums beating the charge, some 16,000 infantrymen stepped off with cries of *"Vive l'Empereur!"* The attack began from the left, with Donzelot's men stepping off first followed by Quiot's, then Marcognet's and finally, after only a few minutes, Durutte's. The troops had to cross 1,200 meters of farmland covered with standing wheat and rye to reach Wellington's lines. The grand battery gave support as long as it dared, taking advantage of the fact that elevation permitted it to fire over the heads of the troops, while light cavalry covered the flanks to shield them from enemy horsemen. On they came, closer and closer to the Allied lines. The skirmishers of both armies clashed, and Wellington's fell back. Not until they were within 500 meters did Wellington order his artillery into play. The Allied shells tore great gouges in the ranks of the three closely packed divisions, though Durutte's men got off rather lightly. Despite their losses, despite the muddy ground and the tangled rye, the troops never faltered, moving forward inexorably. On the left Donzelot's men smashed up against La Haie Sainte, driving the men of the K.G.L. 2nd Light Battalion out of the orchard and into the farm buildings. The cuirassiers, supporting Donzelot on his left, helped isolate the little garrison and beat back an attempt to reinforce by the Hanoverian Field Battalion Luneburg, which was virtually shattered. But then the steady fire of the German troops began to tell on the dense ranks. Unable to deploy, Donzelot's attack faltered, though Travers' cuirassiers forced the Hanoverians and K.G.L. battalions holding the main line into square. Meanwhile on the far right, Durutte's men rapidly drove Saxe-Weimar's Nassauers out of Papelotte, La Haie and Frischermont, pushing them back towards the ridge line. But it was in the center that the attack achieved its greatest success. Quiot's and Marcognet's men swarmed up the forward

A recent view of the Ohain Road, near Papelotte, about where the brigades of Vivian, Vandeleur, and Winke began the battle, looking much as it did back in 1815. North (i.e., the Allied side) is to the right. Note that the ground is rather muddy, as it was in 1815, but that the crops are young greens rather than mature grains. Photo by Ed Wimble.

slope of the ridge, forcing the companies of the 95th Foot posted in the Sandpit to fall back to the main line and then smashed right into the most vulnerable of all of Wellington's troops, Bijlandt's Dutch-Belgian brigade. Already battered by the bombardment, having suffered some 750 killed and about 600 wounded—over 40 percent of their 3,200 men, including all officers above the rank of major— Bijlandt's green troops could take no more. They broke to the rear, temporarily disrupting the British 28th Regiment and leaving a gaping hole in Picton's front. The French began to redeploy from columns into line. The moment of victory was at hand! Had cavalry been available it might well have secured the day, but there was none, for Travers' cuirassiers were off to the left. And as d'Erlon's moment

Although not based on an incident which occurred during the battle, this illustration, entitled "Close up the ranks!" depicts a scene which must have occurred many times at Waterloo, as an old sergeant orders the troops to maintain their front, filling in the places of the fallen.

hung in the balance, Picton acted. With the French at 40 meters, he ordered his brigade commanders, Major General Sir Denis Pack and Lieutenant General Sir James Kempt into the fray.

As the British troops rose from their prone positions their officers cried out orders! "Ninety-Second, you must advance!" yelled Pack as he led the Gordon Highlanders forward with the 42nd and 44th close behind, while Kempt's men poured in volley after volley at less than 40 meters range. Picton placed himself at the head of Kempt's brigade, waving his sword and shouting, "Charge! Hurrah! Hurrah!" As Pack's men smashed into d'Erlon's troops at the improbable odds of perhaps 2,000 to 8,000, they faltered momentarily. Picton cried out, "Rally the Highlanders" and then fell dead with a bullet through his famed top hat. Despite his death, the attack gained momentum. Within minutes Lord Uxbridge came up with the Guards Cavalry Brigade under Major General Lord Edward Somerset (Fitzroy Somerset's elder brother) and Major General Sir William Ponsonby's Union Brigade.

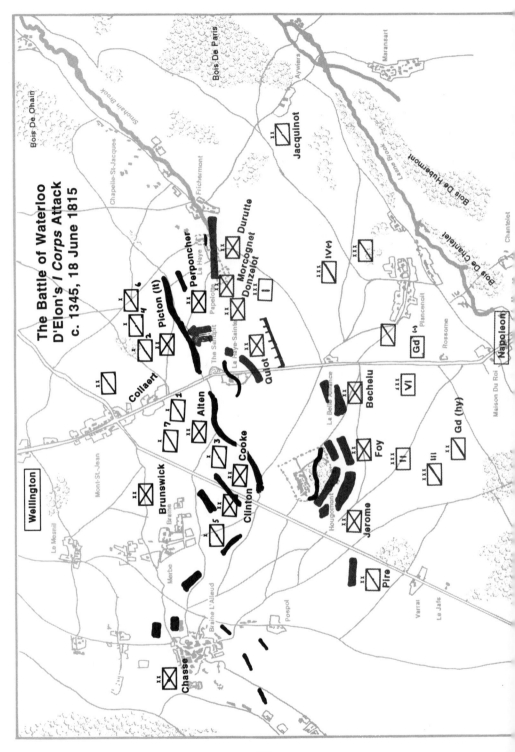

The Battle of Waterloo
D'Elon's I Corps Attack
c. 1345, 18 June 1815

Lieutenant General Sir Thomas Picton, commander of Wellington's 5th Division, who fell at the head of his troops at Waterloo, here uncharacteristically dressed in uniform, rather than his customary dark civilian coat with top hat.

Personally leading up the Life Guards, Wellington said, "Now, gentlemen, for the honor of the Household troops," and 1,400 Guardsmen charged, scattering Travers' cuirassiers before smashing into Donzelot's left flank. Almost simultaneously, Ponsonby's troopers charged through the ranks of the 92nd Highlanders with the Royal Scots Greys in the lead. Catching hold of their countrymen's stirrups, some of the Highlanders joined the charge, crying, "Hurrah, 92nd! Scotland forever!" They plunged together into Marcognet's massed troops. The momentum of the twin charges was enormous. Struck by both cavalry and infantry, the French gave way despite fierce resistance. Within minutes d'Erlon's attack had been broken, the shattered columns swarming back to their own lines, having lost the eagles of the *45th* and the *105th* and leaving behind over a thousand dead and more than 2,000 prisoners. Wellington's front was secure. But the moment of victory is the moment of greatest danger. The enthusiasm of the moment infected the British cavalry: ignoring the call to rally, they

La Haie Sainte (or La Haye-Sainte), under attack by the Baron Quiot's 1st Brigade of the 1st Division, at about 1330, shortly after having overrun the orchard.

pressed on, harrying the French infantry to the rear and advancing on Napoleon's grand battery.

Watching from La Belle-Alliance, Napoleon saw the Scots Greys overrun a part of his grand battery. Calmly remarking, "Those terrible grey horses, how they fight!" and he then launched a swarm of cavalry against them. Two fresh regiments from the *1st Cavalry Division*, the *3rd* and *4th Lancers*, slammed into the Union Brigade, while two more of cuirassiers struck the Guards. The British troopers were virtually surrounded in Napoleon's grand battery. A wild melee ensued, as the tired British tried to cut their way out, aided by the light dragoons of Major General Sir John Vandeleur's 4th Cavalry Brigade and the hussars of Sir Hussey Vivian's 6th. In the end nearly half of those who had charged failed to return, among them Ponsonby himself, who was wounded by repeated lance thrusts. The injured Posonby would be succored by a

*The charge of the Scots Greys, from the painting "Scotland For-
ever," by Lady Butler, painted in the late nineteenth century. Although her husband, the commander of the regiment, arranged for
her to witness an actual charge from the front, Lady Butler's picture is wrong on a number of accounts, most notably in the align-
ment of the troops. Their front is curved, and they are going away
from each other: if they had actually charged in this fashion they
would have had to all begin from a single point, and would soon
have dispersed all over the battlefield.*

French major of the dragoons, Baron de Laussat, whom he
would meet again by chance 19 years later. Thus the
impetuosity of Wellington's troopers marred what would
otherwise have been a signal success. In the end, he had
lost more men than had the French, for to the 4,000 infantry
casualties he had suffered, he now had to add 2,500
cavalrymen lost or rendered useless, for Ponsonby's brigade had been completely shattered and Somerset's badly

The British cavalry attack. The French cuirassiers prepare to deliver their counterattack, the British having charged too far.

mauled. Nevertheless, time had been gained. At about 1430, even as his cavalry was plunging headlong against Napoleon's artillery, Wellington had spotted in the distance some Prussian patrols. As the last troopers streamed back to his lines, at about 1500 Wellington was confident that the Prussians were indeed on their way. Meanwhile there settled over the field a relative calm. Wellington used this lull to good advantage, sending yet another couple of companies of guardsmen to bolster the defenders of Hougoumont, where a fire broke out at about this time as a result of a bombardment with incendiary shells and burned most of the buildings and with them scores of wounded from both armies; Wellington instructed the defenders to hold the ruins as long as defense seemed practical. In the center, while placing Kempt in command of Picton's division, he sent the 95th back into the Sandpit

A modern view of the farm of La Haie Sainte. During the battle the barn door, on the right, was missing, having been burned for firewood by Allied troops the night before the battle. During the fiercest of the fighting for the place, the troops of Major George Baring's 2nd Light Battalion, K.G.L., temporarily blocked the entry with an improvised barrier which included 19 French corpses. Photo by Ed Wimble.

and two companies of the K.G.L. 1st Light Battalion together with some of the Nassauers that had been pulled out of Hougoumont into La Haie Sainte. At the same time he brought into the line Major General Sir John Lambert's 10th Brigade of 2,500, with many veterans of the Peninsula, to replace Bijlandt's brigade, which surprisingly rallied not too far in the rear. On his right he brought forward a battalion each of the K.G.L., Brunswickers and Hanoverians to bolster the Guards Division. Meanwhile, on his left flank, Saxe-Weimar managed to reoccupy Papelotte while the 1,200 hussars and light dragoons of the 1st Light Brigade of the Dutch-Belgian Cavalry Division skirmished with the *3rd* and *4th Lancers* of d'Erlon's *1st*

Cavalry Division, commanded by Baron Jacquinot. While making these dispositions, Wellington also found the time to visit several parts of the front and even popped in on La Haie Sainte and the Sandpit.

The troops were taking a terrible punishment. Sergeant Lawrence of the 40th Foot recalled later that as the 10th Brigade moved up, "a shell from the enemy cut our Deputy Sergeant Major in two, and having passed on to take the head off one of my company of grenadiers named William Hooper, exploded in the rear not more than one yard from me, hurling me at least two yards in the air." Lawrence was lucky. Beyond a scrape on his face he was uninjured, despite the fact that the tassels on his sash were burned and his sword hilt blackened by the blast. As Wellington's troops stood the French pounding and the Duke himself went about his business, across the valley to the south Napoleon too was active.

Even as the last of his cavalrymen streamed back behind the French lines, Napoleon had received a message from Grouchy, dispatched at about 1130. It was a sobering communique, for it made clear that Grouchy was in no position to succor Napoleon on this day, for he was too far away and had effectively lost touch with the bulk of the Prussian Army. The situation was now grim. At this point Napoleon had several options. He could go over to the defense. However, such a course was suicidal, for Wellington would be unlikely to attack until the Prussians were at hand in force, whereupon the French would be so outnumbered as to make defeat certain. He could fall back, effecting a juncture with Grouchy in a day or so, and then try for a rematch. Unfortunately, that would mean abandoning the field, thereby conceding victory to Wellington by default, with possible potent political implications. In addition, it would give Wellington and Blucher time to join forces, which would mean a future engagement would have to be fought against considerably superior numbers. In the end, the third option was the only viable one, to attempt to win the battle before the Prussians arrived. At about 1530 Napoleon issued new orders to Ney, flatly instructing him to seize La Haie Sainte immediately at whatever cost. Ney acted with commendable speed.

1545: The French Cavalry Attacks

Within minutes of receiving Napoleon's order to take La Haie Sainte, Ney had organized an attack. The grand battery opened fire again. Gathering up all of d'Erlon's men who could be rallied quickly, a brigade each from the divisions of Quiot and Donzelot, Ney personally led them forward, ordering some of Milhaud's cuirassiers to follow behind. The storm of shot and shell which now engulfed Wellington's center was heavier even than that which had preceded d'Erlon's assault. Indeed, it was perhaps the most intense bombardment hitherto in history. Seasoned veterans from Spain remarked upon the volume of fire. Several Allied ammunition wagons blew up in spectacular pyrotechnic displays. Ney's two brigades were subject to an intense Allied barrage, but they never faltered, coming up smartly and smashing into the defenders of La Haie Sainte. The heavily outnumbered K.G.L. defenders, no more than 500 or so men against 4,000, gave a good account of themselves in a hot engagement, holding the French at the edge of the orchard. As this action unfolded a series of seemingly inconsequential incidents took place.

Seeing the approaching French, Wellington put his center into squares, pulling some of the battalions back to lower positions on the reverse slope while ordering up additional forces from Chasse's division and Picton's flank. Meanwhile, some of Wellington's troops were escorting groups of prisoners to the rear along with scores of wounded, who were crowded into ammunition wagons. At the same time, one of the cavalry regiments posted to the rear of the line pulled back somewhat to avoid the shower of shot. All of these actions were individually

Marshal Ney, on one of the five horses he would lose during the battle, in a sketch made many years later. A fine commander at one time, by 1815 Ney was long past his prime, and Napoleon ought never to have entrusted him with the direction of so important a battle.

A carbineer, two regiments of which took part in Ney's great cavalry charges during the mid-afternoon. Although there were some details of equipment, uniform, and mission which differed between carbineers — carabiniers — and cuirassiers, of which there were a dozen regiments with the army, both were breast-plated heavy cavalry.

minor in the unfolding drama of the battle. But taken together they had enormous consequences.

From in front of La Haie Sainte, 500 meters or so away, Ney at the head of the *54th* and *55th of the Line* noticed these rearward movements in Wellington's center. Through the smoke, noise and confusion, it appeared to Ney that the Allies were pulling out. He ordered the escorting cuirassier brigade to charge, hoping to turn the retreat into a rout. Baron Delort, commanding the *14th Cavalry Division*, objected, citing the muddy condition of the ground, but Ney demurred, telling him to go in with his whole division. Within minutes Milhaud's other division, General de Division Wathier Comte de St. Alphonse's *13th Cavalry Division*, had been committed as well. Seeing Milhaud's entire corps—some 3,000 cuirassiers—forming up in a dale just in front of d'Erlon's lines, Lefebvre-Desnouettes brought the *Guard Light Cavalry* into position behind them on his own initiative. At about 1600, some 5,000 cavalrymen began moving across the valley. So hastily had the attack been organized that no infantry had been ordered up to support it, nor was the order given for horse artillery to go along. Worse yet, instead of being sent against Picton's front, on Wellington's left, which had already been battered by d'Erlon's attack, the charge was directed against Wellington's center, held by Alten's relatively unscathed British 3rd Division. Moreover, as they advanced, the troopers masked the fire of the grand battery, by now shifted to the west side of the Brussels road, thereby depriving themselves of artillery support. Watching from his observation post at Rossomme, Napoleon could do nothing. The divisions were deployed next to each other with the *Guard Light Cavalry* on the left. Each division had four regiments abreast in squadron columns. As a squadron of about 100 men usually deployed in two lines on a front of about 50 meters, with intervals each division had a front of about 250 meters and a depth of 50

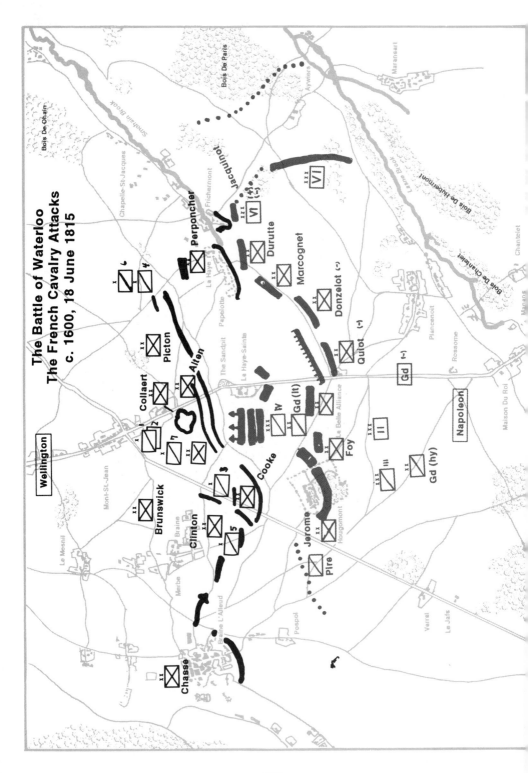

The Battle of Waterloo
The French Cavalry Attacks
c. 1600, 18 June 1815

With Marshal Ney and his staff at their head, the French cuirassiers charge the Allied line, in a scene from the 110 meter cyclorama of the battle in the Musee du Panorama de Waterloo.

to 75. Thus the attacking cavalry had a front of about 750 meters and a depth of perhaps 75.

The charging squadrons moved off obliquely to the Allied front, a direction dictated by the need to avoid flanking infantry fire from Hougoumont and La Haie Sainte. This narrowed the available maneuvering room to but 1,200 meters. The charge was conducted in standard

"Prepare to receive cavalry!" The Duke of Wellington encourages his troops to stand fast, as his gunners get ready to fire their last rounds and seek shelter in the infantry squares.

fashion. During the initial stages the troopers advanced at a walk, only slowly increasing their pace to a trot and then a canter. Not until they had advanced about 800 meters, a matter of five minutes or so, during which they were already receiving the attentions of the Allied artillery, did they wheel somewhat to the right to face directly against Wellington's center. At this point about 500 meters from their objective, the charge actually began. Now, as they attempted to get up a full speed of ideally 20 kilometers an hour, the muddy nature of the ground began to tell. Meanwhile Wellington's troops made ready.

"Prepare to receive cavalry!" rang out in the Allied battalions. The troops sprang into action. In many cases the men had been calmly lying down on reverse slopes. Now they formed ranks, covering the crest and reverse slope of the ridge with 20 squares arranged checkerboard fashion in two rows. Each square—actually more like a rectangle—had four ranks to a side bristling with bayonets; as one row knelt, a second stood at the charge and

An extremely exaggerated depiction of the effects of the "sunken-road" on the French cavalry. In fact, although the road was somewhat lower than the surrounding ground, the difference was by no means as great as shown, and the attacking cavalrymen were only mildly affected by it. In the aftermath of the battle however, apologists for the French, most notably Victor Hugo, made much of the incident.

two others prepared to fire. Between and in front of the squares the Allied gunners stood to their pieces. Behind the squares, partially as a reserve and partially to encourage the fainthearted, Wellington deployed several regiments of light cavalry. As the French came on, the Allied gunners sent round after round into their ranks, towards the last double-shotting the guns with a round of canister atop one of solid shot. The storm of fire swept through the attacking squadrons, killing and wounding scores of men and horses, but not checking their advance. The cuirassiers and lancers and chasseurs swept up the muddy slope. Although some of the French troopers plunged helplessly down the side of the sunken Ohain road, most, tradition to the contrary notwithstanding, negotiated the obstacle and

An officer of **Chasseurs a Cheval** *of the* **Garde.**

pressed on. Getting off one final round, most of the Allied gunners, as ordered, abandoned their pieces and fled to the refuge of the nearest squares, often with the French so close behind that they were forced to lie down beneath the leveled bayonets. But not all did so. Fearing that a battalion of green Brunswickers that he was supporting would break if they saw his men abandon their pieces, Captain Cavalie Mercer held his troop of the Royal Horse Artillery to their work, everyone seeking shelter beneath the guns as the French thundered through their position, unable to reach the gunners with their sabers.

Napoleon saw the movement of the Allied gunners from afar. Thinking that the game was up, he cried, "The English are done for! Their general is an ignoramus!" And indeed, the attack appeared both magnificent and inexorable. Ensign Rees Gronow of the Foot Guards was later to write,

> Not a man present who survived could have forgotten in after life the awful grandeur of that charge. You perceived at a distance what appeared to be an overwhelming, long moving line, which, ever advancing, glittered like a stormy wave of the sea when it catches the sunlight. On came the mounted host until they got near enough, while the very earth seemed to vibrate beneath their thundering tramp. One might have supposed that nothing could have resisted the shock of this terrible moving mass. They were the famous cuirassiers, almost all old soldiers who had distinguished themselves on most of the battlefields of Europe. In an almost incredibly short period they were within 20 yards of us, shouting "*Vive l'Empereur!*"

And at 20 yards the steady infantry delivered a volley. Scores of the attackers fell. The charge faltered. Further volleys followed. The momentum of the attack was broken and the cavalrymen swarmed around the squares of the first row only to wash up against those in the second. The attackers made strenuous efforts to break the solid ranks, riding around and around, firing their carbines and pistols at them, while the lancers attempted to spear their way in. But it was to no avail. In the face of the steady lines of bayonets and the continuous fire, the horses refused to press home. Casualties mounted amongst the attackers and in the squares as well. Ensign Gronow wrote, "It was impossible to move a yard without treading upon a wounded comrade, or the bodies of the dead, and the loud groans of our wounded and dying were most appalling." As men fell they were replaced in the first ranks with men pressed forward by officers and sergeants. Some squares were forced to narrow their frontage, but none admitted the French. With neither infantry to engage nor horse artillery to shoot down the defenders, the French cavalry-men repeatedly attempted to attack, each time being beaten off. Soon Wellington ordered his own cavalry in. Uxbridge committed the British 3rd, 5th and 7th Cavalry Brigades, 4,500 hussars and light dragoons, the Brunswick cavalry, 700 hussars and over 200 uhlans, determined on avenging their fallen duke, and the Heavy Brigade of the Dutch-Belgian Cavalry Division, some 1,200 carabiniers, for a total of nearly 6,000 troopers. The charge helped drive the French back from the line of squares. Cognizant of his earlier failure to rein in the Guards and Union Brigades, Uxbridge kept firm control of his squadrons, and the attack halted when it had ejected the French from the ridge and the troopers pulling back. Wellington's gunners returned to their pieces, which the French had failed to spike, and opened fire once more. Despite this Allied artillery fire, the French rallied at the base of the ridge and renewed the attack. This time they were unable to gain sufficient momentum, and barely reached the crest of the ridge before Wellington's gunners swept them back again. Finally, after four charges and numerous local attacks and suffering casualties, Ney called them back. The battered squadrons turned from the line of squares. As the French rode back down the slope over the bodies of hundreds of dead and wounded men and horses, the Allied guns came once more into play, inflicting further casualties.

Watching the French go, Wellington turned to an aide inquiring as to the time. It was about 1620. He said, "The battle is mine; and if the Prussians arrive soon, there will be an end of the war." And indeed, the Prussians had come, for by 1600 they were skirmishing with the cavalry which Napoleon had posted in front of the Paris Wood on his extreme right flank.

Napoleon observed all this from afar. He was not pleased by what he saw. Turning to Soult, he said, "This movement is premature and may yet have disastrous results on this day. It is an hour too early." But even as his

"The Wounded Cuirassier."

troopers were still hotly engaged, he considered his options. Comte Lobau, guarding his right flank, should be able to hold the Prussians for a while. If he could break Wellington soon he would win the battle before the Prussians could pose a serious threat. Ney's charge had been an error of judgment, but perhaps it had at least strained the defenders. Napoleon decided that a second blow delivered immediately might do the trick. He ordered Kellermann's

III Cavalry Corps up. Kellermann protested, but before he could obtain confirmation of the orders, Baron l'Heritier took matters in his own hands and started his *11th Cavalry Division* off. It was as though every man on horseback had lost his head. The balance of Kellermann's corps joined l'Heritier's men, as did the *Guard Heavy Cavalry*, though Napoleon seems not to have intended them to take part. Soon nearly 6,000 cavalrymen were mustering for a charge. But still more were to join in. As Milhaud's men and those of Lefebvre-Desnouettes fell back at last, they rallied. Anxious to recoup their earlier failure, they fell in behind Kellermann's squadrons. By 1700 thousands of cavalrymen—at least 8,000 and possibly as many as 10,000 depending upon the casualties which Milhaud and Lefebvre-Desnouettes had suffered and how many of their man had rallied—were pounding across the casualty littered field towards Wellington's line of battered squares. Kellermann alone seems to have kept his head. As he joined his troopers, he ordered one brigade to halt, so that 800 carabiniers alone remained uncommitted of the Emperor's entire reserve of cavalry.

Once more the French cavalry rode up the slope on a front of about 500 meters. Once more Wellington's gunners fired until the last and then fled to the safety of the nearest squares. And once more the French tide broke on the steady squares, though many took a severe beating. The attacks were delivered with tremendous elan and dedication, courage so desperate as to elicit admiring comments even from the foes, one British officer exclaiming, "By God, those fellows deserve Bonaparte, they fight so nobly for him!" Like many of the men, Ney, who personally led several of the attacks and lost his fourth horse of the day in the process, seems to have been afflicted by a battle lust: during one attack he was seen beating on a British gun with a broken saber. Nevertheless, however brave they were, no troopers could be expected to break infantry squares unsupported. Once again the French attack had

"The Last Trophies," Allied battle flags being presented to Napoleon, the last such he would ever see.

been poorly made, for no infantry accompanied the cavalry and but a single battery, which, though it wrought great execution against the squares on which it fired, could do little to affect the overall course of the struggle. Nevertheless, Ney tried repeatedly to break the Allied front. In desperation he ordered up even the single brigade of carabiniers which Kellermann had withheld from the fight. Their commander Baron Blanchard protested. "The salvation of France is at stake!" cried the marshal and sent him into action. Altogether eight charges seem to have been made and scores of attacks. Some squares were not hit even once, while one claimed to have been struck 23 times, though the average was seven or eight. Wellington—whose opinion of Napoleon sank during the battle, "Damn the fellow, he's a mere pounder after all."—was seemingly everywhere, moving from square to square with remarkable immunity with men falling all around him. He issued orders calmly, calling up additional units and once personally leading the Life Guards into position for a counterattack. His mere presence was often sufficient to steady a shaken square, as the officers shouted out, "Silence! Stand to your front! Here's the Duke." Casualties were heavy on both sides. Finally, even Ney, the "Bravest of the Brave," had to call it off. By 1730 the shattered squadrons were streaming back down the corpse littered slopes, as the Allied gunners once more sprang to their pieces to fire into their backs.

In the two hours of cavalry attacks the French made two grand assaults for a total of about a dozen charges, committing altogether nearly 10,000 men. The results had been poor. Napoleon's cavalry had suffered greatly, between 30 percent and 40 percent of the men had fallen casualty. To be sure, the Allied line had been seriously battered, with many of Wellington's battalions reduced to ineffectiveness, but none had broken, though perhaps only the presence of the 10th Hussars in their rear had held some of the greener Brunswickers to their duty. Now the Duke was busily shifting men about to strengthen his line. He brought Chasse's division over from Braine l'Alleud to replenish his reserve. He put half the Guards Division into his center, and placed all of Clinton's 2nd Division into the line. Finally he sent the light company of the K.G.L.'s 5th Line Battalion into La Haie Sainte to bolster the dwindling garrison under Major George Baring. This would leave him a bit thin on the ground in some places. But if he had ever held any doubts about winning, he held them no longer, for from the east the sounds of heavy fighting had been audible for some time. The Prussians had arrived.

1700: Plancenoit

Bulow's IV Corps had marched hard through the morning and into the afternoon. Around 1600 elements of Bulow's advanced guard had started skirmishing with pickets from the *3rd Cavalry Division* and outposts of Lobau's *VI Corps* to the east of Plancenoit, a small village little more than a kilometer east of the Charleroi-Brussels road to the southeast of the main Waterloo battlefield. Lobau advanced using a peculiar deployment which placed his two divisions in line one behind the other. Despite this, his veterans pressed forward against light resistance from the somewhat more numerous troops of Bulow's 15th and 16th Infantry Brigades, composed primarily of Landwehr, largely unseasoned militiamen. But as more and more of Bulow's men emerged from the Paris Wood, Lobau's troops were increasingly outnumbered. Then, at about 1630 Blucher himself arrived at Lasne, not far to the rear. Observing Wellington's lines from afar, he decided an immediate attack was necessary, passing the word on to Bulow by the hand of the faithful Nostiz. With two brigades, plus all his cavalry and artillery up, Bulow had over half his corps. He attacked. By 1700 Lobau had fallen back towards Plancenoit. Unable or unwilling to break Lobau's front, Bulow attempted a turning movement around Lobau's right, which would have put him in Napoleon's rear. Lobau fell back on the village which was somewhat lower than the country to its east. He put a brigade into Plancenoit and stretched his other three to the north in an attempt to link up with the right flank of *I Corps*. Surveying the scene, Blucher remarked, "If only we had that damned village," and ordered it taken. In a determined attack, Bulow struck Plancenoit with three batteries and the 16th Brigade—some 6,000 men supported by 24 guns against perhaps 2,000 with no more than 8 pieces—while the 13th and 15th Brigades of 12,000 infantrymen supported by 64 guns—confronted Lobau's three other brigades of 5,500 or so infantry with perhaps 24 guns. Attacking with two battalions each against the right, the center, and the left of the Plancenoit position, Bulow's men ejected Lobau's brigade from Plancenoit. Prussian artillery rounds were soon falling in the vicinity of Napoleon's headquarters and on the Charleroi-Brussels road, Napoleon's only line of retreat. The Emperor reacted swiftly. General de Division Philippe Duhesme and the

Young Guard were thrown in, along with a horse artillery battery of the *Artillery Reserve*, nearly 5,000 men with 6 guns.

Supported by Lobau's artillery, Duhesme's youthful guardsmen swept into Plancenoit. They drove the Prussians from the village and the cemetery beyond in a single furious assault, while Lobau formed a defensive line stretching northwards to link up with the right flank of *I Corps*. But Bulow recovered rapidly. In infantry alone, his incomplete corps outnumbered the defenders of Plancenoit by over three-to-two, some 18,000 to no more than 12,000, and he had nearly twice as much artillery, some 88 guns to 50. He made another attack on the village. As the 16th Brigade struck the village, the 13th and 15th pinned Lobau's attention to its north all along the line to the vicinity of Papelotte, where Lobau's flank abutted that of d'Erlon at 90 degrees. Bulow's second attack on Plancenoit, by six battalions of the 16th Brigade and two of the 14th, was beaten off by the *Young Guard*. It was now nearly 1800. The 14th Brigade having come up, Bulow essayed yet another attempt against Plancenoit, while requesting support from I Corps, which had been reported in the vicinity of Ohain.

For his third try at Plancenoit, Bulow committed five battalions from the 14th Brigade and two from the 16th, with the balance of both brigades rendering fire support. The troops attacked from several directions at once under cover of heavy artillery fire. After a short, fierce fight, the *Young Guard* was ejected from Plancenoit in considerable disorder. It was shortly after 1800. Lobau and Duhesme called for reinforcements. As Prussian shot once more rained down around his headquarters, Napoleon had to face a difficult choice, for Ney was at that same moment calling for more troops from his post in La Haie Sainte for a desperate try at breaking Wellington's center. Of fresh troops, Napoleon had but 15 battalions left, the famed *Old Guard*. The Emperor acted quickly. If he supported Ney, he might break Wellington, but in the process find the Prussians smashing into his army from the rear; while if he supported Lobau and Duhesme he could stabilize the situation on his flank and still have time to crush Wellington. He sent two battalions of guardsmen into Plancenoit on the double, while ordering 11 more to form a line of squares running along the Charleroi-Brussels road from La Belle-Alliance to Rossomme, thus creating a reserve line should disaster befall his troops at Plancenoit, while still being available to support the main front to the north. The remaining two battalions he retained as a general reserve and headquarters guard. This arrangement was a poor compromise, for it committed the entire reserve to Plancenoit, yet only two battalions were actually to fight.

The attack of the *Old Guard* at Plancenoit was a fine example of their skill, courage and dash, fitting testimony to their record as some of the finest troops in history. The two battalions—the *1st* of the *2nd Grenadiers* and the *1st* of the *2nd Chasseurs*, some 1,100 men in all—went into Plancenoit with the bayonet. They swept into the village in two battalion columns without firing a shot. In less than 20 minutes of furious house-to-house fighting the *Old Guard* retook Plancenoit. By about 1830 fully 14 battalions of Prussians, over a third of Bulow's corps, were in flight before them. As the regrouped men of the *Young Guard* resumed their positions in Plancenoit, the *Old Guard* battalions pressed on, clearing some small woods to the east of the village and emerging into open ground. At this point, Bulow launched a counterattack. Caught in the open by superior numbers, the veteran guardsmen fell back. Despite this setback, by 1845 the situation on Napoleon's right had been stabilized. This was good news for Napoleon, for the situation on the main front was becoming critical and he badly needed the battalions which had formed square along the Charleroi-Brussels road for a desperate venture. He began shifting them to the vicinity of La Belle-Alliance.

General Baron Pelet, commander of the **2nd Chasseurs** *of the* **Old Guard,** *attempts to rally the* **Young Guard,** *as his troops come up to bolster the defense of the village in the face of an overwhelmingly superior assault by the Prussian IV Corps.*

While Napoleon was regrouping his increasingly slender reserve, Prussian strength was growing. Zeithen's I Corps, perhaps 20,000 men, had reached the vicinity of Ohain at about 1800. Zeithen had halted there for a time, uncertain as to his next moves. One of his staff officers had observed from afar the Allied lines in front of Mont-St. Jean and, seeing the long column of wounded streaming to the rear, had committed the same error as Ney had made earlier, concluding that Wellington was about to retreat. He passed his information to Zeithen at about 1830, just about when Bulow's request for support had reached him. This put Zeithen in a difficult spot, having to decide whether to continue westward to support Wellington or move southwards to assist Bulow. While he hesitated, Carl von Muffling came up and quickly disabused him of the notion that Wellington was pulling out. This set I Corps on the proper course once more. Meanwhile Generalmajor Georg von Pirch's II Corps, some 15,000 strong, was coming up as well, by 1830 having a brigade at Couture, about two kilometers northeast of Plancenoit.

The struggle for Plancenoit had been a difficult one. Although casualty figures are unavailable save for French officers, these alone tell an interesting tale. Of 486 infantry officers involved in the fighting against Bulow's IV Corps—335 from *VI Corps*, 117 from the *Young Guard* and an estimated 34 from the *Old Guard*—17 had been killed (3.5 percent) and 151 wounded (31.1 percent), which, together with a handful of prisoners, amounted to over a third of the officers involved, a serious loss and indicative of the intensity of the fighting. Despite this great effort, the outcome of the struggle for Plancenoit was not decisive. The combat did not determine the outcome of Waterloo. In a sense Plancenoit was a side show, running its course in relative isolation from the events on Napoleon's principal front, that against Wellington. Nevertheless, Plancenoit did help shape the course of what was to follow. The action at Plancenoit had secured Napoleon's right, though at the cost of most of his infantry reserves. This gained him time, a commodity with which he had been rather careless over the last few days. If the battle could still be won, and there is no evidence that Napoleon despaired that it could, it had to be done soon and it had to be against Wellington. Indeed, even as the struggle for Plancenoit was at its most intense, that to Napoleon's front had grown still more critical. But so too had that on Wellington's front. The Duke's line was thin now, with reserves virtually gone. He was becoming anxious and was heard to mutter, "Would that night or Blucher came." The supreme moment of the battle was at hand.

1800: The Crisis

By 1800 the Emperor's cavalry had been broken and was streaming back from the ridge at Mont-St. Jean, where Wellington was calmly if speedily juggling battalions and brigades around to strengthen his strained center. As Marshal Ney made his way back to the French lines he came upon some fresh troops, Bachelu's *5th Division* and that half of Foy's *9th* which had not been sucked into the cauldron of fire that was Hougoumont, some 6,500 men in all. He led them forward in a hastily organized attack. As the French artillery resumed its fire, the troops advanced in good order, but once more without proper supports. They approached the Allied line between La Haie Sainte and Hougoumont, by chance precisely that portion of the front into which Wellington had just put the best of his dwindling reserves, shoving leftward the battered battalions of Hanoverians and Nassauers and Brunswickers, K.G.L. and Britons which had withstood the cavalry charges. Deployed were Major General Peregine Maitland's 1st Brigade, some 2,000 sturdy guardsmen, and Major General Frederick Adam's 3rd, over 2,500 riflemen and light infantry, the latter in an improvised four-deep line rather than two-deep as was the British custom. As the French infantry advanced they once more masked the fire of the grand battery. Thus relieved of the punishing attentions of the French artillery, the Allied troops could devote themselves fully to the attacking infantry. An enormous volume of musketry and artillery fire greeted the attackers, a "hail of death" in the words of Maximilien Foy, who was grievously wounded in the shoulder. Hundreds fell. Riding by the defending battalions Wellington was heard to mutter to himself, "I believe we shall beat them after all," and ordered what was left of his cavalry into action. There was little of it available. The Dutch-Belgian Heavy Cavalry Brigade, which had done well earlier, now refused to charge. The Duke of Cumberland's Hussars, a contingent of affluent young Hanoverian gentlemen off to enjoy the wars at their own expense, fled the field, their colonel at their head, spreading rumors of defeat all the way back to Brussels. A charge was improvised with troops on hand, a miscellany of British, K.G.L. and Brunswicker stragglers and casuals, which helped beat back the French. Within 10 minutes of the start of the attack, Foy's and Bachelu's men were in retreat, having suffered 1,500 casualties. Wellington's line had held once again. Observing the action, Napoleon noted the importance to the defense of La Haie Sainte, which had delivered devastating rifle fire into the flank of the attackers. He renewed his order of 1530 that the place be taken. Within minutes, Ney was making ready to attack again.

Gathering up a brigade from Donzelot's *2nd Division*, perhaps 2,000 men, Ney added to them a detachment of engineers, a battery of light artillery and some regiments of cavalry. Ordering the balance of *I Corps* to follow him as soon as possible, he led these forward at about 1815 or so. For the first time the French were making a combined arms attack, coordinating the different arms to work in concert. Under cover of a heavy artillery barrage Ney advanced in a relatively open order behind a screen of skirmishers with his flanks covered by light cavalry. The attackers crossed the 500 meters from the grand battery to the orchard in about 6 minutes. Defensive fire was surprisingly light. Among the farm buildings Major George Baring's garrison, although comprising 9 companies of the King's German Legion and a contingent of Nassauers, had been reduced to about 375 men. Some of the defenders had been fighting all day and the supply of ammunition was dangerously low, most troops having but 4 or 5 rounds left out of the 60 with which they had started. Nor could they scavenge ammunition from the numerous dead and dying French troops about them, for, save for the Nassauers, they were armed with Baker rifles, requiring special ammunition. Somehow in the chaos of battle no one had heeded Baring's repeated calls for ammunition. Nevertheless, despite the desperate shortage, the troops were a grimly determined lot, one man even telling Baring, who was British, "No man will desert you, we will fight and die with you."

The French rapidly gained control of the orchard and pressed up to the farm buildings. While some of them struggled to climb through windows and over walls, a sapper lieutenant battered down the main gate with an axe and led a party into the enclosure. A ferocious hand-to-hand fight ensued, with heavy losses on both sides. Finally, Baring ordered his men to abandon the place. By 1830 it was over, only 45 of the garrison making it back to the security of the Allied lines, barely 400 meters to the rear. La Haie Sainte was finally in Ney's hands.

Having taken the vital farm, Ney did not rest on his laurels. He summoned up the other divisions of *I Corps*. Meanwhile a battery was posted in the garden behind the farmhouses. Its guns quickly began to bombard the battered survivors of Kempt's 8th and Lambert's 10th Brigades, deployed on the main front just east of the Brussels road. If anything, the fighting grew more intense. As Sergeant Lawrence of the 40th stood next to his company commander, "a cannon shot came and took the captain's head clean off," saturating him with the man's blood, then with 14 color sergeants already down "and officers in proportion," the regimental standard was entrusted to his reluctant hands. Nevertheless, Lawrence survived virtually unscathed. Meanwhile, under the intense fire the

Sandpit was evacuated, the troops adding their rifles to the defense of the main line. The French mustered for an attack on the thin line of British troops. Observing the situation, Lieutenant General Charles Alten, commanding the wreck of his own division and several additional units on the front just west of the Brussels road, ordered Baron Ompteda's 2nd K.G.L. Brigade to strike an advancing French column, the balance of Donzelot's division, just then beginning to move into action. Aware that a regiment of French cuirassiers was posted just west of the farm, Ompteda wisely chose to disregard these instructions. But at that very moment the Prince of Orange came up and flatly ordered him to put his two battalions, the 5th and 8th, into line and attack. His protests overruled by the brave but inept Prince, Ompteda entrusted the safety of his two teenage nephews to his second-in-command, put himself at the head of his troops and advanced. The French cuirassiers struck the two battalions on their right flank. They were cut to pieces, the 8th losing its colors and Ompteda himself being numbered among the dead. Colonel Frederick Arentschildt, commanding the 7th Cavalry Brigade, threw the 3rd Hussars of the K.G.L. into the flank of the French cuirassiers, driving them off and enabling the few survivors of the debacle to regain the security of the ridgeline.

Further to the right, Wellington was observing the action from among the guardsmen of Maitland's 1st Brigade. Skirmishers from Quiot's *1st Division* had advanced part way up the ridge and were beginning to cause injury to Maitland's and Adam's troops. A more determined attack against Adam's front gained some ground, thus threatening to isolate Hougoumont. Seeing this, Wellington put the Guards into a line four men deep and told them, "Drive those fellows away." The Guards proceeded to do just that, chasing the French off the ridge. But then they were attacked by some French cavalry. Forming square, they beat off the charge and fell back to the security of the ridge.

By now most of *I Corps* was in action once more. Marcognet's *3rd Division* was trading volleys with Pack's British 9th Brigade and Best's Hanoverian 4th, though not pressing the action. Over on the Allied far left, Durutte had committed his *4th Division* against Saxe-Weimar's Nassauers clinging to the farmsteads of Frischermont, La Haie and Papelotte. The fighting there became intense, and each side made several attacks and counterattacks, both displaying fine tactical skill. But the position was naturally strong and Saxe-Weimar was able to keep Durutte from gaining control of any of the buildings for long. Nevertheless, by about 1845 the situation grew desperate for Saxe-Weimar, who had to give up all three places. However, Durutte was unwilling to occupy Frischermont, for he was becoming aware of the presence of the Prussians on his right and was soon forced to break off the action against Saxe-Weimar. Thus, though shaken and driven back, Wellington's left flank was secure. It was in his center that the situation was approaching a crisis.

By 1830 Wellington's center was becoming extraordinarily thin. Though Kempt, Pack and Lambert were holding their own just east of the Brussels road, the 400 or 500 meters between the road and Maitland's Guards were being held by the remnants of four badly battered brigades—Ompteda's, Kielmansegge's, Kruse's and Sir Colin Halkett's—plus odd bits and pieces of the Brunswickers. Ammunition was low, as was morale. Alten had been wounded and command of the 3rd Division had devolved on Kielmansegge, who was having difficulties enough keeping his own two green battalions of Hanoverians on the line. Wellington was informed of this critical situation and did what he could. Since the situation on his left was beginning to turn out quite well, Wellington began to strip troops away from the left, pulling the Hanoverian 5th Brigade out, as well as Vandeleur's 4th Cavalry Brigade and Vivian's 6th—which had already begun such a movement on its commander's own initiative, bringing them towards the center. His far right being relatively unscathed as well, he ordered the last of Chasse's 3rd Dutch-Belgian Division up. Then he personally led five battalions of Brunswickers—their average age 17—from their position in reserve behind Maitland into line with Alten's battered 3rd Division. Even as he did so, Ney was desperately calling upon his Emperor for more troops.

Napoleon received Ney's call for some reinforcements at about 1830. The Emperor's response was, "Some troops! Where do you expect me to get them from! Do you want me to make some?" Yet he did have substantial forces available, the 15 battalions of the *Garde Imperial* in the vicinity of Plancenoit. If he had committed half of these—4,000 men—to Ney's support he might well have broken through Wellington's enfeebled center. But he did not do so. To some extent his failure is understandable. Considering Ney's performance since operations began on the 15th, Napoleon certainly had reason to doubt the latter's judgment. At the same time the message had arrived just as the situation at Plancenoit was becoming critical, as could be seen by the rain of Prussian shot around his own headquarters, threatening to cut his only line of retreat. In the end, Napoleon had chosen to send two battalions of the *Old Guard* into Plancenoit and then strung most of the rest of them in squares along the Charleroi-Brussels road between La Belle-Alliance and Rossomme to serve as a final reserve line should Plancenoit turn into a disaster. Clearly this had been a compromise. But it was a compromise which left much to be desired. Over a dozen of his finest and freshest battalions were committed to doing nothing during the most critical moments of the battle. Nor can his ignorance of the situation confronting Ney be used as an excuse, for he had made no real effort during the course of the day to ascertain the true situation at the front, sticking pretty much to the vicinity of his command post, from which little could be seen due to the enormous volume of smoke which hung over the field. Thus, in a very real sense, Napoleon let slip the most critical moments of the battle by doing nothing. And Ney, desperately clinging to his toe hold in the Allied center, was left to his own resources.

Ney's last attacks by mingled elements from the divisions of Quiot and Donzelot were delivered at about 1845. Under cover of the fire of the grand battery—which never ceased to bombard the Allied line save when masked by attacking troops—the infantry went forward for one last try, driving right for the Brunswickers whom Wellington had led into the line moments before. Perhaps only the presence of the Duke, or possibly the line of light cavalry which Vivian drew across their rear, lent these green boys the courage to stand firm, but stand they did. A hasty counterattack was organized, the Prince of Orange himself gathering up the remnants of Kruse's Nassauers to drive the French back, suffering a wound in his shoulder in the process. The line had held.

Now virtually alone, for almost all his staff officers had fallen, many at his side, such as Fitzroy Somerset, who lost an arm, Wellington visited his troops. Dead and wounded men and horses lay everywhere. All of his front line units had been badly handled. Many batteries had lost most of their guns. His battalion squares were horribly reduced, being but "little specks" in the words of Captain William Hay of the 12th Light Dragoons. Several officers asked if their battalions could not be relieved. The Duke, his ashen face the only evidence of the strain which he was under, would answer, "They must hold their ground to the last man....Wait a little longer, my lads, you shall have them presently....We must not be beat, what would they say in England?...Impossible...." different words, yet all with the same message: "Standfast!" Invariably the response from the troops and officers was the same, "Very well, my Lord." A bare three kilometers to the east large masses of troops could be seen forming up, Zeithen's Prussians come up at last. Only time was needed now, as the crisis having been reached, had not yet passed. For as Wellington well knew, Napoleon's ultimate resource the *Garde Imperial* had yet to be encountered.

1900: *La Garde!*

Napoleon decided to commit the *Imperial Guard* shortly after his right flank had been secured by the retaking of Plancenoit, and even as Ney's regiments were heavily engaged along the ridge of Mont-St. Jean. Of the 23 battalions of the *Guard*, two of the *Old Guard* and all eight of the *Young Guard* were in Plancenoit and one of the *Old Guard* was at Le Caillou to secure his headquarters. This left 12 battalions. He decided to commit nine battalions to an attack, holding out three as a final reserve. Shortly before 1900 he got on his white horse and led his cheering grenadiers and chasseurs forward. At La Haie Sainte, within 550 meters of Wellington's center, he relinquished command to Ney, who would lead the attack. While General de Division Antoine Drouot, overall commander of the *Imperial Guard*, and General de Division Louis Friant, commanding the *Grenadiers*, organized the attack, Napoleon ordered Rielle and d'Erlon to support it with whatever they had. A rumor having begun to spread that the Prussians had arrived, Napoleon instructed de la Bedoyere to spread the word that the oncoming troops were Grouchy's. The news fired the men with enthusiasm. Cries of *"Vive l'Empereur"* and *"Voila Grouchy!"* and *"En avant!"* arose from thousands of throats. But then, even as the grand battery renewed its bombardment of the Allied center, cannon fire could be heard from the rear. Elation turned to confusion. Yet determination and discipline held.

The *Guard* formed for the attack in a single "close column of grand divisions," with all nine battalions deployed in echelon to the left, each one next to and slightly to the rear of that to its right. Each battalion deployed on a two company front, roughly 75 men—about 75 meters—

Having ordered them to win his battle for him, Napoleon salutes the veterans of the **Old Guard.**

wide and nine men—18 meters—deep. Between each pair of battalions were two 6-pounders or 5.5-inch howitzers, so that the entire "column"—actually a diagonal line—of some 5,000 men and 16 guns stretched for nearly a kilometer in width as it mustered under the partial shelter of a gentle swale just below La Haie Sainte. On the right were the two battalions of the *3rd Grenadiers*, then came the single battalion of the *4th*, the two battalions of the *3rd Chasseurs* and the two of the *4th*, while the two battalions of the *1st Grenadiers*—the core of the *Old Guard*—were on the left. At about 1910 the attack began.

Wellington had begun making arrangements to meet the attack of the *Imperial Guard* even as Napoleon was deciding that it should be undertaken. This was not necessarily a stroke of genius on his part. By 1830 it was clear that the battle could not last much longer and that all his troops had to do to win was hang on a bit more, for if the Allied army was strained to the breaking point, so too was Napoleon's. The latter had but two choices, to break off the action and retreat south or to throw in the *Garde*, the best and most successful troops in Europe. Wellington's resources were thin. His front was by now held by battered bits and pieces of units: the 300 meter stretch between the Brussels road and Maitland's 1st Brigade was held by the remnants of no less than 21 battalions, British, K.G.L., Hanoverian, Brunswicker and Nassauer. By 1900 Wellington had brought up his last intact infantry unit, 6,800 men of Chasse's Dutch-Belgian 3rd Division, and posted it along the Ohain road, about 400 meters behind the center of his right wing, where Maitland's guardsmen and Adam's light infantrymen and riflemen lay, partially concealed by standing grain and the reverse slope. In addition to Chasse's men, Wellington had in reserve 3,000 relatively fresh cavalrymen, the brigades of Vivian and Vandeleur, plus the remnants of the five other British cavalry brigades, the now unreliable Dutch-Belgian cavalry and the Hanoverian 5th Infantry Brigade. It was not much with which to meet a French attack, but it was all he had. He ordered his artillery to cease fire. Meanwhile, the activity in the French lines had attracted Wellington's notice. In addition, some skirmishers from the 52nd Light Infantry had captured a deserter, a captain of carabiniers who had approached them on horseback with his hands in the air. Between expressions of loyalty to Louis XVIII and outbursts of curses upon Napoleon, the man had spoken freely to Lieutenant Colonel Sir Augustus Frazer, commanding Wellington's horse artillery. An attack was definitely being organized. Having done what he could to meet it, all Wellington could do was wait, standing calmly with Maitland's guardsmen. He did not have to wait long. Soon the French drummers could be heard beating the "*pas de charge.*"

The battle of Waterloo has been likened to a play, unfolding in five grand acts. To press the analogy further, it is very much a Greek tragedy, with an obvious, inevitable and unavoidable end, for the outcome of the climactic

Forming the two right flank battalions of the attack, the **3rd Chasseurs** *of the* **Garde** *advance in two hollow squares.*

event of the battle, the attack by the *Imperial Guard*, seems somehow preordained. Curiously there is much which is obscure about this final attack.

Amid cries of *"Vive l'Empereur!"* the nine battalions of the *Garde Imperial* stepped off, a grim-faced Ney at their head. As d'Erlon's divisions renewed their struggle with Wellington's left along the length of the ridge, the attacking battalions moved almost directly against Wellington's right center, advancing somewhat at an angle from the Brussels road. Ney told off the two left hand battalions to screen Hougoumont, which was still stoutly resisting, despite being in flames and closely beset by Jerome and Foy. As the remaining seven battalions advanced, the cohesion of their echeloned line began to unravel, due partially to the unevenness of the ground and partially to the dense clouds of smoke which hung over the area. The

David Hendrik Chasse

David Hendrik Chasse, baron, luitenant generaal (1765-1849), was of Dutch bourgeois origins. He entered the service of the United Provinces as an aspiring cadet in 1775, but political indiscretions forced him to flee to France, where he became a captain in 1792. He remained there for several years, passing to the Batavian Republic in 1795, becoming a generaal majoor when the republic became the Kingdom of Holland in 1806, and transferring into French service as a general of brigade when Napoleon annexed Holland in 1810. Until 1808 onward he saw relatively little active service. From 1808 his career became more distinguished. He commanded Dutch troops in the Peninsula, during the Wagram campaign, in Spain again, and during the campaign of 1814, becoming a baron. After Napoleon's first abdication he entered the service of the Netherlands. He commanded the 3rd Dutch-Belgian Division with some distinction during the Waterloo campaign and later the Anglo-Allied I Corps during the opening phases of the occupation of France. From 1819 he was commandant of the fortress of Antwerp, which he successfully defended against Belgian forces in 1830, but in 1832 was forced to surrender to a French army under Marshal Maurice Etienne Gerard who in 1815 had commanded Napoleon's *IV Corps*. He later retired from military service and was a member of the Estates-General of the Netherlands for several years.

Chasse was typical of a generation of middle ranked officers who learned their trade in the French armies during the Revolution and the Empire, and who after the Liberation War of 1813-1814 became prominent in the armies of many of the minor European powers.

attackers split into two, then three and apparently finally four columns, while the two battalions of the *1st Grenadiers* on the left halted about half-way across the field to form a final reserve. From the British lines they looked irresistible. Like many others, Ensign Gronow, lying down in the ranks of the 1st Foot Guards near where stood Wellington watching the progress of the attack, recalled that the approaching troops were "the heroes of many memorable battles." Nearby, his comrade Captain Harry Powell remembered that never had an attack by the *Garde* failed. As the French emerged from the smoke, Wellington's artillery came into play. Cannon balls cut through the ranks, looking, wrote Lieutenant George Pringle of the Royal Artillery, like standing corn being blown in the wind. Yet on they came, never wavering, crying *"Vive l'Empereur!"* as they dressed ranks repeatedly to close the gaps left by the killing and maiming of their comrades. Ney's mount was killed, his fifth of the day, but the "Bravest of the Brave" struggled to his feet to march sword in hand at Friant's side. The sturdy battalions marched on, ascending the slope as Allied fire increased. Then they struck, with a final cry of *"Vive l'Empereur!"*

The *3rd Grenadiers*, on the French right, were the first to hit the Allied line, going up against two battalions of Brunswickers and Major General Sir Colin Halkett's 5th Brigade. The Brunswickers fell back, the 30th and the 73rd wavered. The *4th Grenadiers* came up next, hitting Halkett's other two battalions, the 33rd and the 69th, and they too wavered. From his position some hundreds of meters to the west, Wellington cried out, "See what's wrong there!" and dispatched an aide. Halkett was shot in the mouth, but bravely held his men to their duty as Wellington galloped over to bring forward again the Brunswickers, who had been steadied by the presence of Vandeleur's cavalry in their rear, while Chasse threw the 2,800 men of his 1st Brigade into a counterattack. Striking hard, Chasse's men drove the French back down the ridge as Wellington raced back to Maitland's brigade.

The *3rd Chasseurs* came next. Ascending the ridge just where Maitland's guardsmen where lying, they found it apparently undefended save for some guns from which the crews were hastily falling back. When they were within 55 meters of the Ohain road Wellington called out, "Now, Maitland, now's your time!" Perhaps half a minute later, with the French within 30 meters, Wellington cried out, "Stand up, Guards!" Nearly 2,000 men rose amidst the tall grain. Maitland's voice rang out, "Make ready! Fire!" and

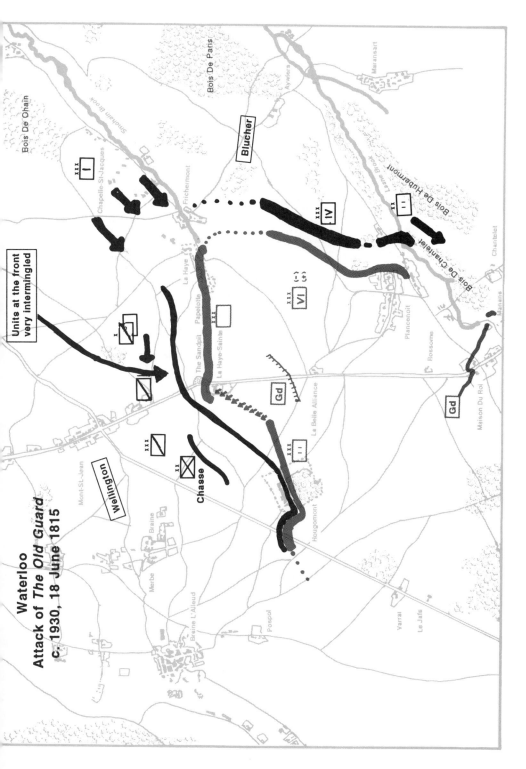

Waterloo
Attack of *The Old Guard*
c. 1930, 18 June 1815

Units at the front
very intermingled

Wellington

Chasse

Blucher

I

IV

II

VI (?)

Gd

Gd

Gd

Bois De Ohain

Bois De Paris

Bois De Hubermont

Bois De Chantelet

Chapelle-St-Jacques

Smohain Brook

Frichermont

La Haye

Papelotte

The Sandpit

La Haye-Sainte

La Belle Alliance

Hougomont

Mont-St-Jean

Braine

Merbe

Braine L'Alleud

Pospol

Plancenoit

Rossome

Maison Du Roi

Manans

Chantelet

Lasne Brook

Aywiers

Maransart

Varrat

Le Jafs

247

Lieutenant General David Henri Chasse leads the 1st Brigade of his Dutch-Belgian 3rd Division into a bayonet charge against the **4th Grenadiers** *of the* **Garde.**

the first of four ranks of guardsmen discharged their muskets. The shortness of the range, perhaps 20 meters, caused terrible casualties in the ranks of the *3rd Chasseurs*, perhaps 300 falling. The startled chasseurs halted, attempting to deploy into line. Within seconds a second volley was delivered. Some of Halkett's men, steadier now, joined in, pouring fire into the French from the flank. A few minutes more and the chasseurs broke, turning to flee. As the *3rd Chasseurs* dissolved, the British guardsmen suddenly found themselves in a difficult position, for they had also crossed the front of the final French column, that of the *4th Chasseurs*, which now threatened them on their left. However, Maitland's battalions made an orderly, if hasty withdrawal, while the *4th Chasseurs* ignored them to advance grimly on Adam's brigade.

Seeing the *4th Chasseurs* coming, Lieutenant Colonel Sir John Colborne of the 52nd Light Infantry ordered the 1,050 men of his battalion—the strongest in Wellington's army—out of the tall grain, wheeled them to the left and deployed them parallel to the French line of advance. Adam rode up, inquiring as to what Colborne was about. "To make that column feel our fire," came the reply. Adam confirmed Colborne's initiative with a laconic, "Move on." Colborne then sent a company forward to skirmish with the French. The chasseurs halted, executing a right wheel to engage the threat to their flank, losing all momentum for the attack. Within minutes, as his men were trading fire with the *4th Chasseurs*, Colborne received orders from Wellington to execute that very maneuver he had just completed. The balance of Adam's brigade joined in the fire fight, followed soon after by elements from Halkett's and Kielmansegge's brigades. Wellington rode up to the 95th Rifles to order a bayonet attack. As the men began to cheer him he replied, "No cheering, my lads, but forward and complete your victory!" Even as the 95th advanced, Colborne's men were already at work, driving the French back in a furious bayonet charge. The 52nd soon advanced beyond the support of other Allied forces and Colborne was about to order a halt when the Duke rode up, crying, "Well done, Colborne! Well done! Go on. Never mind, go on, go on. Don't give them time to rally. They won't stand." Nor did they. By 1940 the *Garde* was in full flight. And in the ranks of the French army there arose the never before heard cry, "*La Garde recule*—The Guard retreats!"

Evening: Disaster

As the shattered battalions of the *Garde* streamed back, many things began to happen at once. Over on Wellington's left the lead elements of Zeithen's I Corps had come up even as the *Garde* was making its attack. After an unfortunate exchange of fire with Saxe-Weimar's brigade (Dutch-Belgian uniforms were similar to French ones) Zeithen's men stormed into Papelotte and La Haie, ejecting Durutte's troops and incidently breaking Napoleon's flank open by driving between d'Erlon and Lobau. D'Erlon began to curl his right flank around to deny it to the

Berthier: The Man Who Wasn't There

The most important French general during the Waterloo campaign may well have been Marshal Louis-Alexandre Berthier, whose principle contribution was not being there at all.

When the French Revolution broke out, Berthier was already a lieutenant colonel in the *Royal Army*, experienced both in conventional soldiering and military engineering, and had served with Rochambeau at Yorktown during the American Revolution.

Throwing in his lot with the new regime, Berthier had modest success at first, until assigned to serve under Napoleon Bonaparte in the Italian campaign of 1796, where he, as did many others, finally stepped irreversibly into the pages of history.

Berthier's talent did not lie in actually commanding troops in the field, but rather in being the ultimate chief of staff. He kept various branches of Napoleon's army coordinated to a degree unusual for the time, leaving the Emperor free to move troops about on the actual battlefield. Napoleon's tactics depended on keeping the armies of his foes apart, holding one enemy force at bay with a minimum number of his own troops, while concentrating the rest of his forces to overwhelm his remaining opponent. These tactics required careful timing and the prompt delivery of accurate messages to his various units in the field. To this end, Berthier was followed about by a small army of mounted messengers, specially organized guides and aides-de-camp as well as young officers from the chasseur and hussar regiments. Berthier normally sent out a half-dozen riders with the same message to avoid the frequent 1815 experience of a single messenger getting lost or arriving with a message too late to be of use.

Even staff officers in Napoleon's time had to remain within eyesight, and firing range of the enemy. Berthier had the unique ability, sadly lacking in 1815, to rapidly translate the Emperor's terse and often cryptic orders into understandable instructions for his subordinates, sometimes while under fire. Messages that had passed through the hands of Berthier would not have created the confusion experienced by Ney and Grouchy during the Hundred Days.

It is estimated that Berthier and Napoleon spent less than two weeks' total time apart in all the years from 1795 to 1814. Berthier was known in the *Grand Army* as the "Emperor's Wife." No one else knew the Emperor's mind as well. No one else knew what he *meant* to say when he issued an order on the battlefield. When Napoleon created the marshals of the Empire in 1804, Berthier was the first created, taking precedence even over the heroes of the Revolution. He was to be wounded numerous times over the years, but received a new honor or title for virtually every injury.

By 1814 Berthier and other marshals had wearied of Napoleon's endless wars. After the first abdication, Berthier accepted some honors and appointments from the restored monarchy. When Napoleon escaped from Elba, Berthier was one of those that escorted Louis XVIII to safety in Belgium, but he declined the offer to join the Royalist cause and went into self-imposed exile in Bavaria, where his wife was a princess.

Although Berthier was among those Napoleon ordered struck from the rolls of the marshals on 10 April 1815 (an order that was in fact never carried out), many believed the Emperor hoped Berthier would eventually rejoin him. Such was not to be. The one marshal whom Napoleon could never fully replace fell to his death from the third story of the castle at Bamburg, Bavaria on 1 June 1815.

The first trained observer to reach Berthier's body was Anselm von Feuerbach, a noted jurist, an important official in the Napoleonic kingdom of Bavaria and the father of the philosopher Ludwig Feuerbach. After having the marshal's body removed to a nearby chapel, Feuerbach conducted an investigation. Feuerbach's testimony has apparently been ignored by those who offer the more bizarre explanations for Berthier's death. Feuerbach determined that Berthier had been standing by a window watching Russian soldiers advancing on France. He had been melancholy and drinking heavily in exile, including a bottle of champagne consumed the morning of his death. The window was high off the floor, about chest-high for an average man. Feuerbach was told by officials of the palace that a chair was found near the window. Feuerbach was less impressed by some townspeople who thought they heard Berthier cry *"Oh mon Dieu!"* as he fell. Feuerbach clearly felt that Berthier's death had been an accident, although he left open the possibility of suicide. Tales of mysterious masked assassins would appear to be romantic invention.

Berthier's body was fearfully battered by bouncing off three story's worth of crenelations and balustrades before hitting the ground, but was still quite recognizable when Feuerbach reached it. We thus have a detailed description of the clothing Berthier was wearing at the time of his death, which tells us more than Feuerbach realized. Berthier was wearing a civilian coat of green cloth, the color of Napoleon's personal livery. In the buttonhole of the green coat was the rosette of the Royalist Order of St. Louis, the gift of Louis XVIII. Perhaps this seemingly contradictory choice of attire reflected Berthier's mixed feelings in the last year of his life.

"In for a penny, in for a pound." Wellington, on the right, orders his army to attack.

Prussians. Wellington, having just returned to his stately elm at the Mont-St. Jean crossroads spotted the movement. He stood in his stirrups, trying for a better view. A moment later a staff officer came pounding up, "The day is ours! The Prussians have arrived!" As all eyes turned on Wellington a last ray of sunlight touched his face. Some officers urged caution. Wellington thought for a moment, then said, "Oh, damn it! In for a penny, in for a pound." Taking off his cocked hat he waved it in the direction of the French three times. A cheer swept the ranks. Vivian's and Vandeleur's light cavalry swept forward, followed by the nearest infantry regiments. Wellington was making his first and only offensive move of the day, to sweep the French from the field.

The cry of *"La Garde recule!"* had unnerved the French troops. Now, with Zeithen eroding away their right and Wellington's troops advancing to their front, other cries were heard: *"Nous sommes Trahis*—We are betrayed!", *"Suave qui peut*—Every man for himself!" and *"Trahison*—Treason!" Men who had endured all through the long, hard battle now lost heart. Wellington's infantry ejected the French from La Haie Sainte. One of the retreating battalions of the *Garde* attempted to form square, only to be ridden down by 7th and 10th Hussars, though not before inflicting heavy losses. The 18th Hussars pressed on to La Belle Alliance itself, seizing two batteries. The fire of the grand battery slackened and then virtually ceased. One of the last French balls to come over flew right between Wellington's body and Copenhagen's neck as they stood just below La Haie Sainte. Uxbridge, standing next to the Duke cried out, "By God! I've lost my leg!" Putting down his telescope, Wellington absent-mindedly said, "Have you, by God?" Then, seeing that the ball had shattered Uxbridge's knee, he held him up until help could come. Moments later he spotted a group of French troops who had rallied on a nearby hill. He ordered Adam's brigade to dislodge them. Within a few minutes the French had been driven from the hill. Organized resistance was becoming rare in the French ranks, but some men reacted with desperate courage.

As panic set in, the French troops began to melt away, closely pressed by the advancing Allies. Wellington followed his men closely, ignoring enemy fire. Admonished that he was taking unnecessary risks he replied, "Never mind, let them fire away. The battle's won, my life is of no consequence now."

All across the field the French were in flight as Wellington's light cavalry regiments harried them back, supported by those of his infantry battalions which could advance, while Major Edward Whinyates sent dozens of Congreve rockets streaking overhead to hasten the French on their way. Meanwhile Zeithen's Prussians pushed d'Erlon's flank back. As a Prussian band played "God Save the King" and a British one *"Nun denket Alle Gott,"* the armies met and mingled on the Brussels road, just south of La Haie Sainte. More importantly, the lead brigades of Pirch's II Corps had come up on Napoleon's extreme right and

"Come, see how a marshal of France dies." Ney, broken sword in hand, urges the 95th of the Line *to join him in a final do-or-die attack to stem the Allied tide.*

gone into action near Plancenoit. As one brigade attempted to turn the French position at the village, a second drove directly on Le Caillou, Napoleon's headquarters on the Charleroi-Brussels road, the main French line of retreat. But this was where Napoleon had the hard core of his army. The 10 battalions of the *Garde* in Plancenoit denied their flank, keeping Pirch's men from making any gains. At Le Caillou the *1st Battalion* of the *1st Chasseurs*, some 650 men, advanced into the wooded ground to the east and met and drove back a force five times their number. Whatever happened to their front, the French flank was still secure, sheltering their slender line of retreat.

Marshal Ney, wounded in the head, his uniform torn and filthy, an epaulet hanging loose, his face blackened from smoke and sweat, a broken sword in his hand, seemed everywhere attempting to rally troops, leading local counterattacks, trying to hold back the Allied tide and perhaps trying to fall gloriously, "Come, see how a Marshal of France dies," d'Erlon reported him as saying. But just as victory had eluded him, so did death. Finally, unable to find his demise or rally the troops, Ney too joined the stream of fugitives. Napoleon formed his last reserve, three battalions of the *Old Guard*—the *2nd* of the *2nd Grenadiers*, the *2nd* of the *1st Chasseurs* and the *2nd* of the *2nd Chasseurs*—into a row of squares just above La Belle-Alliance in an effort to stem the Allied tide.

Allied troops came up, pausing before the resolute squares. A call to surrender was given. General de Brigade Pierre Cambronne of the *1st Chasseurs* by legend gave the answer, *"Merde!"* traditionally rendered as "The Guard dies, but never surrenders!" For a moment Napoleon stood once more in the midst of his *Old Guard*. Then, after a few minutes, he got into his traveling coach, and escorted by the *Lancers of the Guard* fled southwards. Tradition holds that the three squares of the *Old Guard* marched to the rear with awesome discipline and dignity under a shower of Allied fire. Actually Cambronne and his regiment surrendered to Colonel Hew Halkett's 3rd Hanoverian Brigade, composed entirely of militia battalions, a humiliating end for the Emperor's *grognards*.

At about 2100—just as the 10 battalions of the *Guard* in Plancenoit finally gave up the burning village, having done all they could to protect the army's line of retreat— Wellington met Blucher on the Brussels road between Rossomme and La Belle-Alliance. In the fading twilight the Old Hussar cried out, *"Mein lieber Kamerad*—My old comrade!" and leaned over to kiss Wellington, adding, *"Quelle affaire*—What an affair!" Conversing in French, of which Blucher had but poor command, the two agreed that the relatively fresher Prussians should undertake the pursuit. Blucher's chief of staff Wilhelm Gneisenau had already thrown himself enthusiastically into the task. Personally leading 4,000 troopers on what he called "a hunt by moonlight" he harried the disorganized French all the way to Frasnes. There, in the small hours of the morning, the exhausted cavalrymen gave up, bedding down to rest their tired horses. The battle of Waterloo was over.

That night, as his friend and aide Colonel Alexander

"Brave Frenchmen, surrender!" An English officer — probably Major General Peregine Maitland of the Guards Brigade— calls upon the last squares of the **Garde** *Imperial to yield. By tradition General of Brigade Pierre Cambronne of the* **1st Chasseurs** *replied, "Merde!" and the troops drew off in good order. Actually, the last three battalions of the* **Garde** *surrendered.*

Gordon lay dying in his bed, Wellington took a melancholy supper at his headquarters in Waterloo. Though a heavy table was laid, only one officer joined him, his Spanish aide Lieutenant General Miguel de Alava, virtually all the other members of his staff being dead or wounded. The two spoke little. During their meal a list of the slain and wounded was brought to the Duke. He looked it over, remarking, "Well, thank God I don't know what it is to lose a battle. But nothing can be so painful as to gain one with the loss of so many friends." Around midnight Muffling, the Prussian liaison officer, joined them, remarking that Blucher intended to call the battle after "La Belle-Alliance," a double entendre referring not only to the village which lay in Napoleon's center but also to the alliance of Britain and Prussia. Soon after the Duke noted, "The hand of Almighty God has been upon me this day." He drank

"Quelle affaire," Blucher greets Wellington at La Belle-Alliance at about 2130 hours.

one toast with Alava and then went to bed. By 0300 he was astir again, penning his report of the battle, which he dubbed "Waterloo," realizing what English pronunciation would make of "Mont-St. Jean" or "La Belle-Alliance."

Napoleon spent most of the night of 18-19 June on the run. When he left the field of Waterloo he made for Genappe, where he hoped to rally the army. At Genappe it became clear that there was little which could be done. The narrow streets were full of fugitives, making passage almost impossible. The Emperor swapped the comfort of his *berline* for a charger and, with the lancers forcing a way through the panic, continued his flight. He reached Quatre Bras at about 0100 on the 19th. There he briefly considered making a stand, if the *7th Division*, some 4,500 men, could be brought up from Ligny, where it had spent the last two days policing the old battlefield. But it soon became clear that the division was not to be found and he resumed his flight. Not until 0500, as Wellington was still at work on his report, did he call a halt, having reached Charleroi nearly

30 kilometers to the south. After a brief rest, he reached Philippeville, a further 30 kilometers, by afternoon. There he dictated a letter to his brother Joseph, Regent of France and *soi disant* king of Spain. He reported the events of the last five days in a few sentences and his optimism—or megalomania—undiminished, then added "...all is not lost" and issued a detailed set of instructions concerning the raising of yet more troops. But indeed, Waterloo had been a decisive blow.

Waterloo was an unusually bloody affair even by the standards of the age. Surveying the field the next day, Wellington said, "I hope to God that I have fought my last battle!" and later he wrote, "Next to a battle lost, the greatest misery is a battle won." Over 180,000 men had been engaged; some 72,000 French, perhaps 70,000 British and Allies and at least 40,000 Prussians. Of these, some 86,000 had become casualties of one sort or another, killed, wounded, fled or captured, nearly 50 percent of those engaged. Wellington's army had lost about 17,000 in killed and wounded and some 10,000 temporarily absent, leaving him with little more than 43,000 organized troops by the battle's end. Virtually his entire staff had been wiped out, nearly all of his aides and staff officers becoming casualties, many at his side. Even Blucher's Prussians had suffered 7,000 casualties. But Napoleon's magnificent *Armee du Nord* had been shattered, losing perhaps 44,000 men in killed, wounded, captured and fled, nearly 60 percent of the number engaged, he had also lost 220 pieces of artillery in the bargain, over 80 percent of those which he had brought to the field.

There were many reasons for the French disaster at Waterloo: Napoleon's failure to control the battle; Wellington's grim determination, courage and serene demeanor; the surprising brittleness of French morale; the unexpected steadiness of Allied troops; the timely arrival of Blucher's Prussians; the unfortunate morning rains, and more. Of these, perhaps the most serious was Napoleon's failure to control the fight more closely. For most of the battle he let his subordinates do pretty much what they wanted: his inept brother Jerome became entangled in the fight for Hougoumont, thereby denying him the use of an entire army corps; d'Erlon deployed his corps in what may have been the worst possible formation; Ney's repeated attacks with both cavalry and infantry were ill timed, ill coordinated and conducted over different ground each time; and Grouchy never quite understood what his mission was supposed to be, thereby permitting the Prussians to elude his pursuit. The extraordinary calm with which Wellington conducted the defense, his instinctive grasp of where the post of danger lay and his well-timed counter blows all helped turn French errors into serious reverses. And then there was Blucher's gallant decision to go to the aid of his allies whatever the cost. In the end, the battle degenerated into an inelegant slugfest: "He just moved forward in the old style," Wellington would write some weeks later, "and was driven off in the old style." After the battle, Napoleon thought that he still had a chance, but he would have to work hard to reverse the effects of Waterloo.

La Garde Imperial

One of the premier fighting forces of history, Napoleon's *Imperial Guard* began in an almost casual fashion. Under the Republic, generals commanding armies were authorized small detachments of mounted escorts for their personal security. Soon after young citizen Bonaparte was sent to command the *Armee d'Italie* in 1796, he created a small squadron of *Guides* under Captain Jean Baptiste Bessiers. The *Guides* served General Bonaparte well over the next few years. However, when he took control of France in 1799 as First Consul, Napoleon saw the need for a larger escort. He took two other escort formations, the infantry battalions which had guarded the Directors and the Legislative Assembly, he combined them with his *Guides* to form the *Consular Guard* on 2 December 1799, consisting of two infantry regiments, the *Grenadiers* and the *Light Infantry*, two of cavalry, the *Light Cavalry* (later the *Grenadiers a Cheval*) and the *Chasseurs*, and a battery of light artillery. This relatively modest force (perhaps 1,300 men and eight guns), soon began to grow, so that at Marengo (it numbered about 2,100 men with eight guns, by late 1804, when it was redesignated the *Garde Imperial*, it was about 8,000 men and 24 guns, and the following year it reached about 12,000 men. This gradual growth continued through the years of Napoleon's greatest power, 1806-1812. Relatively, however, the *Garde* was still a fairly modest-sized force,

numerically an almost insignificant element in Napoleon's *Grand Armee*: in early 1812 the *Garde* totalled only about 25,000 men, in an army that approached a million, all theaters considered.

Of course the importance of the *Garde* was far out of proportion to its size. The *Garde* formed a genuine *corps d'elite* in the French Army. It was recruited from veterans of high intelligence, excellent character, and proven courage. Although normally withheld from combat, when it went into action it invariably proved successful. The *Garde* served as a mark against which regular units could measure themselves, it functioned as an officer and NCO training school, and it gave Napoleon a highly reliable reserve. So although guardsmen earned more pay and cost more to maintain than did line troops, they were certainly worth the small additional price. Things began to change with the disastrous campaign in Russia.

Napoleon's military system relied heavily upon veteran troops, men who knew what to do and did it. His campaigns before Russia were relatively cheap in terms of manpower losses, and the veterans could readily season recruits in camp and on the march, so that the latter rather quickly began to behave like veterans themselves. But losses in Russia were horrendous, numbering in the hundreds of thousands, and had come on top of the alarming drain caused by "the Spanish ulcer" since 1808. Then came the disastrous losses of 1813. These losses short-circuited Napoleon's training system, for the veterans, who had formerly always outnumbered the recruits, now were outnumbered by them. To try to get some reliable troops in the field quickly, Napoleon began to cull the very best men from among the new recruits and funnel them into the *Garde*. The result was a marked increase in the size of the *Garde*. When Napoleon went into Russia in June of 1812 the *Garde* had about 25,000 men. After the Russian disaster he more than doubled the *Garde*, so that about 56,000 were available for the campaign of 1813. Following the disaster at Leipzig Napoleon once again increased the *Garde*, so that during the campaign of 1814, which ended in April, it totalled about 112,500 men. To put it another way, the *Garde* had increased from less than 0.5 percent of his army in June of 1812, to about 9 per-

cent by mid-1813, to about 17 percent by March of 1814. There was a payoff to this rapid increase in strength, for the *Garde* did a lot of serious fighting during 1813-1814. But this payoff came at the expense of the line, which was starved of valuable manpower, and particularly of junior troop leaders.

During the Waterloo campaign, the *Garde* was back down to more manageable proportions, roughly 19,700 men in the *Armee du Nord* (16 percent) and another 5,000 or so scattered about the rest of France, so that overall the *Garde* totalled no more than about 4 percent of his 600,000 strong armies.

The *Garde* performed well during the Waterloo campaign, most notably at Ligny on the 16th and at Placenoit on the 18th. But the defeat of the grand assault of the *Grenadiers* and *Chasseurs* on the evening of the 18th signalled the dissolution of the army.

Infantry

1st Grenadiers, 1st & 2nd Bns with Napoleon (1040 officers and men)
2nd Grenadiers, 1st & 2nd Bns with Napoleon (1100)
3rd Grenadiers, 1st & 2nd Bns with Napoleon (1180)
4th Grenadiers, 1st Bn with Napoleon (530)
1st Chasseurs, 1st & 2nd Bns with Napoleon (1310)
2nd Chasseurs, 1st & 2nd Bns with Napoleon (1165)
3rd Chasseurs, 1st & 2nd Bns with Napoleon (1065)

4th Chasseurs, 1st & 2nd Bns with Napoleon (1075)
Provisional Battalion of the Old Guard, at Paris (400)
1st Tirailleurs, 1st & 2nd Bns with Napoleon (1100)
2nd Tirailleurs, 1st & 2nd Bns in the Vendee (775)
3rd Tirailleurs, 1st & 2nd Bns with Napoleon (990)
4th Tirailleurs, 1st Bn forming at Paris (410)
5th Tirailleurs, 1st Bn forming at Paris (175)

6th Tirailleurs, 1st Bn forming at Rouen (265)

7th Tirailleurs, 1st Bn forming at Paris (100)

8th Tirailleurs, 1st Bn forming at Lyon (150)

1st Voltigeurs, 1st & 2nd Bns with Napoleon (1220)

2nd Voltiguers, 1st & 2nd Bns in the Vendee (940)

3rd Voltigeurs, 1st & 2nd Bns with Napoleon (970)

4th Voltigeurs, 1st & 2nd Bns at Paris (740)

5th Voltigeurs, 1st Bn forming at Paris (205)

6th Voltigeurs, 1st Bn forming at Amiens (130)

7th Voltigeurs, 1st Bn forming at Amiens (205)

8th Voltigeurs, 1st Bn forming at Amiens (185)

Note: The *Provisional Battalion*, which was authorized 200 men each from the *1st Grenadiers* and *1st Chasseurs*, was apparently intended to form the cadre for additional battalions, but it is not clear that it was actually formed. The *4th Tirailleurs* and *4th Voltigeurs* formed a brigade which was intended to reinforce Napoleon's army during the campaign, but it only reached the *Armee du Nord* during the retreat from Waterloo. The *Young Guard* formations in the Vendee formed a brigade in Brayer's Division. Volunteer battalions organizing at Bordeaux and Lyon had been promised places in the *Young Guard* as a reward for their enthusiasm: it is possible that these are included in the *Voltinguer* or *Tirailleur* regiments shown as forming.

Cavalry

Grenadiers a Cheval, 1st, 2nd, 3rd, & 4th Sqns with Napoleon (800)

Dragoons de la Imperatrice, 1st, 2nd, 3rd, & 4th Sqns with Napoleon (815)

Chasseurs a Cheval, 1st, 2nd, 3rd, 4th, & 5th Sqns with Napoleon (1200)

Mamelukes, one platoon with the *Chasseurs a Cheval* (26)

Lanciers de la Garde, 1st, 2nd, 3rd,

4th, & 5th Sqns with Napoleon (900)

Husards de la Garde, 1st, 2nd, 3rd, & 4th Sqns forming at Paris (???)

Eclaireurs de la Garde, 1st, 2nd, 3rd, & 4th Sqns forming at Paris (???)

Gendarmerie d'Elite, 1st Coy with the Grandiers a Cheval (110)

Gendarmerie d'Elite, 2nd Coy at Paris (120)

Note: The *Lanciers polonaise* formed the first squadron of the *Lanciers de la Garde*.

Artillery

Old Guard Foot Artillery, six Bttys with Napoleon (730, 48 pieces)

Old Guard Horse Artillery, four Bttys with Napoleon (400, 32 pieces)

Young Guard Foot Artillery, three Bttys with Napoleon (300, 24 pieces)

Young Guard Foot Artillery, two Bttys en route (200, 16 pieces)

Old Guard Train, ten Coys with Napoleon (925)

Note: The two batteries en route appear to have joined the *Armee du Nord* during its retreat from Waterloo.

Miscellaneous

Engineers of the Guard, one company with Napoleon (112)

Mariners of the Guard, one company with Napoleon (107)

Artisans, several companies existed at depots and Paris (???)

All the cavalry except the newly forming *Husards* and *Eclaireurs* (a cossack-style scout-lancer regiment), plus the foot *Grenadiers* and *Chasseurs* were formally known as the *Old Guard,* although the *3rd* and *4th Regiments* were sometimes informally referred to as the *Middle Guard.* The other regiments were all *Young Guard.* Note that although *Marins de la Garde* is usually translated as "marines," *marins* more accurately means "sailors," hence use of "mariners."

The organization of the *Garde* was peculiar. In the field it did not form an actual army corps, but rather a pool into which the Emperor might dip for troops as circumstances dictated. While the cavalry was organized into divisions, the infantry was maintained as a pool as well, which explains how Napoleon tossed odd battalions of the *Garde* into action at Placenoit. On paper the *Grenadiers* and *Tirailleurs* formed a single corps, as did the *Chasseurs* and *Voltigeurs,* so that although there were numerous infantry regiments in the *Garde,* there were actually only two eagles, one for *Grandiers* and one for *Chassuers.*

Napoleon the Commander

Few generals can be compared favorably with Napoleon. Before his time perhaps only Alexander, Hannibal, Caesar, Belisarius, Ghengis Khan, Gustavus Adolphus and Frederick the Great can be considered his peers. Certainly none since his time approach his reputation even remotely. A deadly foe, Napoleon sought to destroy his enemies by bringing them to battle at the earliest opportunity. To be sure he had a superb military instrument, brought to perfection by the Revolution. But the armies of Revolutionary France lacked adequate direction and guidance. It was Napoleon who provided that.

Looking back upon Napoleon's career, it is difficult to compare his campaigns. He personally appears to have viewed that of 1809 as his finest effort. Yet, while the quality of the French Army had begun to slip and the Austrians proved a doughty foe, one must dismiss this evaluation. The consensus among historians is that Napoleon was at his peak during the Italian campaign of 1796-1797 and again during the campaign in France in 1814. In both, but particularly in the latter, he faced a considerably superior foe with inferior resources within the framework of an unfavorable political and strategic situation. The Italian campaign, of course, turned out successfully, while that in France did not. Nevertheless, on balance, the campaign of 1814 must be considered the most brilliant demonstration of Napoleon's mili-

tary talents. That he lost should not obscure its remarkable conduct.

For a perfect campaign, we need look no further than that of 1806. The French Army, honed to a fine edge by the brilliantly conducted campaign of 1805 in Germany and Bohemia, secured the total annihilation of the Prussian army and state in precisely one month, from 6 October to 6 November. It was a remarkable demonstration of what the French military system could accomplish under Napoleon's guidance. But the achievement was flawed in that the foe was ill led and poorly prepared for a struggle to the death.

Napoleon had an enormous capacity for hard work, a remarkable ability to comprehend his opponents' intentions through the fog of war, a tremendous ability to develop and carry out highly sophisticated, yet eminently practical plans of campaign, an instinctive ability to inspire his troops and a marvelous skill at leading, all combined with an incredible ambition to pursue his destiny. In the end, of course, it was this ambition which brought him low. Intoxicated by his victories, he failed to fully understand the limitations of France's physical and spiritual resources, the character and motivation of Britain, his principal foe, and the nationalist nature of the force which the French Revolution had unleashed and which he himself had helped to spread throughout Europe.

Moreover, Napoleon appears to have been unable to understand his own physical and intellectual limitations. The long years of war had taken their toll. By 1815 he was stout, suffered from several ailments (apparently including ulcers, hemorrhoids and venereal disease) and was no longer capable of the sustained physical efforts which saw him through his earlier campaigns. Although on 15 June he managed to spend about 17 hours in the saddle, over the next few days his physical resources diminished rapidly and he was even seen to doze in the saddle at times when he ought to have been observing operations. Concerning a commander's physical and intellectual abilities, he had once observed, "We have but a short time for war." By 1815 Napoleon's time had past. Yet despite his final defeat, Napoleon remains one of the most successful commanders in history.

It's All in the Name

A study of French dispatches and memoirs of the Hundred Days suggests that, had victory gone to the French or the course of battle shifted a few hundred yards in a different direction, not only history, but the whole terminology of the campaign would have been changed.

The area around Ligny was initially referred to by French commanders as "Fleurus," a village of comparable size just south of Ligny itself. The area was so designated by Marshal Soult in dispatches to General Reille of 15 June at 1000 and to Marshal Ney of 16 June, 0930. Napoleon referred to Fleurus in his Army Bulletin of 15 June, his letter to Joseph Bonaparte of 16 June, and in his dispatches to both Ney and Grouchy of 16 June. The Fleurus designation was also used by General Berthezene of the 11th Division, Ney's senior aide-de-camp Colonel Heymes, Captain Coignet the baggage-master of the army, and many others.

Fleurus appears in French communications at about the time the *Armee du Nord* crossed the Sambre at Charleroi. Two roads go north from Charleroi, the first due north through La Belle-Alliance and Waterloo to Brussels, the second goes slightly northeast to Fleurus, Ligny and points beyond. It may be that Fleurus was simply the name the French saw on the road sign in Charleroi.

The center of the battle on June 16 gradually shifted north from the original focus of French attention at Fleurus to Ligny. The name of Ligny quickly became established in French dispatches and early accounts of the battle. The term became particularly well-entrenched in accounts written in later years, when it became apparent that Ligny was destined to be the last victory of Napoleon's armies.

There was some initial confusion regarding the proper designation of Quatre Bras ("Four Arms"), with some on both sides referring to it as Quatre Chemins ("Four Roads"). Napoleon used the name Quatre Chemins in his dispatch to Ney of 16 June. The term was used by a few others, including Captain Francois of Grouchy's *30th Line*, and even appears in some English accounts.

"Mont-St. Jean" would very likely have been Napoleon's official name for the battle of Waterloo if it had proven a French victory. The Emperor used the term in his order to corps commanders the morning of 18 June. Soult refers to Mont-St. Jean in his dispatch to Ney later at 1100, but two hours later he uses the names Waterloo and Mont-St. Jean equally in his dispatch to Grouchy.

It is thus possible that a slight shift in the fortunes of war or the tide of battle would have transformed Ligny-Quatre Bras-Waterloo into Fleurus-Quatre Chemins-Mont-St. Jean. Wavre apparently would always have been Wavre.

The name Mont-St. Jean was used frequently during the reign of Napoleon III and is still encountered in French writing today, but to the victor goes the spoils, including the right of naming the victory.

CHAPTER X

The End

19 June-15 July

*I*n a sense Napoleon did have some cause for optimism on the afternoon of 19 June. Wellington and Blucher had both suffered grievously, both armies being reduced to a combined strength of no more than 120,000 as a result of the series of battles between 15 and 19 June. Napoleon believed he could yet draw upon France's resources to reinforce his battered ranks. As he wrote to his brother Joseph, "When I reassemble my forces, I shall have 150,000 men. The *federes* and the National Guards (such as are fit to fight) will provide 100,000 men, and the regimental depots another 50,000. I shall thus have 300,000 soldiers ready at once to bring against the enemy. I will use carriage horses to drag the guns; raise 100,000 men by conscription, arming them with muskets taken from Royalists and from National Guards unfit for service; organize a mass levy in Dauphiné, Lyonnais, Burgundy, Lorraine, Champagne; and overwhelm the foe....I have heard nothing of Grouchy. If he has not been captured, as I rather fear, that will give me 50,000 men within three days....Above all, steadfastness and courage!" But Napoleon's optimism was misplaced. As he hurried south from Philippeville he left Marshal Soult to rally the remnants of the *Army of the North*. The marshal managed to concentrate no more than

Napoleon's Correspondence During the Hundred Days

Napoleon was a tireless dispatcher of letters and orders, accompanied even in the field by as many as six secretaries. An official edition of his correspondence was published by orders of his successor Napoleon III in the 1860s. Volume XXVIII of the *Correspondance*, which covers the Hundred Days, contains 386 letters, orders and dispatches, and does not include a number of documents which have surfaced in subsequent years.

Napoleon's pre-occupation with matters military is obvious from the fact that the great majority of the communications are to the solid and dependable Marshal Davout, then serving as Minister of War. Although careful to refer to active marshals as *mon cousin*, the Emperor's correspondence usually has a clipped and peremptory tone, often consisting largely of "you do this-and-that," and "you send this-and-that," the words of a man to whom giving commands has become second nature.

A comparative study of Volume XIX of the *Correspondance*, covering the Wagram campaign of 1809, shows a similar set of priorities, although communications to the minister of war do not outnumber those to the minister of foreign affairs quite so heavily. Dispatches to the indispensable Fouché and the always faithful Admiral Decres are just as common in 1809, demonstrating the persistent importance of internal security and naval and colonial matters to the Napoleonic regime. It is also evident that Carnot's predecessors as minister of the interior did not receive the kind of attention in 1809 that Carnot did in 1815, suggesting that this Revolutionary hero's reputation as the "Organizer of Victory" was more important to Napoleon than his actual government position.

The survival of Napoleon's extensive correspondence with Davout is

27,000 men. These he brought into Soissons by 24 June. Meanwhile, Marshal Grouchy had not been heard from since the 17th.

Grouchy did not learn of the debacle at Waterloo until about 1030 on 19 June, as he was resting his troops after finally seizing Wavre and Limale from the Prussians. Some of his officers suggested falling on the Allied rear as they pursued Napoleon southwards, but Grouchy rejected this

owed largely to Madame Davout, who saved all of her husband's papers, even on the driest military matters, which enabled them to be recovered by Napoleon III's editors.

Napoleon's Correspondance in 1815		
Person	Title	no. of communication
Davout	minister of war	195
Carnot	minister of the interior	21
Decres	minister of the navy and the colonies	21
Gaudin	minister of finance	10
Caulaincourt	minister of foreign affairs	9
Fouce	minister of the police	8
Soult	army chief of staff	8
Joseph Bonaparte	exiled King of Spain and president of the cabinet	7
Drouot	commander of the Imperial Guard	5
Mollien	minister of the public treasury	5
Montalivet	steward of royal property	3
Ney	marshal of France	3
Total		386

notion as overly rash. Correctly reasoning that the critical thing to do was to save what he could from the disaster, he decided to retreat back to France through Namur. Grouchy's troops quickly broke contact with the Prussians and began to fall back. Marching rapidly—far more rapidly than they had marched on the 17th and 18th—they seized Namur after a brief skirmish at about 1600. There they camped for the night. The next morning elements of

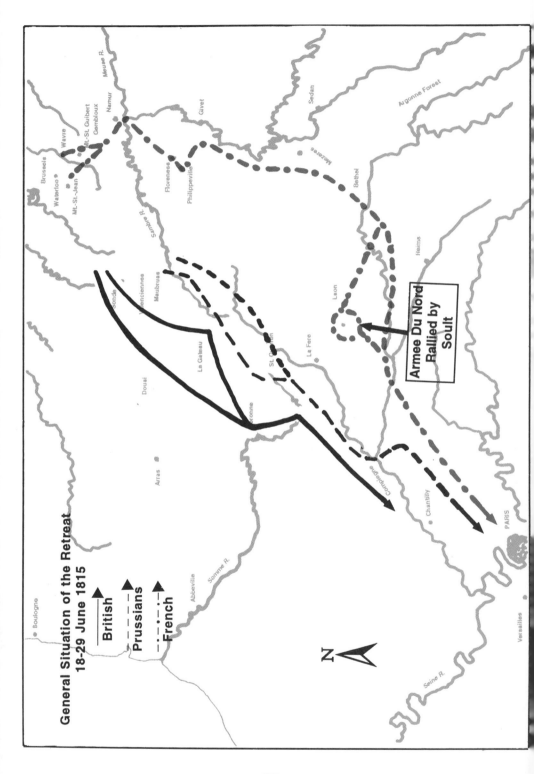

General Situation of the Retreat
18-29 June 1815

British
Prussians
French

Armee Du Nord Rallied by Soult

N

Boulogne
Abbeville
Somme R.
Arras
Douai
Conde
Valenciennes
Maubruas
Le Cateau
Bouchonne
Compiegne
Chantilly
PARIS
Versailles
Seine R.
St. Quentin
La Fere
Leon
Reims
Bethel
Mezeres
Sedan
Argonne Forest
Givet
Philippeville
Floreness
Sambre R.
Gembloux
Mt.-St. Guilbert
Namur
Meuse R.
Wavre
Brussels
Waterloo
Mt.-St.-Jean

the Prussians II Corps attacked, but were beaten off. They essayed another attack later that day, as the French were pulling out of the town, but were once again repulsed by a well-handled rear guard, and suffered about 1,500 casualties. This defeat convinced the Prussians to leave Grouchy's little army alone and it was not pursued. The next morning, 21 June, Grouchy brought his relatively unscathed command into Philippeville. Finding that the remnants of the *Army of the North* had already abandoned the place, he marched on. On 25 June Grouchy reached Soissons, where Marshal Soult was trying to reorganize the army, by then reinforced to somewhat more than 30,000 men due to a trickle of reinforcements. Grouchy brought over 30,000 undefeated troops with him—not the 50,000 which Napoleon had averred in his optimism—all relatively fresh and with their morale intact. Thus there were perhaps 62,000 men who could be salvaged from the debacle. Grouchy assumed command and commenced a retreat on the 26th.

The Allies, of course, were by no means idle during these days. After the battle Wellington's army was reduced to only about 52,000 battle-ready men, and Blucher's to perhaps 66,000. With Wellington following behind, the Prussians took up the pursuit. A series of small, sharp actions occurred as French rear guards repeatedly clashed with the Prussian advanced guards. Most of these actions were small affairs, but at Compiegne and Crespy on the 27th and at Villers-Cotterets on the 28th they turned into fairly sizeable combats, though neither side was really interested in a major clash. In these actions the French gave as well as they received, but they continued to fall back on Paris.

Grouchy brought the remnants of the army into Paris on 29 June. Added to the considerable garrison already present, this made an army of upwards of 120,000 men, at least on paper, albeit that many of the troops were ill trained and morale was poor. Late that night Blucher

The War at Sea

The long wars of Revolutionary and Napoleonic France saw Britain victorious at sea most of the time. Between 1793 and 1815 France lost 91 ships-of-the-line, including 41 which were subsequently commissioned in the Royal Navy, while Britain lost 33, only five of them to enemy action. Despite these losses, Napoleon kept building new liners. By the time of his first abdication in 1814, the *Imperial Navy* had about 100 ships-of-the-line, while the Royal Navy possessed nearly 250, about half of which were regularly in commission. Figures for frigates were not much different. With the apparent end of the wars, the Royal Navy and the French *Royal Navy* drastically reduced personnel, while putting a lot of older ships up for scrap. As a result, by the time of Napoleon's escape from Elba the Royal Navy had only about 220 liners available, no more than a quarter of which were in commission, while the French had only about 70, few of which were in commission.

Realizing that the impending campaign would be short, Napoleon made little effort to prepare the fleet for war. Almost immediately he transferred about 70,000 naval personnel to serve as fortress troops, thereby releasing better trained men for service with the army in the field. This left the *Imperial Navy* with few men capable of taking a ship to sea. This was just as well, for almost as soon as word of Napoleon's escape from Elba reached London, the Royal Navy began recommissioning ships, and British squadrons soon reappeared before French ports, while British frigates once more began to sweep the seas of French shipping.

There were few naval actions during the Hundred Days, most of them minor and all of them British victories, and they had no impact on the course of the campaign of Waterloo. But had the war lasted longer, had Napoleon managed to secure a victory in Belgium, the effects of British maritime supremacy would have begun to tell.

approached and essayed an assault on the northern defenses of the city. Marshal Louis Davout, an excellent field commander whom Napoleon had been forced to assign as war minister, directed the defense. A major action threatened before Blucher decided to pull back and await Wellington, who was by then more than 30 kilometers behind him.

While all of this was going on, Napoleon was fighting

the last battle of his career, a political one, and one in which he failed completely to take part. Reaching Paris on 21 June, he immediately took a bath and then went to sleep, rather than seize the reins of government. As he slept, he lost control of France. The Chambers decided France had had enough of war. Calling out the *National Guard*, they declared that any attempt to dissolve the legislature would be considered treason and requested Napoleon's abdication. He acceded to their demand on the 22nd. For some days Napoleon moped around Paris, while representatives of the Chambers immediately began negotiations with the Allies. The situation was delicate. Despite Napoleon's optimism, France was in dire straits. To be sure, on paper, enormous armies might yet be concentrated. However, the country was war weary. Moreover, not only was the political situation unchanged, but the military situation had worsened as a result not merely of Waterloo, but also of Allied activities on France's other frontiers. Blucher and Wellington were to the north of Paris, enormous Allied forces were pressing into Alsace and Lorraine, still other Allied forces were advancing from Italy. Though Davout urged Napoleon to seize power, it was clearly impossible. The best that might be accomplished militarily was another drawn-out campaign like that of 1814. On 25 June Napoleon left Paris for Malmaison, where he hung about for four days before leaving incognito for the coast.

Meanwhile, the Allies were proving somewhat confused in their demands on France, partially because they themselves had no clear policy. Some sought a restoration of the Bourbons under Louis XVIII, others believed his less reactionary cousin Louis Philippe might fit the bill and there were even some who suggested that Napoleon's infant son be installed as Napoleon II. Then there were new territorial demands to be made and met, minor ones to be sure, as well as occupation terms and reparations. And through it all, Allied forces—notably Prussians—

Napoleon sails to England aboard **H.M.S. Bellerophon.**

were rampaging across northern France. Military force is designed to serve a political purpose and on 1 July Davout acted to remind the Allies that while France might not be able to win a renewed war, she might make the cost of the Allied demands uncomfortably high. About a thousand hussars of the 2nd Cavalry Brigade of the Prussian II Corps were raiding west of Paris in the direction of Versailles. Davout ordered Comte Exelmans' *II Cavalry Corps* rebuilt to about 3,000 men, supported by elements of the *14th Division* to deal with them. At Rocquencourt, just west of Paris, Exelmans ambushed and annihilated the entire Prussian brigade. Then Davout offered an armistice, agreeing to accept Louis XVIII in return for an amnesty under threat of carrying on the war. The armistice was concluded on 4 July.

Even as these events were unfolding, Napoleon had reached Rochefort. He toyed with the idea of taking ship for the United States, but was unable to secure passports and a safe conduct from the Royal Navy, which had the port under tight blockade. He considered various schemes. The frigate *La Saale* was placed at his disposal. Although his brother Joseph urged him to take the chance, he decided it was too dangerous. On 15 July he boarded HMS *Bellerophon*, throwing himself "like Themistocles" on the mercy of his most determined enemy. The next day he reached England. He had calculated his chances fairly well—though not perfectly, as Joseph reached the United States by slipping through the blockade—for the British knew not what to do with him. Almost any other of his enemies would probably have had him shot. While diplomatic negotiations raged Napoleon spent 21 days in England, an object of intense curiosity. Finally a decision was reached. On 7 August Napoleon was placed aboard HMS *Northumberland*. He disembarked at St. Helena on 17 October, spending his first nights on the island in a cottage in which the Duke of Wellington had once briefly resided. He ended his days there on 5 May 1821.

Back in Europe the aftermath of the Hundred Days was rather anticlimactic, although the restored Bourbons took their petty revenge on some. Ney and de la Bedoyere were shot, but surprisingly others, most of those accused of "treason" by the Royalists, got off with minor penalties and rustication, or were spirited out of the country, often with the connivance of Allied officers. Less fortunate were the many ordinary citizens who had supported Napoleon and now found themselves the object of attack by the "White Terror." Unknown numbers suffered the loss of their livelihoods, their property and sometimes their lives at the hands of ultra-Royalist mobs before Louis XVIII managed to bring things under control. As for the Allies, they exacted some additional territories and some additional reparations from France, but Britain, mindful of upsetting the balance of power in Europe, kept these additional penalties small, and in the end the outcome was but little more severe than the terms already imposed. By 1818 the last of the Allied occupation forces were gone.

Losses During the Waterloo Campaign

This table attempts to give a breakdown of the daily casualty rate—killed, wounded and missing—for the four days of the campaign, along with an indication of French losses as a proportion of Allied ones. Figures are for the most part estimated on the basis of fragmentary information, notably so for the French, and include men who "temporarily" deserted the colors but returned to duty within a day or so. This was a particular problem for the Prussians (the losses shown for them on the 17th being largely deserters and stragglers) and the Anglo-Allied Army (which lost about 10,000 men to desertion during the battle of Waterloo.) In both cases, however, the troops in question were returned to duty within a few days, so that actual losses of the Anglo-Allied Army were about 22,600 men and those of the Prussians about 30,200, which makes French losses for the campaign about 122.3 percent of Allied losses.

In round figures, Napoleon lost slightly more than half his army during the four-day campaign, while Wellington lost about 20 percent and Blucher about 23 percent; in all three cases stragglers who rejoined the colors within a few days are not included.

Note that the figures given on the table following do not always agree with those in the main text, since these lump losses to straggling, desertion and minor actions into those for the principal engagements on the 16th and 18th.

Losses of artillery appear to have been quite small. The Prussians seem to have lost 6 pieces in the fighting along the Sambre on the 15th and a further 21 at Ligny, for a total of 28. The Dutch-Belgians lost

---

Meanwhile, almost from the very start, Waterloo began to assume mythic proportions, a development to which Napoleon and his most enthusiastic supporters made enormous contributions. In scores of writings, "The Exile" and his supporters gradually reshaped the story of the battle to throw virtually the entire onus for defeat upon Grouchy, Ney and others, while polishing still further the already formidable Napoleonic myth.

In retrospect, the Waterloo campaign was a glorious and spectacular episode, but hardly a decisive one. The decision had already been reached in 1813 and 1814, when, in consequence of the twin disasters of the Russian campaign

six pieces in the fighting at Quatre Bras, but otherwise no British or Allied gun appears to have been lost permanently. Likewise, the French lost a number of pieces temporarily during the series of battles, most notably when the Household Cavalry overran a portion of Napoleon's Grand Battery at Waterloo; no French guns were permanently lost until after the collapse of the *Armee du Nord* on the evening of 18 June, when about 120 pieces were abandoned.

Losses During the Waterloo Campaign						
Date (June)	Action	French	Anglo-Allied	Prussian	Total	Ratio Fr:AA/Pr
		(Thousands of Men)				
15		0.6	0.1	2.0	2.1	28.6
16	Ligny	13.7	18.7	18.7	73.2	
	Quatre Bras	4.1	5.2	5.2	78.8	
	Total	17.8	5.2	18.7	23.9	74.4
17		0.1	0.2	10.0	10.2	0.1
18	Waterloo	43.7	27.1	7.0	34.1	128.1
	Wavre/ Limale	2.4	2.5	2.5	96.0	
	Total	46.1	27.1	9.5	36.6	125.9
	Total	64.6	32.6	40.2	72.8	88.7

and the ongoing "ulcer" in Spain, it became clear that France could not stand against the combined powers of Europe, even with Napoleon in command. Napoleon's last bid for power was virtually foredoomed. The best that could have been hoped for militarily was to draw out the campaign as long as possible in the hope that the Allies would become war weary. But none of the countries aligned against him was likely to collapse before France herself did. Napoleon could not himself be everywhere, and thus could not ensure that France would win every battle. Indeed, he could not even be certain that he himself could win every battle. So in a protracted war, a war of attrition, the Allies would have the upper hand. The last chance to preserve the Empire politically had passed in 1813 or even 1814, when Napoleon had spurned quite reasonable, indeed generous, terms from the Allies which would have left France with greatly expanded frontiers. But Napoleon wanted it all, the Grand Empire as it had existed in 1810, and pressed for a military solution. The campaign of 1815 was Napoleon's third effort to seek a military solution to a political problem that would no longer permit one. In a sense, then, the campaign of 1815 was a foregone conclusion. Yet as Wellington put it to a friend, the battle of Waterloo, with which the campaign reached its climax, had been "...a damned nice thing—the nearest run thing you ever saw in your life....By God! I don't think it would have been done if I had not been there." It had been so dramatic a fight that Napoleon's dreams of victory seemed almost possible. And that is perhaps the reason the Waterloo campaign has such an enormous hold on the imagination.

Some Waterloo Alumni

Many illustrious men fought in Belgium in 1815. Yet the mere presence of Napoleon and Wellington, Blucher and Ney, and all the other notable commanders, often obscures the fact that their armies were mostly made up of young men, literally hundreds of thousands of them. And among these faceless multitudes there were a few who would later achieve some measure of fame in their own right.

A number of later famous—or infamous—British officers served at Waterloo in various junior positions. Undoubtedly the most well known of these was Lieutenant ′ Colonel Fitzroy Somerset, Wellington's young aide who lost an arm at Waterloo. A generation later, as Lord Raglan, he would ineptly command the British Army in the Crimean War (1854-1856), by which time he was so advanced in age that he tended to forget who the enemy was, referring to them occasionally as "the French," much to the embarrassment of his French allies. Another British veteran of Waterloo who was to prove less than competent had already done so during the campaign, Lieutenant Colonel William K. Elphinstone of the 33rd. He was arguably the worst battalion commander in any of the armies during the campaign, and later went on to become quite possibly the most indecisive officer ever to command an army in the field, a dubious distinction which he acquired during the First Afghan War (1839-1842). There he dithered on so heroic a scale that of an army of some 4,000 troops and 10,000 camp followers, only one man did not escape death or capture! Not all alumni of the Waterloo campaign were so inept.

Despite the loss of his left hand due to wounds received at Ligny, Lieutenant Colonel Sir Henry Hardinge, Wellington's liaison officer at Blucher's headquarters, later held many important civil and military posts, including governor general of India, in which capacity he took the field during the First Sikh War, voluntarily placing himself under the command of an officer of lesser seniority, Sir Hugh Gough, ending his days as a field marshal and viscount.

Harry Smith, the quartermaster of Wellington's 6th Division, later went on to a distinguished career, winning the battle of Aliwal (28 January 1846) during the First Sikh War, defeating the Boers at the battle of Boomplaats (29 August 1848) and becoming the victor in the Eighth Kaffir War (1850-1853). He had two brothers also at Waterloo, one of whom, Lieutenant Thomas Smith of the 95th, was the first British officer to enter Paris at the end of the pursuit of the French.

There were a number of Frenchmen active during the campaign who later rose to some fame. General de Division Louis de Bourmont, the Royalist officer who deserted Napoleon's army on the very morning of the first day of the campaign of Waterloo, went on to a distinguished career in the Bourbon government, beginning with service as one of the prosecutors at the trial of Marshal Ney and eventually rising to become an inept governor of Algeria, minister of war and a marshal. One of Napoleon's fellow-Corsicans, Colonel Jean Sebastiani, commanded a brigade in the *II Corps* during the campaign and later went on to serve as commanding officer of the French volunteers in the Greek War for Independence, eventually becoming a lieutenant general, deputy and peer of France. His brother Colonel Horace Sebastiani commanded a *National Guard* unit during the campaign and later went on to serve as a noted liberal in the Chamber of Deputies and ended his days as a marshal.

There were several men active on the minor fronts who rose to considerable distinction in later years. Lieutenant Colonel Thomas Bugeaud de la Piconnerie commanded the *14th of the Line* with great skill in the Alps under Marshal Suchet, being principally responsible for the flank attack which resulted in the defeat of the Austrians at Conflans. In 1836 Bugeaud was sent to Algeria, where he conducted a masterful series of campaigns which led to the French annexation of the country, and ended his days as a marshal. Emile Deschamps, a lieutenant in the garrison of the Fortress of Vincennes,

later became a noted romantic critic, poet, author and translator. His commanding officer at Vincennes was one of the most distinguished of Napoleon's middle-ranking officers, General de Brigade Pierre Daumesnil. One of the earliest officers of the *Garde Imperial*, Daumesnil had covered himself with glory on many a field, but was seriously wounded in 1812 and thereafter assigned to command Vincennes which he did with great determination; he did not haul down the Imperial tricolor until mid-August of 1815 and, in connivance with French Royalist authorities, refused to admit Allied troops into the fortress until 15 November! Colonel Charles Fabvier organized guerrilla operations against Allied forces in northeastern France during the campaign and did not surrender until August. He later returned to active duty, while remaining politically prominent as a liberal and eventually becoming commandant of Paris after the Revolution of 1830, inspector general of France and chief of staff to both the Greek and Danish armies at various times, ending his days as a deputy during the Second Republic. Lieutenant Aimable Jean Jackques Pelissier, who served under Rapp in Alsace, later served with some distinction in North Africa and became one of the most noted officers of the Second Empire, earning a baton in the process.

The Other Fronts

The central drama of Waterloo necessarily dominates any treatment of the Hundred Days. It is thus easy to forget that there were military operations on all of the frontiers of France during the Waterloo campaign, and a serious internal security problem in the Vendee as well.

The Vendee. Almost as soon as Napoleon returned to Paris there were serious outbreaks against him all over France. In most areas these were put down rather handily. Not so, however, in the the Vendee, the area roughly at the base of the Breton peninsula. The Vendee had remained staunchly Royalist through the long years of both the Republic and the Empire, despite considerable repression. When Napoleon returned to power the Vendee burst into open revolt once more. Royalist leaders there planned to recruit some 56,000 peasants, who would be equipped as an army and transported by Britain's Royal Navy. This estimate was optimistic, for the rebels never numbered more than 16,000 men, few of whom were trained. Worse yet, the local Royalist leaders failed to organize a central command for their forces, so that there were four separate Royalist columns operating in the area, each under a totally independent commander. The rising was doomed from the start. Nevertheless, Napoleon took it quite seriously, reasoning that it had to be suppressed as quickly as possible lest it fester and grow.

To accomplish this task he organized the *Army of the Loire*. This force totalled about 15,000 men, including a brigade of the *Young Guard* and sizable contingents from regiments of Napoleon's own *Army of the North*. The Bonapartist troops made short work of the rebels and their sympathizers, operating with great brutality. Their superior power was never in doubt, as the imperial forces defeated the rebels in a series of bloody, one-sided encounters, culminating in the annihilation of the largest surviving Royalist force at Roche-Servien on 16 June. This released about half the troops in the Vendee for service on other fronts. However, by that time it was already too late. So in a perverse way the Royalist rebels helped to topple Napoleon, for they tied up what amounted to an entire army corps, a force which could have been put to much better use elsewhere.

The Pyrennes. The quietest of France's frontiers during the Hundred Days was that bordering Spain. To cover this frontier Napoleon assigned two "corps of observaton." By mid-June each of these forces amounted to about 15,000 men and could call upon local *National Guards* in an emergency. Such an emergency never arose. The Spanish army was hardly a formidable fighting force, nor could the guerrilleros, who had sustained Spain's military honor during the long Peninsular campaign (1808-1814), readily operate inside France. Spain was able to concentrate no more than about 24,000 men for duty on her frontier with France, and even given time no more than 12,000 additional troops would have been available (plus a small contingent of excellent Portuguese troops, provided various diplomatic niceties could be worked out between the two mutually suspicious Iberian powers). At best these forces would have been adequate to do no more than conduct some cross-border raids. They did even less than that, permitting some of the troops assigned to the *IV Corps of Observation* to assist in the Vendee.

The Alpine Front. The Italian frontier was held by two forces, which by mid-June numbered some 33,000 men. Along the alpine frontier the very capable Marshal Louis Suchet commanded the 23,600-strong *Army of the Alps*. Supporting him on the coast were an additional 10,000 men in the *II Var Corps of Observation* under the very experienced Marshal Guillaume Brune, long out of favor with Napoleon for his republican sentiments, but a good man to have around given the Royalist leanings of Provence. In addition, there were some 3,000 troops ensconced in various fortified places. These forces were expected to do little more than impede the advance of the Austro-Italian forces in Italy, which could be expected ultimately to number as many as 120,000 men. The odds against the Imperial forces were soon increased when Suchet gallantly sent 7,000 men in support of the forces covering the Jura. Realizing that he had

little chance if the enemy came after him, Suchet decided to act as aggressively as possible.

On 14 June Suchet launched a series of small, sharp attacks against Austrian and Piedmontese forces holding various alpine passes as far north as Geneva. By 21 June he had succeeded in securing several of these, but had been repulsed at others. By this time the Austro-Piedmontese Army of Upper Italy, under General Johann von Frimont, had begun to move. Supported by the Blockade Corps of the Allied Army of the Rhine, Frimont slipped his I Corps through Switzerland so that it descended on the Jura passes, cutting Suchet's lateral links with French forces further north. Frimont's II Corps had tougher going. As II Corps attempted to cross the Alps, Suchet disputed its passage virtually every step of the way, thus preventing Frimont from registering any significant gains. A considerable number of minor though sharp engagements occurred over the next week, some open field actions and others sieges and assaults of the many fortified places in the area.

But even as operations had opened on this front, matters were coming to a head in Belgium. Learning of Napoleon's defeat at Waterloo, Suchet decided to offer an armistice in order to avoid further bloodshed. Frimont refused, demanding complete surrender. Unwilling to totally open France to invasion, Suchet gambled. On 28 June, at Conflans, he launched a determined counterattack against Frimont's II Corps, inflicting serious damage on it at relatively little cost. He then once more offered an armistice, which this time the chastened Frimont was willing to accept. Under its terms, Suchet was able to pull his army back on Lyons. It was there that the end of the war found him.

The operations on the Italian Front had developed predictably. Suchet's conduct of the campaign in the Alps had been a masterpiece of rear-guard operations. Perhaps only he could have brought it off, which is why Napoleon sent him there in the first place.

The Jura. France's alpine frontier with Switzerland was held by the small *I Jura Corps of Observation*. Initially numbering only about 8,400 men, it was reinforced by 7,000 more from Suchet's army on the Italian frontier. There was little this tiny force could do when, on 25 June, the left wing of the Allied Army of the Rhine, some 100,000 men or more, crossed into France from the vicinity of Basel. Nevertheless, the French, under general LeCourbe, did their best. Sharp rear-guard actions were fought at Donnemarie and Chabannes before LeCourbe retired on heavily fortified Belfort, there to await the end of the war.

The Rhine. At the beginning of June, Allied forces in the Rhineland held a front of over 350 kilometers, stretching from the Moselle to the Swiss border at Basel, employing over 300,000 men, with a further 157,000 Russians within a few days march. To hold back this enormous host, Napoleon put over 20,000 men into the many fortresses with which Alsace and Lorraine were liberally seasoned, and backed them up with 23,000 more in the *Army of the Rhine* under Division de General Jean Rapp, a loyal campaigner. The odds against Rapp were considerable, but his skills were great and his foes less than energetic.

Allied forces were divided into three groups. There was a sizable North German Corps in the valley of the Moselle. This fortunately moved with great lethargy and had barely begun to annoy the garrisons of the French frontier fortresses when the campaign came to an end. At the other extreme, the left wing of the Allied Army of the Rhine became enmeshed with LeCourbe's *Jura Corps* and elements of Suchet's *Army of the Alps*. This left Rapp to confront only the right wing of the Army of the Rhine, which comprised a Bavarian Corps of some 57,000 men under Field Marshal Karl Wrede along with a South German Corps of 44,000 strong under the Prince of Wurttemberg and 10,000 Advanced Guard of the Russian Army. On 10 June Wrede's Bavarians, with some Russians in tow, crossed into France after a sharp engagement at Sarrebrucken. The force wandered into the heart of Lorraine, accomplishing little of military importance, while stirring up guerrilla activity among the Bonapartist peasantry through various depredations. By the end of the campaign Wrede —of whom Napoleon had once said, "I made him a count, but even I could not make him a general" — was on the out-skirts of Nancy, having advanced about 100 kilometers in 18 days.

Crossing into France near Lan-dau on 23 June, Wurttemberg's corps proved a more dangerous foe. Local French forces withdrew into Landau and elsewhere. Rather than attempt to besiege these many little places, Wurttemberg wisely put them under blockade, while press-ing his forces up the valley of the Rhine towards Strassbourg. Rapp retreated slowly, coming off the worse for it in two moderate-sized engagements on the 26th. But two days later, at La Souffel, Rapp, with but 18,000 men present, inflicted a sharp repulse on Wurttemberg, who greatly outnumbered him. De-spite this creditable success, Rapp then fell back on nearby Strass-bourg, with Wurttemberg following cautiously, to establish a fairly close blockade over the next few days. Rapp's situation after La Souffel was by no means a good one, for over 150,000 Russians under Field Marshal Prince Mikhail Barclay de

Tolly had begun crossing the Rhine even before that battle. Had the campaign lasted a few weeks more the Russians would have been upon him. On the other hand, had Napo-leon triumphed at Waterloo, the Em-peror and his victorious *Army of the North* would have been marching up at just about the same time. This would have saved Rapp, at least temporarily. But then Napoleon would have had to contend with Al-lied forces of perhaps two or three times his own strength.

Conclusion. In general the opera-tions on the frontiers of France had not gone unfavorably for the French. No one, least of all Napo-leon, had expected any of the fron-tier armies to secure stunning victories over their foes. Each had done pretty much what had been ex-pected: hold the line until a decision could be reached in Belgium. In this, they had not failed their Em-peror. But the outcome in Belgium was not what Napoleon anticipated. Thus, it mattered little what tran-spired on the frontiers of France.

Guide for the Interested Reader

This is not intended to be a comprehensive survey of the literature of the Waterloo Campaign, but rather a guide to assist readers who are interested in pursuing the subject further.

Books. In the enormously voluminous literature of Napoleon and his age, Waterloo is one of the most-written about events in military history. Donald Howard's *Napoleonic Military History: A Bibliography* (New York and London: 1986) lists over 2,000 pieces on the campaign and is undoubtedly incomplete.

For a short general introduction to the art of war in the period see the present writer's *Napoleon at War: Selected Writings of F. Loraine Petre* (New York: 1984) or Gunther Rothenberg's *The Art of Warfare in the Age of Napoleon* (Bloomington, Ind. and London: 1978). A weightier and more serious treatment is David Chandler's *The Campaigns of Napoleon: the Mind and Method of History's Greatest Soldier* (New York and London: 1966), which may be usefully supplemented by his *Dictionary of the Napoleonic Wars* (New York and London: 1979, 1993).

Ugo Pericoli's *1815: The Armies at Waterloo* (London: 1973) is the best short introduction to the nature and organization of the armies which fought the battle. H.C.B. Rogers' *Napoleon's Army* (New York and London: 1974) is the best short introduction to Napoleon's war machine, but John R. Elting's much weightier *Swords around a Throne* (New York and London: 1988) is superior. For the *Garde Imperial* nothing has surpassed Henry Lachoque's *The Anatomy of Glory: Napoleon and His Guard* (London and Providence, RI: 1961; London and New York: 1978). There is no comparable recent treatment of Wellington's army, but see Charles W. C. Oman's old but very valuable *Wellington's Army, 1809-1814* (London: 1913/London: 1986), which has a good many errors, but remains the best treatment the British Army of the period has ever had. No works in English are of comparable value for the Allied armies or the Prussians.

There are numerous general works on the Waterloo Campaign. Although very old, William Siborne's *History of the Waterloo Campaign* (London: 1847; London: 1991) remains indispensable despite some errors, as is also *Waterloo Letters: A Selection from Original and Hitherto Unpublished Letters Bearing on the Operations of the 16th, 17th, and 18th June, 1815, by Officers Who Served in the Campaign*, edited, with explanatory notes by Major-General H.T. Siborne (London, 1891; London: 1993), which contains hundreds of the letters which the elder Siborne solicited from participants in the battle during his research. For some spirited, although perhaps not always accurate, criticisms of Siborne, see D.C. Hamilton-Williams, "Captain William Siborne," *Journal of the Society for Army Historical Research*, Vol. 66 (1988). Also old, but of considerable value, are Henry Houssaye's *1815: Waterloo* (Kansas City: 1905, but several reprints since) and A.F. Becke's *Napoleon and Waterloo* (London: 1939). Anthony Brett-James' *The Hundred Days* (London: 1964) and David Chandler's *Waterloo: The Hundred Days* (London: 1980) are more recent, and have valuable insights to offer. An unusual look at the campaign is to be found in *Waterloo* (New York and London: 1980) edited by Lord Chalfont and containing integrated accounts of the battle by French,

Allied and Prussian authors. A most unusual treatment of Waterloo is John Keegan's *The Face of Battle* (New York and London: 1976), which attempts to look at the battle from the perspective of the men who fought it.

There are innumerable biographies of Napoleon, but that contained in Chandler's *The Campaigns of Napoleon* is perhaps most useful to the student of military history. Wellington has been the subject of several good biographies, of which the most notable are Elizabeth Longford's *Wellington: The Years of the Sword* (London: 1969), and Arthur Bryant's *The Great Duke* (New York and London: 1972). Jac Weller's *Wellington at Waterloo* (New York and London: 1967; London: 1992) focusses on the Duke's activities during the battle and is immensely useful as a result. Roger Parkinson's *The Hussar General: The Life of Blucher* (London: 1975) is a good treatment of that wonderfully curious man. Most of the subordinate commanders in the campaign have not received much attention. However, Raymond Horricks' *Marshal Ney: The Romance and the Real* (New York: 1982) is an interesting book. Napoleon's marshals are the subject of several works, of which David Chandler's *Napoleon's Marshals* (New York and London: 1988) is perhaps the best, but Peter Young's *Napoleon's Marshals* (New York and London: 1978) and R.F. Delderfield's *The March of the Twenty-Six* (London: 1962) are both of considerable value.

There were numerous memoirs by participants in the campaign, from Napoleon, who lied wonderfully, on down to private soldiers, mostly in the British Army, but not exclusively. Anthony Brett-James has collected a number of first-hand sources in his *Napoleon's Last Campaigns from Eye-witness Accounts* (London: 1964). Among the more interesting memoirs are Captain Cavalie Mercer's *Journal of the Waterloo Campaign* (London: 1870; London:1985) and Friedrich Karl Ferdinand von Muffling's *History of the Campaign of 1815*.

The best published order of battle for the campaign is

Scott Bowden's *Armies at Waterloo* (Arlington, Tex: 1983), which is extremely detailed, but with which the present writer does not always agree.

The campaign of 1815 figures in a number of novels and short stories right up to the present, but there have never been better treatments of the battle than Victor Hugo's *Les Miserabiles*, despite the Bonapartism which leads him into several errors, Napoleonic veteran Stendahl's *The Charterhouse of Parma* and Arthur Conan Doyle's short story "The Return of Gerard."

Simulation Games. The Waterloo Campaign has probably been the subject of more wargames than any other military operation. Undoubtedly the best of the many Waterloo games was *Napoleon at Waterloo* (Simulations Publications, 1974), a simple, well balanced, and quite realistic recreation of the battle which is long out of print. The very first commercial game on the subject, Avalon Hill's *Waterloo* is surprisingly good, and still in print after nearly 30 years. Another older game, *Wellington's Victory* (SPI/TSR) is a remarkably accurate recreation of the nature of the battle on a "monster" scale. A number of more recent games are quite good, notably *Empires in Arms* (Avalon Hill) and *Napoleon's Latter Battles* (3-W), as is the series *The Emperor Returns*, *La Bataille de Ligny*, *La Bataille de Quatre Bras* and *La Bataille de Mont Saint Jean* (Clash of Arms). There exist numerous miniatures rules for the Waterloo period, of which the best probably are *Napoleon's Battles* (Avalon Hill) and *Empire* (Scott Bowden).

Film. Waterloo figures at least peripherally in a number of motion pictures. In most of them the treatment is superficial, and often silly. However, Sergei Bondarchuk's Italo-Russian *Waterloo* (1971), with Rod Steiger as Napoleon, Christopher Plummer as Wellington, and Vittorio Gassman as Blucher was quite good. Not only did the confusion of the battle come across very effectively, but some attention was paid to appropriate tactics. Although their shape was inaccurate, aerial shots of Wellington's squares demonstrated how the cavalry swarmed between them ineffectively: interestingly, the Soviet troops who impersonated the Allied infantrymen "broke" several times during rehearsals of the French cavalry charges. Research for this picture eventually was incorporated in the Ugo Pericoli book cited above.

Touring the Battlefield. The sites of the campaign of 1815 are in many cases extremely well preserved. Indeed, the field of Waterloo itself is very little changed from what it was in 1815.

The principal changes in the area have been the result of roadbuilding and the creation of the Lion Monument, a tall earthen mound dedicated to the memory of the Dutch-Belgian troops. Road construction has altered the width, though not the location, of most of the roads in the area. The movement of earth for the mound has greatly altered the terrain immediately in front of the center of Wellington's lines. This is partially compensated by the wonderful panorama of the field which one gets from the top.

The area immediately behind Wellington's front lines, where he held his reserves, has been rather built up. However, aside from the earth that was removed for the Lion Monument the area in front of the Allied lines is virtually unchanged. Indeed, much of the area is still working farmland, just as it was in 1815. The principal buildings which figured in the battle—Hougoumont, La Haie Sainte, and the rest—are still there with little change: they are mostly private property however, and may not usually be visited. As a result of the relative lack of development southward from Wellington's lines it is possible to view the area of the main battle, across to where Napoleon's army deployed more or less as it was in 1815. And likewise, it is possible to view the Allied lines from Napoleon's.

Knowing a good thing when they see one, the citizens of the Waterloo area have provided a number of amenities, including several excellent small museums, in addition to various souvenir stands and restaurants dedicated to separating the tourist from his money. One event not to be missed is the regular demonstration by a fife and drum corps which very effectively points out the efficacy of these instruments in conveying instructions across the battlefield.

Under no circumstances should the visitor miss the film that is shown in the theater at the visitor's center immediately behind the Lion Monument, as it is one of the most effective cinematic recreations of a battle ever made.

Order of Battle

The Waterloo Campaign

15 June 1815

This order of battle covers the principal armies at the start of the campaign in Belgium in some detail, with an outline of the composition for the forces in other theaters. It is important to realize that there was some shifting of regiments and brigades among divisions and corps during the the campaign, and even at its start minor elements of some units were on detached service with other formations. Names appearing in parentheses are those of commanding officers; where the name is the same as that of the country, a member of the ruling family was in command. The roman numerals after the names of certain German commanders were a contemporary means of avoiding confusion among officers with identical names.

Figures given for manpower reflect the strength of units on the eve of the campaign, rather than the number actually brought into action, which are those used in the text. These numbers are approximate and in some cases have been estimated: where subordinate unit totals do not equal higher unit totals, the difference is to be attributed to staffs, engineers, train personnel and other service forces attached, which are not actually shown here. Despite often heroic efforts, determining the precise strength and composition of an army is virtually an impossible task. Official returns often omit various people, such as most medical and staff personnel, servants and casual hangers-on, such as Pierre in *War and Peace*, while stragglers, deserters and details are often included. Thus, it is not possible to gain more than an approximate notion of the strength of the armies which fought in 1815, nor is the matter of some hundreds of men either way of much consequence when dealing with armies in the scores of thousands.

Battalion numbers are in some cases uncertain or based on circumstantial evidence. British regiments with only one battalion were customarily listed merely as, for example, "The 33rd of Foot," but are here given as "1st Bn, 33rd Ln," an anachronism introduced to clarify the number of battalions present.

Note that there is some uncertainty about the identity of units and commanders in the case of some smaller formations.

Abbreviations and conventions are: *Art.*, artillery; *Au*, Austrian; *Bav*, Bavarian; *Bde*, brigade; *Bn*, battalion; *Br*, British; *Btty*, battery of artillery, called a "field brigade" in the British Army and usually a "troop" in the horse artillery; *Cav.*, cavalry; *Coy.*, company; *DB*, Dutch-Belgian; *Div*, division; *Elms*, elements, a detachment or detail; *Engrs.*, engineers; *Inf.*, infantry, sometimes referred to as "Foot"; *Gd.*, Guards; *Han.*, Hanoverian; *Hvy*, heavy; *hwtzr*, howitzer; *KGL*, "King's German Legion," German troops regularly enlisted in British service; *Ln.*, of the Line; *Lt.*, Light; *LW*, Landwehr, German states' militia; *Mixed*, a formation composed of contingents from the minor German states; *NGd*, French National Guard troops; *pdr*, pounder; *pieces*, pieces of artillery; *Pion.*, pioneers, an alternate name for combat engineers; *Res*, reserve; *R.F.A.*, the Royal Foot Artillery; *Rgt*, regiment; *R.H.A.*, Royal

Horse Artillery; *Sqn*, squadron. For artillery, the usage "6x12 pdrs" means "six 12-pounder cannon." Unless otherwise noted, a unit is always considered a regiment. If no type is indicated, the troops in question are considered infantry. Note that some anachronisms have been introduced to make terminology and usage more familiar to persons in the late twentieth century.

The Armies in Belgium

The French

The Army of the North (Napoleon)
(122,600 with 368 pieces)

Imperial Guard (Drouot, *vice* Mortier) (20,700 with 110 pieces)
  Grenadiers (Friant)(4,500 in 7 Bns)
    1st Grenadiers (Petit)(1,040 in 2 Bns)
    2nd Grenadiers (Christiani)(1,100 in 2 Bns)
    3rd Grenadiers (Poret de Morvan)(1,180 in 2 Bns)
    4th Grenadiers (Harlet)(530 in 1 Bn)
  Chasseurs (Morand)(5,000 in 8 Bns)
    1st Chasseurs (Cambronne)(1,310 in 2 Bns)
    2nd Chasseurs (Pelet)(1,165 in 2 Bns)
    3rd Chasseurs (Mallet)(1,065 in 2 Bns)
    4th Chasseurs (Henrion)(1,075 in 2 Bns)
  Young Guard **(Duhesme) (4,800 in 8 Bns)**
  [1st *Young Guard Div* (Barrois)]
    1st Bde (Chartrand)(2,340 in 4 Bns)
      1st Tirailleurs (Trappier)(1,110 in 2 Bns)
      1st Voltigeurs (Secretan)(1,220 in 2 Bns)
    2nd Bde (Guye)(1,970 in 4 Bns)
      3rd Tirailleurs (Pailhes)(990 in 2 Bns)
      3rd Voltigeurs (Hurel)(970 in 2 Bns)
  Heavy Cavalry **(Guyot) (2,000 in 8.5 Sqns & 2 Bttys, with 12 pieces)**
    Grenadiers a Cheval (Dubois)(800 in 4 Sqns)
    Dragoons (Ornano, absent)(815 in 4 Sqns)
    1st Coy, Gendarmerie d'Elite (Dyonnet)(110 in 1 Sqn)
    Light Cavalry (Lefebvre-Desnouettes)(2,100 in 10 Sqns)
    Chasseurs (Lallemand)(1,200 in 5 Sqns, plus one troop of 26
      Mamelukes)
    Lancers (Colbert)(900 in 5 Sqns, one of Poles)
  Artillery **(Desvaux de Saint-Maurice) (3,200 in 13 Foot and 5 Horse
    Bttys, with 134 pieces)**
    Old Guard Foot Artillery (Lallemand)(730 in 6 Bttys, probably 36x6-
      pdr & 12x6" hwtzrs)
    Old Guard Horse Artillery (Duchand)(400 in 4 Bttys, with 24x6-pdr
      & 8x6" hwtzrs)

Young Guard Foot Artillery (Lallemand)(300 in 3 Bttys, probably with 18x12-pdrs & 6x6" hwtzrs)

Line Foot Artillery (Dubuard-Maruin)(430 in 4 Bttys, probably with 24x12-pdrs & 8x6" hwtzrs)

Line Horse Artillery (Laurent)(75 in 1 Btty, with 4x6-pdrs & 2x6" hwtzrs)

> *Old Guard Train* (??)(925 in 10 Coys)
> *Line Train* (?7)(615 in 5 Coys)
> *Engrs of the Guard* (Bergeres)(112)
> *Mariners of the Guard* (Preaux)(107)

I Corps (D'Erlon) (19,800 with 46 pieces)

1st Div (Allix, replaced by Quiot) (4,200 in 8 Bns & 1 Btty, with 8 pieces)

1st Bde (Quiot)(2,110 in 4 Bns)
> 1st & 2nd Bns, 54th Ln (960)
> 1st & 2nd Bns, 55th Ln (1,150)

2nd Bde (Bourgeois)(1,880 in 4 Bns)
> 1st & 2nd Bns, 28th Ln (900)
> 1st & 2nd Bns, 105th Ln (980)

Arty (Hamelin) (184 in 1 Btty, with 8 pieces)
> 20th Btty, 6th Foot Arty (Hamelin)(85 with 6x6 pdrs & 2x6" hwtzrs)
> 5th Coy, 1st Train Sqn (Paleprat)

2nd Div (Donzelot) (5,300 in 9 Bns & 1 Btty, with 8 pieces)

1st Bde (Schmitz)(2,925 in 5 Bns)
> 1st, 2nd, & 3rd Bns, 13th Lt (1,875)
> 1st & 2nd Bns, 17th Ln (1,050)

2nd Bde (Aulard)(2,200 in 4 Bns)
> 1st & 2nd Bns, 19th Ln (1,030)
> 1st & 2nd Bns, 51st Ln (1,170)

Arty (Cantin)(185 in 1 Btty, with 8 pieces)
> 10th Btty, 6th Foot Art (Cantin)(90 with 6x6 pdrs & 2x6" hwtzrs)
> 9th Coy, 1st Train Sqn (Vaillant)

3rd Div (Marcognet) (4,100 in 8 Bns & 1 Btty, with 8 pieces)

1st Bde (Nogues)(1,930 in 4 Bns)
> 1st & 2nd Bns, 21st Ln (1,040)
> 1st & 2nd Bns, 46th Ln (890)

2nd Bde (Grenier)(1,975 in 4 Bns)
> 1st & 2nd Bns, 25th Ln (975)
> 1st & 2nd Bns, 45th Ln (1,000)

Arty (Emon)(180 in 1 Btty, with 8 pieces)

19th Coy, 6th Foot Art (Emon)(85 with 6x6 pdrs & 2x6" hwtzrs)
2nd Coy, 1st Train Sqn (Cosgueterre)
4th Div (Durutte) (4,000 in 8 Bns & 1 Btty, with 8 pieces)
1st Bde (Pegot)(2,135 in 4 Bns)
1st & 2nd Bns, 8th Ln (985)
1st & 2nd Bns, 29th Ln (1,150)
2nd Bde (Brue)(2,730 in 4 Bns)
1st & 2nd Bns, 85th Ln (630)
1st & 2nd Bns, 95th Ln (1,100)
Arty (Bourgeois)(180 with 8 pieces)
9th Btty, 6th Foot Art (Bourgeois)(90 with 6x6 pdrs & 2x6" hwtzrs)
3rd Coy, 1st Train Sqn (Drulin)
1st Cav Div (Jacquinot) (1,700 in 11 Sqns & 1 Btty, with 6 pieces)
1st Bde (Bruno)(910 in 6 Sqns)
7th Hussars (495)
3rd Chasseurs (415)
2nd Bde (Gobrecht)(800 in 6 Sqns)
3rd Lancers (460)
4th Lancers (340)
Arty (Bourgeois)(160 in 1 Horse Btty, with 6 pieces)
2nd Btty, 1st Horse Art (Bourgeois)(75 with 4x6 pdrs & 2x6" hwtzrs)
4th Coy, 1st Train Sqn (Daux)
Art Res (Dessales) (200 in 1 Btty, with 8 pieces)
11th Btty, 6th Foot Arty (Charlet)(90 with 6x12 pdrs & 2x6" hwtzrs)
6th Coy, 1st Train Sqn (Didier)(120)
Engrs (Garbe)(355)
2nd Coy, 1st Engineers (350)

II Corps (Reille) (25,150 with 46 pieces)
5th Div (Bachelu) (4,300 in 9 Bns & 1 Btty, with 8 pieces)
1st Bde (Husson)(2,005 in 4 Bns)
1st & 2nd Bns, 3rd Ln (1,145)
1st & 2nd Bns, 61st Ln (860)
2nd Bde (Campy)(2,105 in 5 Bns)
1st & 2nd Bns, 72nd Ln (995)
1st, 2nd, & 3rd Bns, 108th Ln (1,110)
Arty (Deshailles)(190 in 1 Btty, with 8 Pieces)
18th Btty, 6th Foot Art (Deshailles)(90 with 6x6 pdrs & 2x6" hwtzrs)
3rd Coy, 1st Train Sqn (Valette)(100)

6th Div (Jerome Bonaparte) (8,000 in 13 Bns & 1 Btty, with 8 pieces)
 1st Bde (Bauduin)(4,230 in 7 Bns)
  1st, 2nd, & 3rd Bns, 1st Lt (2,340)
  1st, 2nd, 3rd, & 4th Bns 2nd Lt (1,890)
 2nd Bde (Soye)(3,590 in 6 Bns)
  1st, 2nd, & 3rd Bns, 1st Ln (1,795)
  1st, 2nd, & 3rd Bns, 2nd Ln (1,795)
 Arty (Meunier)(200 in 1 Btty, with 8 Pieces)
  2nd Btty, 2nd Foot Art (Meunier)(95 with 6x6 pdrs & 2x6"
  hwtzrs)
  1st Coy, Equipment Train (Fivel)(105)
7th Div (Girard) (4,600 in 9 Bns & 1 Btty, with 8 pieces)
 1st Bde (Sebastiani)(2,030 in 4 Bns)
  1st & 2nd Bns, 11th Lt (955)
  1st & 2nd Bns, 82nd Ln (1,075)
 2nd Bde (Piat)(2,390 in 5 Bns)
  1st, 2nd, & 3rd Bns, 12th Lt (1,190)
  1st & 2nd Bns, 4th Ln (1,200)
 Arty (Barbaux)(180 in 1 Btty, with 8 pieces)
  3rd Btty, 2nd Foot Arty (Barbaux)(75 with 6x6 pdrs & 2x6"
  hwtzrs)
  1st Coy, 1st Train Sqn (??)(60)
  2nd Coy, [4th? 5th?] Train Sqn (??)(45)
9th Div (Foy) (5,000 in 11 Bns & 1 Btty, with 8 pieces)
 1st Bde (Tissot)(2,040 in 4 Bns)
  1st & 2nd Bns, 92nd Ln (1,070)
  1st & 2nd Bns, 93rd Ln (970)
 2nd Bde (Jamin)(2,755 in 6 Bns)
  1st, 2nd, & 3rd Bns, 4th Lt (1,635)
  1st, 2nd, & 3rd Bns, 100th Ln (1,120)
 Arty (Tacon)(190 in 1 Btty, with 8 pieces)
  1st Btty, 6th Foot Art (Tacon)(90 with 6x6 pdrs & 2x6" hwtzrs)
  3rd Coy, 1st Train Sqn (??)(100)
2nd Cav Div (Piré) (2,300 in 15 Sqns & 1 Btty, with 6 pieces)
 1st Bde (Hubert)(1,175 in 8 Sqns)
  1st Chasseurs (550)
  6th Chasseurs (620)
 2nd Bde (Wathiez)(940 in 7 Sqns)
  5th Lancers (450 in 3 Sqns)
  6th Lancers (480 in 4 Sqns)
 Arty (Gronnier)(165 in 1 Horse Btty, with 6 Pieces)
  2nd Btty, 4th Horse Atry (Gronnier)(80 with 4x6 pdrs & 2x6"
  hwtzrs)

> *2nd Coy, 5th Train Sqn* (??)(85)

Art Res (le Pelletier) (215 in 1 Btty, with 8 pieces)

> *7th Btty, 2nd Foot Arty* (le Pelletier)(100 with 6x12 pdrs & 2x6" hwtzrs)
>
> *7th Coy, 1st Train Sqn*(Gayat)(115)

Engrs (Richemont) (435)

> *1st Coy, 1st Engineers* (Repecaud)(430)

III Corps (Vandamme) (17,600 with 38 pieces)

8th Div (Lefol) (5,300 in 11 Bns & 1 Btty, with 8 pieces)

> *1st Bde* (Billiard) (2,955 in 6 Bns)
>
> > *1st, 2nd, & 3rd Bns, 15th Lt* (1,740)
> >
> > *1st, 2nd, & 3rd Bns, 23rd Ln* (1,215)
>
> *2nd Bde* (Corsin) (2,105 in 5 Bns)
>
> > *1st, 2nd, & 3rd Bns, 37th Ln* (1,175)
> >
> > *1st & 2nd Bns, 64th Ln* (930)
>
> *Arty* (Chauveau)(195 in 1 Btty, with 8 Pieces)
>
> > *7th Btty, 6th Foot Arty* (Chauveau)(90 with 6x6 pdrs & 2x6" hwtzrs)
> >
> > *? Coy, 1st Train Sqn* (??)(90, plus 12 men of the *1st* Coy)

10th Div (Habert) (4,800 in 12 Bns & 1 Btty, with 8 pieces)

> *1st Bde* (Gengoult)(1,760 in 6 Bns)
>
> > *1st, 2nd, & 3rd Bns, 34th Ln* (1,440)
> >
> > *1st, 2nd, & 3rd Bns, 88th Ln* (1,320)
>
> *2nd Bde* (Dupeyroux)(2,825 in 6 Bns)
>
> > *1st, 2nd, & 3rd Bns, 22nd Ln* (1,460)
> >
> > *1st & 3rd Bns, 70th Ln* (955)
> >
> > *? Bn, 2nd Foreign [Swiss]* (410)
>
> *Arty* (Guerin)(185 in 1 Btty, with 8 pieces)
>
> > *18th Btty, 2nd Foot Arty* (Guerin)(95 with 6x6 pdrs & 2x6" hwtzrs)
> >
> > *4th Coy, 5th Train Sqn* (Lecocq)(95)

11th Div (Berthezene) (4,800 in 8 Bns & 1 Btty, with 8 pieces)

> *1st Bde* (Dufour)(2,490 in 4 Bns)
>
> > *1st & 2nd Bns, 12th Ln* (1,210)
> >
> > *1st & 2nd Bns, 56th Ln* (1,275)
>
> *2nd Bde* (Logarde)(2,050 in 4 Bns)
>
> > *1st & 2nd Bns, 33rd Ln* (1,135)
> >
> > *1st & 2nd Bns, 86th Ln* (915)
>
> *Arty* (Lecorbeiller)(195 in 1 Btty, with 8 pieces)
>
> > *17th Btty, 2nd Foot Arty* (Lecorbeiller)(100 with 6x6 pdrs & 2x6" hwtzrs)
> >
> > *5th Coy, 5th Train Sqn* (Cheanne)(95)

3rd Cav Div **(Domon) (1,200 in 9 Sqns & 1 Btty, with 6 pieces)**
   1st Bde (Dommanget)(740 in 6 Sqns)
      4th Chasseurs (350)
      9th Chasseurs (390)
   2nd Bde (Vinot)(365 in 3 Sqns)
      12th Chasseurs(365)
   Arty (Dumont)(185 in 1 Horse Btty, with 6 pieces)
      4th Btty, 2nd Horse Arty (Dumont)(80 with 4x6 pdrs & 2x6"
      hwtzrs)
      3rd Coy, 5th Train Sqn (??)(105)
  Art Res **(Doguereau) (205 in 1 Btty, with 8 pieces)**
      1st Btty, 2nd Foot Arty (Vollee)(100 with 6x12 pdrs & 2x6"
      hwtzrs)
      6th Coy, 5th Train Sqn (Lestrat)(105)
  Engrs **(Nempde) (155)**
      1st & 2nd Coys, 2nd Bn, 2nd Engineers (??)(150)

IV Corps **(Gerard) (15,350 with 36 pieces)**
  12th Div **(Pecheux) (4,350 in 10 Bns & 1 Btty, with 8 pieces)**
   1st Bde (Rome)(2,895 in 6 Bns)
      1st, 2nd, & 3rd Bns, 30th Ln (1,455)
      1st, 2nd, & 4th Bns, 96th Ln (1,440)
   2nd Bde (Schaeffer)(1,880 in 4 Bns)
      1st, 2nd, & 3rd Bns, 63rd Ln (1,270)
      1st Bn, 3rd Lt (610)
   Arty (Fenouillat)(200 in 1 Btty, with 8 pieces)
      2nd Btty, 5th Foot Arty (Fenouillat)(100 with 6x6 pdrs & 2x6"
      hwtzrs)
      6th Coy, 2nd Train Sqn (??)(100)
  13th Div **(Vichery) (4,100 in 8 Bns & 1 Btty, with 8 pieces)**
   1st Bde (LaCapitaine)(2,115 in 4 Bns)
      1st & 2nd Bns, 59th Ln (1,060)
      1st & 2nd Bns, 76th Ln (1,055)
   2nd Bde (Desprez)(2,000 in 4 Bns)
      1st & 2nd Bns, 48th Ln (880)
      1st & 2nd Bns, 69th Ln (1,120)
   Arty (Saint-Cyr)(200 in 1 Btty, with 8 pieces
      1st Btty, 5th Foot Arty (Saint-Cyr)(100 with 6x6 pdrs & 2x6"
      hwtzrs)
      2nd Coy, 7th Train Sqn (Thomas)(95)
  14th Div **(Hulot, *vice* Bourmont) (4,600 in 8 Bns & 1 Btty, with 8
    pieces)**
   1st Bde (Hulot)(2,340 in 4 Bns)

      1st & 2nd Bns, 9th Lt (1,260)
      1st & 2nd Bns, 111th Ln (1,080)
    2nd Bde (Toussaint)(1,600)
      1st & 2nd Bns, 44th Ln (980)
      1st & 2nd Bns, 50th Ln (615)
    Arty (Tortel)(165 in 1 Horse Btty, with 6 pieces)
      3rd Btty, 3rd Horse Arty (Tortal)(85 with 4x6 pdrs & 2x6"
       hwtzrs)
      2nd Coy, 2nd Train Sqn (??)(80)
  6th Cav Div **(Maurin) (1,500 in 12 Sqns & 1 Btty, with 6 pieces)**
    1st Bde (Vallin)(815 in 6 Sqns)
      6th Hussars (415)
      8th Chasseurs (400)
    2nd Bde (Berruyer)(810 in 5 Sqns)
      6th Dragoons (230 in 2 Sqns)
      16th Dragoons (580 in 3 Sqns)
    Arty (?)(160 in 1 Horse Btty, with 6 pieces)
      ?th Btty, 2nd Horse Arty (??)(80 with 4x6 pdrs & 2x6"hwtzrs)
      ?th Coy, 2nd Train Sqn (??)(80)
  Art Res **(Baltus) (250 in 1 Btty, with 6 pieces, with pontoon troops)**
    11th Btty, 5th Foot Arty (Francois)(90 with 4x12 pdr & 2x6"
     hwtzrs)
    ?th Coy, 2nd Train Sqn (Raes)(90)
    4th Coy, 1st Pontoon Rgt (Moutonnet)(70)
  Engrs **(Valaze) (210)**
    3rd, 4th, & 5th Coys, 2nd Bn, 2nd Engineers (??)(205)

VI Corps **(Lobau) (10,450 with 38 pieces)**
  19th Div **(Simmer) (4,150 in 9 Bns & 1 Btty, with 8 pieces)**
    1st Bde (Bellair)(1,850 in 4 Bns)
      1st & 2nd Bns, 5th Ln (950)
      1st, 2nd, & 3rd Bns, 11th Ln (1,195)
    2nd Bde (Jamin)(1,760 in 4 Bns)
      1st & 2nd Bns, 27th Ln (820)
      1st & 2nd Bns, 84th Ln (940)
    Arty (Parisot)(245 in 1 Btty, with 8 pieces, with service units)
      1st Btty, 8th Foot Arty(Parisot)(85 with 6x6 pdrs & 2x6" hwtzrs)
      1st Coy, 7th Train Sqn (Laude)(55)
      4th Coy, 8th Train Sqn(??)(40)
      Elms, 1st Coy, 3rd Service Sqn (??)(12)
      3rd Coy, Auxiliary Service Corps of the Oise (??)(52)
  20th Div **(Jeanin) (3,300 in 6 Bns & 1 Btty, with 8 pieces)**
    1st Bde (Bony)(1,810 in 4 Bns)

      1st & 2nd Bns, 5th Lt (875)

      1st & 2nd Bns, 10th Ln (930)

   2nd Bde (Tromelin)(735 in 2 Bns)

      1st & 2nd Bns, 107th Ln (735)

   Arty (Paquet)(260 in 1 Btty, with 8 pieces, with service units)

      2nd Btty, 8th Foot Arty (Paquet)(90 with 6x6 pdrs & 2x6" hwtzrs)

      3rd Coy, 8th Train Sqn (Langlois)(105)

      Elms, 1st Coy, 3rd Service Sqn (??)(12)

      3rd Auxiliary Service Coy of the Aisne (??)(52)

21st Div **(Teste) (2,700 in 5 Bns & 1 Btty, with 8 pieces)**

   1st Bde (Laffitte)(940 in 2 Bns)

      1st & 2nd Bns, 8th Lt (940)

   2nd Bde (Penne)(1,485)

      1st Bn, 65th Ln (505)

      1st & 2nd Bns, 75th Ln (980)

   Arty (Duverrey)(200 in 1 Btty, with 8 pieces)

      3rd Coy, 8th Foot Arty (Duverrey)(95 with 6x6 pdrs &2x6" hwtzrs)

      4th Coy, 6th Train Sqn (Etienne)(70)

      Elms, 1st Coy, 3rd Service Sqn (14)

      Elms, 4th Auxiliary Service Coy of the Aisne (14)

Art Res **(Noury) (225 in 1 Btty, with 8 pieces)**

      4th Btty, 8th Foot Arty (Noseda)(95 with 6x12 pdrs & 2x6" hwtzrs)

      5th Btty, 8th Train Sqn (??)(130)

Engr **(Sabatier) (200)**

      1st & 3rd Coys, 1st Bn, 3rd Engineers (??)(195)

I Res Cav Corps **(Pajol) (3,000 with 12 pieces)**

   4th Cav Div **(P. Soult) (1,500 in 12 Sqns & 1 Btty, with 6 pieces)**

   1st Bde (Saint-Laurent)(900 in 8 Sqns)

      1st Hussars (525)

      4th Hussars (475)

   2nd Bde (Ameil)(430 in 4 Sqns)

      5th Hussars (430)

   Arty (Cotheraux)(160 in 1 Horse Btty, with 6 Pieces)

      1st Btty, 1st Horse Arty (Cotheraux)(75 with 4x6 pdrs& 2x6" hwtzrs)

      3rd Coy, 1st Train Sqn (??)(85)

   5th Cav Div **(Subervie) (1,500 in 11 Sqns & 1 Bttys, with 6 pieces)**

   1st Bde (Colbert)(840 in 8 Sqns)

      1st Lancers (415)

2nd Lancers (420)
2nd Bde (Merlin)(380 in 3 Sqns)
    11th Chasseurs (375)
Arty (Duchemin)(170 in 1 Horse Btty, with 6 Pieces)
    3rd Btty, 1st Horse Arty (Duchemin)(75 with 4x6 pdrs& 2x6"
    hwtzrs)
    4th Coy, 1st Train Sqn (??)(90)

II *Res Cav Corps* (Exelmans) (3,400 with 12 pieces)
9th Cav Div (Strolz) (1,850 in 15 Sqns & 1 Bttys, with 6 pieces)
1st Bde (Burthe)(925 in 7 Sqns)
    5th Dragoons (505 in 3 Sqns)
    13th Dragoons (425 in 4 Sqns)
2nd Bde (Vincent)(765 in 8 Sqns)
    15th Dragoons (415)
    20th Dragoons (445)
Arty (Godet)(120 in 1 Horse Btty, with 6 pieces)
    4th Btty, 1st Horse Arty (Godet)(60 with 4x6 pdrs & 2x6"
    hwtzrs)
    6th Coy, 1st Train Sqn (Hubert)(60)
10th Cav Div (Chastel) (1,550 in 12 Sqns & 1 Btty, with 6 pieces)
1st Bde (Bonnemains)(1,010 in 6 Sqns)
    4th Dragoons (565)
    12th Dragoons (540)
2nd Bde (Berton)(700 in 6 Sqns)
    14th Dragoons (375)
    17th Dragoons (325)
Arty (Bernard)(135 in 1 Horse Btty, with 6 pieces)
    4th Btty, 4th Horse Arty (Bernard)(60 with 4x6 pdrs & 2x6"
    hwtzrs)
    1st Coy, 2nd Train Sqn (??)(75)

III *Res Cav Corps* (Kellermann) (3,900 with 12 pieces)
11th Cav Div (l'Heritier) (2,100 in 13 Sqns & 1 Btty, with 6 pieces)
1st Bde (Picquet)(1,100 in 7 Sqns)
    2nd Dragoons (580 in 4 Sqns)
    7th Dragoons (515 in 3 Sqns)
2nd Bde (Guiton)(775 in 5 Sqns)
    8th Cuirassiers (450 in 3 Sqns)
    11th Cuirassiers (325 in 2 Sqns)
Arty (Marcillac)(160 in 1 Horse Btty, with 6 pieces)
    3rd Btty, 2nd Horse Arty (Marcillac)(80 with 4x6 pdrs & 2x6"
    hwtzrs)
    3rd Coy, 2nd Train Sqn

12th Cav Div **(Roussel d'Hurbal) (2,085 in 12 Sqns & 1 Btty, with 6 pieces)**
 1st Bde (Blanchard)(840 in 6 Sqns)
  1st Carabiniers (435)
  2nd Carabiniers (410)
 2nd Bde (Donop)(785 in 6 Sqns)
  2nd Cuirassiers (315 in 2 Sqns)
  3rd Cuirassiers (465 in 4 Sqns)
 Arty (Leneau)(160 in 1 Horse Btty, with 6 pieces)
  2nd Btty, 2nd Horse Arty (Leneau)(80 with 4x6 pdrs & 2x6" hwtzrs)
  4th Coy, 2nd Train Sqn (Manzat)(80)

IV Res Cav Corps **(Milhaud) (3,100 with 12 pieces)**
 13th Cav Div **(Wathier) (1,350 in 11 Sqns & 1 Btty, with 6 pieces)**
 1st Bde (Dubois)(760 in 7 Sqns)
  1st Cuirassiers (450 in 4 Sqns)
  4th Cuirassiers (310 in 3 Sqns)
 2nd Bde (Travers)(415 in 4 Sqns)
  7th Cuirassiers (170)
  12th Cuirassiers (250)
 Arty (Duchet)(160 in 1 Btty, with 6 pieces)
  5th Btty, 1st Horse Arty (Duchet)(80 with 4x6 pdrs & 2x6" hwtzrs)
  8th Coy, 1st Train Sqn (??)(80)
 14th Cav Div **(Delort) (1,700 in 13 Sqns & 1 Btty, with 6 pieces)**
 1st Bde (Farine)(810 in 6 Sqns)
  5th Cuirassiers (520 in 3 Sqns)
  6th Cuirassiers (285 in 3 Sqns)
 2nd Bde (Vial)(770 in 7 Sqns)
  9th Cuirassiers (410 in 4 Sqns)
  10th Cuirassiers (360 in 3 Sqns)
 Arty (?)(165 in 1 Horse Btty, with 6 pieces)
  4th Coy, 3rd Horse Arty (Jacques)(85 with 4x6 pdrs & 2x6" hwtzrs)
  ?th Coy, 3rd Train Sqn (??)(80)

Notes to the Order of Battle for the French Army in Belgium

1. The artillery with the *Garde* is very confusing. Units and figures given here are based on French returns of about a week before the

Waterloo Campaign actually began. It is probable that these are the numbers officially assigned. The actual number brought northwards is more difficult to acertain. It is likely that no more than about 124 pieces were available at the opening of the campaign, one *Young Guard* battery not having come up on time, and that several batteries may never have gotten across the Sambre, which would have left only about 96 pieces, in only 13 batteries. Also, note that the *3rd Grenadiers*, *4th Grenadiers*, *3rd Chasseurs* and *4th Chasseurs* were informally known as the *Middle Guard*.

2. One battery in III Corps may have been short 2x6" howitzrs.

3. Over 70 percent of the *Army of the North* was composed of infantry, nearly 20 percent of cavalry, and the balance of artillerymen, engineers, and various service personnel, plus staffs, ambulancemen, and other personnel not listed here. Although the army was built around a solid core of seasoned veterans, there were many green men in the ranks, particularly in the cavalry, which partially accounts for the relatively poor performance of the mounted arm during the campaign. A further problem was a certain difficulty of command and communication resulting from the fact that less than a week before the campaign opened Napoleon made a number of significant organizational changes in the army, particularly in the cavalry.

The Allies

The Anglo-Allied "Army of the Low Countries" (Wellington) (112,000 with 203 pieces)

I Corps (Prince William of Orange) (38,400 with 56 pieces)

Br 1st [Guards] Div (Cooke) (4,500 in 4 Bns & 2 Bttys, with 12 pieces)

Br 1st [Guards] Bde (Maitland) (2,000 in 2 Bns)
    2nd & 3rd Bns, 1st Guards (975 & 1,020)
Br 2nd [Guards] Bde (Byng)(2,065 in 2 Bns)
    2nd Bn, Coldstream Gds (1,005)
    2nd Bn, 3rd Guards (1,060)
Arty (Adye) (435 in 2 Bttys, with 12 pieces)
    Sandham's Btty, R.F.A. (200 with 4x9-pdr & 2x5.5" hwtzrs)
    Kuhlmann's Horse Btty, K.G.L. (200 with 5x6-pdr & 1x5.5" hwtzr)

Br 3rd Div (Alten) (7,400 in 13.5 Bns & 2 Bttys, with 12 pieces)

Br 5th Bde (Halkett) (2,300 in 4 Bns)
    2nd Bn, 30th Ln (615)
    1st Bn, 33rd Ln (560)
    2nd Bn, 69th Ln (515)
    2nd Bn, 73rd Ln (560)
K.G.L. 2nd Bde (Ompteda)(1,540 in 4 Bns)
    1st K.G.L. Lt Bn (425)
    2nd K.G.L. Lt Bn (340)
    5th K.G.L. Ln Bn (380)
    8th K.G.L. Ln Bn (390)
    Elms 6th & 7th K.G.L. Ln Bns (14)
    Elms 1st Foreign Bn (2)
Han 1st Bde (Kielmansegge)(3,150 in 6 Bns)
    Bremen Field Bn (520)
    Verden Field Bn (555)
    York Field Bn (510)
    Grubenhagen Lt Bn (620)
    Luneburg Lt Bn (595)
    Field Jager Corps (320)
Arty (Williamson)(400 in two Bttys, with 12 Pieces)
    Lloyd's Btty, R.F.A. (200 with 4x9-pdr & 2x5.5" hwtzrs)
    Cleeves' Btty, K.G.L. (200 with 4x9-pdr & 2x5.5" hwtzrs)

DB 2nd Div (Perponcher-Sedlnitzky) (8,200 in 10 Bns & 2 Bttys, with 16 pieces)
1st Bde (Bijlandt)(3,300 in 5 Bns)
7th Line Rgt (700 in 1 Bn)
27th Jager Bn (800)
5th Militia Bn (480)
7th Militia Bn (675)
8th Militia Bn (560)
2nd Bde (Saxe-Weimar)(4,300 in 5 Bns)
1st, 2nd, & 3rd Bns, 2nd Nassau Inf (2,750)
1st & 2nd Bns, the Regiment of Orange-Nassau (1,550)
Arty (Opstal) (500 in two Bttys, with 16 pieces)
Stievenart's DB Btty (250 with 6x6-pdrs & 2 5.5" hwtzrs)
Bijleveld's DB Horse Btty (250 with 6x6-pdrs & 2 5.5" hwtzrs)
DB 3rd Div (Chasse) (7,200 in 12 Bns & 2 Bttys, with 16 pieces)
1st Bde (Detmers)(3,100 in 6 Bns)
2nd Line Rgt (470 in 1 Bn)
35th Jager Bn (605)
4th Militia Bn (520)
6th Militia Bn (490)
17th Militia Bn (535)
19th Militia Bn (470)
2nd Bde (d'Aubreme)(3,580 in 6 Bns)
3rd Line Rgt (630 in 1 Bn)
12th Line Rgt (430 in 1 Bn)
13th Line Rgt (665 in 1 Bn)
36th Jager Bn (635)
3rd Militia Bn (590)
10th Militia Bn (630)
Arty (Smissen)(480 in 2 Bttys, with 16 pieces)
Lux's DB Foot Btty (240 with 6x6-pdrs & 2x5.5" hwtzrs)
Krahmer's DB Horse Btty (240 with 6x6-pdrs & 2x5.5" hwtzrs)

II Corps (Hill) (27,300 with 40 pieces)
Br 2nd Div (Clinton) (7,250 in 12 Bns & 2 Bttys, with 12 pieces)
Br 3rd Bde (Adam)(2,625 in 4 Bns)
1st Bn, 52nd Ln (1,050)
1st Bn, 71st Ln (800)
2nd & 3rd Bns, 95th Ln (585 & 188)
KGL 1st Bde (Du Plat)(1,760 in four Bns)
1st K.G.L. Ln Bn (410)
2nd K.G.L. Ln Bn (440)
3rd K.G.L. Ln Bn (495)

4th K.G.L. Ln Bn (415)
Han 3rd Bde (Halkett)(2,450 in 4 Bns)
    Bremervorde LW Bn (630)
    Osnabruck LW Bn (610)
    Quackenbruck LW Bn (590)
    Salzgitter LW Bn (620)
Arty (Gold)(400 in 2 Bttys, with 12 pieces)
    Bolton's Btty, R.F.A. (200 with 4x9-pdr & 2x5.5" hwtzrs)
    Sympher's Horse Btty, K.G.L. (200 with 5x9-pdr & 1x5.5" hwtzr)

Br 4th Div (Colville) (7,450 in 12 Bns & 2 Bttys, with 12 pieces)
Br 4th Bde (Mitchell)(1,570 in 3 Bns)
    3rd Bn, 14th Ln (570)
    1st Bn, 23rd Ln (450)
    1st Bn, 51st Ln (550)
Br 6th Bde (Johnstone)(2,400 in 4 Bns)
    2nd Bn, 35th Ln (570)
    1st Bn, 54th Ln (540)
    2nd Bn, 59th Ln (460)
    1st Bn, 91st Ln (825)
Han 6th Bde (Lyon)(3,050 in 5 Bns)
    Calenburg Field Bn (635)
    Lauenberg Field Bn (535)
    Bentheim LW Bn (610)
    Hoya LW Bn (630)
    Nienburg LW Bn (625)
Arty (Hawker)(400 in 2 Bttys with 12 pieces)
    Brome's Btty, R.F.A. (200 with 5x9-pdr & 1x5.5" hwtzr)
    Rettberg's Han Horse Btty (200 with 4x9-pdr & 2x5.5" hwtzrs)

DB 1st Div (Stedman) (6,700 in 11 Bns & 1 Btty. with 8 pieces)
1st Bde (D'Hauw)(3,270 in 6 Bns)
    4th Line Rgt (550 in 1 Bn)
    6th Line Rgt (430 in 1 Bn)
    16th Jager Bn (490)
    9th Militia Bn (555)
    14th Militia Bn (585)
    15th Militia Bn (660)
2nd Bde (Eerens)(3,170 in 5 Bns)
    1st Line Rgt (682 in 1 Bn)
    18th Jager Bn (794)
    1st Militia Bn (591)
    2nd Militia Bn (582)
    18th Militia Bn (515)

Arty (Wynands) (240 in 1 Btty, with 8 Pieces)
  Wynands' DB Btty (240 with 4x6-pdrs & 2x5.5" hwtzrs)
Netherlands Indian Bde (Anthing)(3,215 in 4 Bns & 1 Btty, with 8 pieces)
  1st & 2nd Bns, 5th East Indies Ln (1,540)
  Flankers (535 in 1 Bn, converged from the 19th & 20th Ln Bns)
  10th East Indies Jager Bn (705)
  11th East Indies Jager Bn (720)
  Riesz' DB Btty (240 with 6x6-pdrs & 2x5.5" hwtzrs)
DB Arty Reserve (??) (1,070 in 2 Sqn & 2 Bttys with 16 pieces)
  Guides (Heineken)(70 in 1 Sqn
  Constabulary (Leutner)(60 in 1 Sqn)
  Kaemfher's DB Btty (315)(with 6x6-pdrs & 2x5.5" hwtzrs)
  Severyns' DB Btty (555)(with 6x12-pdr & 2x5.5" hwtzrs)
  Sapper Coy (Esau)(70 in 1 Coy)

Reserve (Wellington) (36,900 with 64 pieces)
Br 5th Div (Picton) (7,600 in 12 Bns & 2 Bttys, with 12 pieces)
Br 8th Bde (Kempt)(2,480 in 4 Bns)
  1st Bn, 28th Ln (560)
  1st Bn, 32nd Ln (660)
  1st Bn, 79th Ln (705)
  1st Bn, 95th Ln (550)
Br [Highland] 9th Bde (Pack) (2,175 in 4 Bns)
  3rd Bn, 1st Ln (605)
  1st Bn, 42nd Ln (525)
  2nd Bn, 44th Ln (455)
  1st Bn, 92nd Ln (590)
Han 5th Bde (Vincke)(2,520 in 4 Bns)
  Gifhorn LW Bn (620)
  Hameln LW Bn (670)
  Hildesheim LW Bn (620)
  Peine LW Bn (610)
Arty (Heisse)(400 in 2 Bttys, with 12 pieces)
  Rogers' Btty, R.F.A. (200 with 5x9-pdr & 1x5.5" hwtzr)
  Braun's Han Btty, (200 with 4x9-pdr & 2x5.5" hwtzr)
Br 6th Div (Cole) (5,600 in 8 Bns & 2 Bttys, with 12 pieces)
Br 10th Bde (Lambert)(2,570 in 4 Bns)
  1st Bn, 4th Ln (670)
  1st Bn, 27th Ln (700)
  1st Bn, 40th Ln (760)
  2nd Bn, 81st Ln (440)
Han 4th Bde (Best)(2,580 in 4 Bns)

Luneberg LW Bn (625)
Munden LW Bn (660)
Osterode LW Bn (675)
Verden LW Bn (620)
Arty (Bruckmann)(410 in 2 Bttys, with 12 pieces)
Unett's Btty, R.F.A. (200 with 5x9-pdr & 1x5.5" hwtzr)
Sinclair's Btty, R.F.A. (210 with 5x9-pdr & 1x5.5" hwtzr)

Brunswick Corps (Brunswick) (6,850 in 8 Bns, 5 Sqns, & 2 Bttys, with 16 pieces)

Adv Gd Bn (672)
Light Bde (Buttler)(2,680 in 4 Bns)
1st Lt Bn (672)
2nd Lt Bn (672)
3rd Lt Bn (672)
Line Bde (Specht)(2,680 in 4 Bns)
1st Ln Bn (672)
2nd Ln Bn (672)
3rd Ln Bn (672)
Attached: Royal Gd (670)
Cavalry: (??)(950 in 5 Sqns)
"Hussars of Death" Rgt (700 in 4 Sqns))
"Black Lancers" Uhlan Sqn (240 in 1 Sqn)
Arty (Lubeck)(510 in 2 Bttys, with 16 pieces)
Field Btty (Moll) (255 with 6x6 pdrs & 2x5.5" hwtzrs)
Horse Btty (Heinemann) (255 with 6x6 pdrs & 2x5.5" hwtzrs)

Hanoverian Res Corps (Decken) (9,350 in 13 Bns)

1st Bde (Bennigsen)(2,155 in 3 Bns)
Bothmer Field Bn (720)
Bremerlehe LW Bn (720)
Mollen LW Bn (710)
2nd Bde (Beaulieu)(2,150 in 3 Bns)
Ahlefeldt LW Bn (715)
Nordheim LW Bn (715)
Springe LW Bn (715)
3rd Bde (Bodecken)(2,150 in 3 Bns)
Ottendorf LW Bn (715)
Ratzeburg LW Bn (715)
Zelle LW Bn (715)
4th Bde (Wissel)(2,865 in 4 Bns)
Diepholz LW Bn (715)
Hanover LW Bn (690)

Neustadt LW Bn (715)
Velzen LW Bn (690)
Nassau Res Contingent (Kruse)(2,850 in 3 Bns)
1st Bn (950)
2nd Bn (945)
Nassau LW Bn (950)
Art Res (Drummond) (1,200 in 5 Bttys, with 30 pieces)
Hutchesson's Btty, R.F.A.(230 with 4x18-pdr)
Ilbert's Btty, R.F.A.(230 with 4x18-pdr)
Morrison's Btty, R.F.A.(230 with 4x18-pdr)
Beane's Horse Btty, R.H.A.(230 with 5x6 pdr & 1x5.5" hwtzr)
Ross' Horse Btty, R.H.A.(230 with 4x9 pdr & 2x5.5" hwtzr)

Cav Corps (Uxbridge) (16,500 with 43 pieces)

Br 1st [Guards] Cav Bde (Somerset)(1,280 in 9 Sqns)
1st Life Guards (243 in 2 Sqns)
2nd Life Guards (247 in 2 Sqns)
Royal Horse Guards, The Blues (260 in 2 Sqns)
1st Dragoon Guards (530 in 3 Sqns)
Br 2nd [Union] Cav Bde (Ponsonby)(1,180 in 9 Sqns)
1st Royal Dragoons (391)
2nd Dragoons (The Scots Greys) (391)
6th Inniskilling Dragoons (396)
Br 3rd Cav Bde (Dornberg)(1,270 in 11 Sqns)
23rd Lt Dragoons (390 in 3 Sqns)
KGL 1st Lt Dragoons (460 in 4 Sqns)
KGL 2nd Lt Dragoons (420 in 4 Sqns)
Br 4th Cav Bde (Vandeleur)(1,179 in 9 Sqns)
11th Lt Dragoons (390)
12th Lt Dragoons (390)
16th Lt Dragoons (390)
Br 5th Cav Bde (Grant)(1,340 in 10 Sqns)
7th Hussars (380 in 3 Sqns)
15th Hussars (390 in 3 Sqns)
KGL 2nd Hussars (565 in 4 Sqns)
Br 6th Cav Bde (Vivian)(1,300 in 10 Sqns)
10th Hussars (390 in 3 Sqns)
18th Hussars (395 in 3 Sqns)
KGL 1st Hussars (495 in 4 Sqns)
Br 7th Cav Bde (Arentschildt)(1,010 in 7 Sqns)
13th Lt Dragoons (390 in 3 Sqns)
KGL 3rd Hussars (620 in 4 Sqns)

DB Cav Div (Collaert) (3,700 in 23 Sqns & 1 Btty, with 8 pieces)
 DB 1st Cav Bde (Trip)(1,250 in 9 Sqns)
  1st [Dutch] Carbineers (460)
  2nd [Belgian] Carbineers (390)
  3rd [Dutch] Carbineers (390)
 DB 2nd Cav Bde (Ghigny)(1,090 in 7 Sqns)
  4th [Dutch] Lt Dragoons (650 in 4 Sqns)
  8th [Belgian] Hussars (440 in 3 Sqns)
 DB 3rd Cav Bde (Merlen)(1,080 in 7 Sqns)
  5th [Belgian] Lt Dragoons (440 in 3 Sqns)
  6th [Dutch] Hussars (640 in 4 Sqns)
 Arty (??)(?? in 2 Horse Half-Bttys (with 8 pieces)
  Gay's DB Horse Half-Btty (?? with 3x6-pdrs & 1x5.5" hwtzr)
  Petter's DB Horse Half-Btty (?? with 3x6-pdrs & 1x5.5" hwtzr)
 Hanoverian 1st Cav Bde (Estorff)(1,685 in 12 Sqns)
  Bremen und Verden Hussars (590)
  Cumberland Hussars (500)
  Prince Regent's Hussars (595)
Cav Art Res (Frazer) (1000 in 6 Bttys, with 35 pieces & 1 rocket section)
  Bull's Hwtzr Btty, R.H.A. (200 with 6x5.5" hwtzrs)
  Gardiner's Btty, R.H.A. (200 with 5x6-pdr & 1x5.5" hwtzrs)
  Mercer's Btty, R.H.A. (200 with 5x9-pdr & 1x5.5" hwtzr)
  Ramsay's Btty, R.H.A. (200 with 5x9-pdr & 1x5.5" hwtzr)
  Webber-Smith's Btty, R.H.A. (200 with 5x6-pdr & 1x5.5" hwtzr)
  Whinyates' Btty, R.H.A. (200 with 5x6-pdr & a rocket section)

Notes to the Order of Battle for the Anglo-Allied Army

Only about 28,000 of Wellington's troops (c. 38.0 percent) were actually British. A further 7,700 or so (c. 10.0 percent) were from the King's German Legion, a veteran corps long in British service. About 25,000 (c. 30.0 percent) were Hanoverians, from King George III's "other" kingdom, while about 21,000 (28.5 percent) were Dutch and Belgian, and some 6,100 (c. 8.2 percent) were Brunswickers. Of his 53,000 infantry, only about a third—20,200 men (38.1 percent)—could be termed both veteran and reliable: some 11,000 of the Britons (c. 50 percent of their infantry), 4,000 of the King's German Legion (100 percent of their infantry), 4,000 or so Hanoverians (c. 16 percent of their infantry), and perhaps 1,200 of the Brunswickers (c. 20 percent of their infantry). There were, to be sure, many veterans among the Dutch-Belgian units, but these had received their training and seasoning in Napoleon's service and could not be relied upon. In the event, of course, many of these troops gave exellent service, particularly the Naussauers, but this was not predictable in advance. About 70 percent of Wellington's troops were infantrymen, 25 percent cavalry, and the balance artillerymen, engineers, medical, and staff personnel. Figures for numbers of troops with Allied artillery batteries are estimated. The odd designation of the "Netherlands Indian Brigade" derives from the fact that it was raised for service in the Dutch East Indies. This brigade and the Dutch-Belgian 1st Division technically constituted the III Corps, under the command of Prince Frederick of the Netherlands, the younger and even more inept brother of the Prince of Orange, who was assisted by a staff of no less than 17 officers! Fortunately, these troops, as well as the British 6th Brigade, plus some forces not included in Wellington's army (such as the Dutch-Belgian 12-pdr battery and the French Royal "Army of Alost") were posted to the west of the actual theater of operations and saw no action during the campaign, as did the 2nd Battalion of the British 81st Foot, which constituted the garrison of Brussels, and the 2nd K.G.L. Hussars, which remained at Courtrai. In addition, the British 18-pdr artillery batteries (aside from some ammunition supply details which were present in the field) and the Hanoverian Reserve Corps were held in the vicinity of Antwerp, possibly to form the core of a garrison in the event that the army had to retreat.

The Prussian "Army of the Lower Rhine" (Blucher) (123,000 with 296 pieces)

I Corps (Zeithen) (31,800 with 80 pieces)

1st Bde (Steinmetz)(7,900 in 9.5 Bns, 4 Sqns, & 2 Bttys, with 16 pieces)
- 12th [2nd Brandenburg] Inf (2,370)
- 24th [4th Brandenburg] Inf (2,410)
- 1st Westphalian [Cleves] LW (2,680)
- 2nd & 3rd Coys, Silesian Rifle Bn (c. 150)
- 7th Light Btty (Schaale)(140, with 6x6-pdrs & 2x7" hwtzrs)
- 7th Horse Btty (Richter)(155, with 6x6-pdrs & 2x7" hwtzrs)

2nd Bde (Pirch II)(7,600 in 9 Bns, 4 Sqns, & 1 Bttys, with 8 pieces)
- 6th [1st West Prussian] Inf (2,450)
- 28th [1st Berg] Inf (2,635)
- 2nd Westphalian [Minden & Ravensberg] LW (2,500)
- 3rd Light Btty (Neander)(150, with 6x6-pdrs & 2x7" hwtzrs)

3rd Bde (Jagow)(7,950 in 9.5 Bns & 1 Btty, with 8 pieces)
- 7th [2nd West Prussian] Inf (2,450)
- 29th [2nd Berg] Inf (2,630)
- 3rd Westphalian [Ost Friesland and Lingen] LW (2,410)
- 1st & 2nd Coys, Silesian Rifle Bn (c. 150)
- 8th Light Btty (Hermann)(145, with 6x6-pdrs & 2x7" hwtzrs)

4th Bde (Henckel-Donnersmarck)(4,750 in 6 Bns & 1 Btty, with 8 pieces)
- 19th [2nd Posen] Inf (2,050)
- 4th Westphalian [Munster[LW (2,550)
- 15th Light Btty (Anders)(140, with 6x6-pdrs & 2x7" hwtzrs)

Cav Res (Roeder) (3,310 in 32 Sqns & 1 Btty, with 8 pieces)

1st Cav Bde (Treskow II)(1,610 in 12 Sqns)
- 2nd [1st West Prussian] Dragoons (480)
- 3rd [Brandenburg] Uhlans (500)
- 5th [Brandenburg] Prince William Dragoons (625)

2nd Cav Bde (Lutzow)(1,550 in 20 Sqns)
- 4th [1st Silesian] Hussars (500), assigned to 1st BdeSteinmetz
- 6th Uhlans (505)
- 1st Kurmark LW Cav (230)
- 2nd Kurmark LW Cav (310)
- 1st Westphalian LW Cav (590), assigned to 2nd Bde
- 7th Horse Btty (Borowski)(150, with 6x6-pdrs & 2x7" hwtzrs)

Art Res (Lehmann, *vice* Holzendorf) (1,080 in 6 Bttys, with 48 pieces)

- 2nd Hvy Btty (Siemon)(200, with 6x12-prds & 2x10" hwtzrs)

> 6th Hvy Btty (Reuter)(200, with 6x12-prds & 2x10" hwtzrs)
> 9th Hvy Btty (Holsche)(200, with 6x12-prds & 2x10" hwtzrs)
> 1st Light Btty (Huet)(140, with 6x6-pdrs & 2x7" hwtzrs)
> 10th Horse Btty (Schaffer)(160, with 6x6-pdrs & 2x7" hwtzrs)
> 1st Hwtzr Btty (Voitus)(180, with 8x7" hwtzrs)

Engrs (Giese) (105)
> 1st Field Pion Coy (Giese)(105)

II Corps (Pirch I) (35,100 with 80 pieces)

> 5th Bde (Tippelskirch)(8,000 in 9 Bns & 1 Btty, with 8 pieces)
>> 2nd [1st Pommeranian] Inf (2,950)
>> 25th Inf (2,420)
>> 5th Westphalian [Paderborn] LW (2,455)
>> Field Jager Coy (72)
>> 10th Light Btty (Magenhofer)(135, with 6x6-pdrs & 2x7" hwtzrs)
> 6th Bde (Krafft)(7,250 in 9 Bns & 1 Btty, with 8 pieces))
>> 9th [2nd Pommeranian] Inf (2,600)
>> 26th [1st Magdeburg] Inf (2,000)
>> 1st Elbe LW (2,460)
>> 5th Light Btty (Michaelis)(140, with 6x6-pdrs & 2x7" hwtzrs)
> 7th Bde (Brause)(7,250 in 9 Bns & 1 Btty, with 8 pieces)
>> 14th [3rd Pommeranian] Inf (2,540)
>> 22nd [1st Upper Silesian] Inf (2,100)
>> 2nd Elbe LW (2,460)
>> 34th Light Btty (Lent)(140, with 6x6-pdrs & 2x7" hwtzrs)
> 8th Bde (Bose)(6,950 in 9 Bns & 1 Btty)
>> 21st [4th Pommeranian] Inf (2,500)
>> 23rd [2nd Upper Silesian] Inf (1,840)
>> 3rd Elbe LW (2,460)
>> 12th Light Btty (??)(140, with 6x6-pdrs & 2x7" hwtzrs)

Cav Res (Wahlen-Jurgass) (5,050 in 36 Sqns & 1 Btty, with 8 pieces)
> 1st Cav Bde (Thumen)(1,650 in 12 Sqns)
>> 1st Queen's Own Dragoons (660)
>> 6th [Neumark] Dragoons (530)
>> 2nd [Silesian] Uhlans (450)
> 2nd Cav Bde (Sohr)(1,730 in 12 Sqns)
>> 3rd [Brandenburg] Hussars (600)
>> 5th [Pommeranian] Hussars (600)
>> 11th [2nd Westphalian] Hussars (520), half to 6th Bde
> 3rd Cav Bde (Schulenberg)(1,500 in 12 Sqns)
>> 4th Kurmark [Berlin] LW Cav (465)

5th Kurmark LW Cav (460)
Elbe LW Cav (575), split between the 7th and 8th Bdes
6th Horse Btty (Jenichen)(165, with 6x6-pdrs & 2x7" hwtzrs)
Art Res (Rohl) (1,100 in 7 Bttys, with 56 pieces,
4th Hvy Btty (Meyer)(210, with 6x12-pdrs & 2x10" hwtzrs)
8th Hvy Btty (Junghaus)(195, with 6x12-pdrs & 2x10" hwtzrs)
10th Hvy Btty (Weigand)(155, with 6x12-pdrs & 2x10" hwtzrs)
37th Light Btty (??)(145, with 6x6-pdr & 2x7" hwtzrs)
5th Horse Btty (Witten)(165, with 6x6-pdrs & 2x7" hwtzrs)
14th Horse Btty (Fritze)(150, with 6x6-pdrs & 2x7" hwtzrs)
2nd Hwtzr Btty (Rode)(155, with 8x7" hwtzrs)
Engr (Aster) (175)
6th Pion Coy (Linde)(85)
7th Pion Coy (85)

III Corps (Thielemann) (27,925 with 64 pieces)'
9th Bde (Borcke)(7,850 in 9 Bns, 2 Sqns, & 1 Btty, with 8 pieces)
8th [1st Brandenburg Life Guards] Inf (2,760)
30th Inf (2,475)
1st Kurmark [Berlin] LW (2,200)
1st & 2nd Sqns, 3rd Kurmark LW Cav (230)
18th Light Btty (Sannow)(155, with 6x6-pdr & 2x7" hwtzrs)
10th Bde (Kampfen)(4,780 in 6 Bns & 1 Btty, with 8 pieces)
27th Inf (2,255)
2nd Kurmark LW (2,150)
3rd & 4th Sqns, 3rd Kurmark LW Cav (230)
35th Light Btty (Wangenheim)(140, with 6x6-pdr & 2x7"
hwtzrs)
11th Bde (Luck)(4,850 in 6 Bns)
3rd Kurmark LW (2,330)
4th Kurmark LW (2,315)
1st & 2nd Sqns, 6th Kurmark LW Cav (200)
12th Bde (Stulpnagel)(6,760 in 9 Bns)
31st Inf (2,560)
5th Kurmark LW (2,000)
6th Kurmark LW (2,000)
3rd & 4th Sqns, 6th Kurmark LW Cav (200)
Cav Res (Hobe) (3,260 in 32 Sqns & 1 Btty, with 8 pieces)
1st Cav Bde (Marwitz)(1,610 in 12 Sqns)
7th Uhlans (385)
8th Uhlans (630)
12th [Saxon] Hussars (590)
2nd Cav Bde (Lottum)(1,500)

7th [Rhenish] Dragoons (500)

9th [Rhenish] Hussars (535)

5th Uhlans (455)

20th Horse Btty (Vollmar)(150, with 6x6-pdr & 2x7" hwtzrs)

Art Res (Mohnhaupt)(1100 in 6 Bttys, with 48 pieces)

7th Hvy Btty (Baldauf)(200, with 6x12-pdrs & 2x10" hwtzrs)

11th Hvy Btty (Liebermann)(170, with 6x12-pdrs & 2x10" hwtzrs)

12th Hvy Btty (Stammer)(175, with 6x12-pdrs & 2x10" hwtzrs)

18th Horse Btty (??)(150, with 6x6-pdrs & 2x7" hwtzrs)

19th Horse Btty (Dellen)(150, with 6x6-pdrs & 2x7" hwtzrs)

3nd Hwtzr Btty (Kurgass)(170, with 8x7" hwtzrs)

Engr (Markoff) (90)

5th Pion Coy (Rohwedel)(85)

IV Corps (Bulow) (31,900 with 88 pieces)

13th Bde (Hacke)(6,760 in 9 Bns, 2 Sqns, & 1 Btty, with 8 pieces)

10th [1st Silesian] Inf (2,400)

2nd Neumark LW (2,075)

3rd Neumark LW (2,365)

1st & 2nd Sqns, 2nd Silesian LW Cav (200)

21st Light Btty (Koppen)(155, with 6x6-pdr & 2x7" hwtzrs)

14th Bde (Rijssel)(7,300 in 9 Bns, 2 Sqns, & 1 Bty, with 8 pieces)

11th [2nd Silesian] Inf (2,200)

1st Pommeranian LW (2,460)

2nd Pommeranian LW (2,415)

3rd & 4th Sqns, 2nd Silesian LW Cav (175)

13th Light Btty (Martitz)(150, with 6x6-pdr & 2x7" hwtzrs)

15th Bde (Losthin)(6,200 in 9 Bns, 2 Sqns, & 1 Btty, with 8 pieces)

18th [1st Posen] Inf (2,400)

3rd Silesian LW (1,900)

4th Silesian LW (1,780)

1st & 2nd Sqns, 3rd Silesian LW Cav (175)

14th Light Btty (Hensel)(155, with 6x6-pdr & 2x7" hwtzrs)

16th Bde (Hiller)(6,465 in 9 Bns, 2 Sqns, & 1 Btty, with 8 pieces)

15th Inf (2,445)

1st Silesian LW (1,800)

2nd Silesian LW (1,710)

3rd & 4th Sqns, 3rd Silesian LW Cav (175)

2nd Light Btty (Schmidt)(140, with 6x6-pdr & 2x7" hwtzrs)

Cav Res (Prince Wilhelm of Prussia) (4,480 in 36 Sqns & 2 Bttys, with 16 pieces)

1st Cav Bde (Schwerin)(2,025 in 12 Sqns & 1 Btty, with 8 pieces)

6th [2nd Silesian] Hussars (665)
10th [1st Magdeburg] Hussars (575)
1st [West Prussian] Uhlans (640)
1st Horse Btty (Zincken)(145, with 6x6-pdr & 2x7" hwtzrs)
2nd Cav Bde (Watzdorff)(605 in 4 Sqns & 1 Btty, with 8 pieces)
8th [1st Westphalian] Hussars (450)
11th Horse Btty (Pfeil)(155, with 6x6-pdr & 2x7" hwtzrs)
3rd Cav Bde (Sydow)(1,850 in 20 Sqns)
1st Neumark LW Cav (365)
2nd Neumark LW Cav (425)
1st Pommeranian LW Cav (305)
2nd Pommeranian LW Cav (315)
1st Silesian LW Cav (425)
Art Res (Braun) (1,000 in 5 Bttys, with 40 pieces)
3rd Hvy Btty (Scheffer)(200, with 6x12-pdrs & 2x10" hwtzrs)
5th Hvy Btty (Conradi)(180, with 6x12-pdrs & 2x10" hwtzrs)
13th Hvy Btty (Wocke)(190, with 6x12-pdrs & 2x10" hwtzrs)
11th Light Btty (Mengden)(160, with 6x6-pdrs & 2x7" hwtzrs)
11th Horse Btty (Borchard)(145, with 6x6-pdrs & 2x7" hwtzrs)
Engr (Le Bauld de Nans) (205)
4th Coy, Mansfield Pion Bn (Nauck)(200)

Notes to the Order of Battle for the Prussian Army

1. The 2nd Hwtzr Btty and the 7th Pion Coy may have joined the army after Waterloo, and the 10th Heavy Btty may not have been present at all.

2. Only about 60 percent of the Prussian troops were technically regulars, the balance being landwehr, militiamen. However, there were numerous veterans among the latter, and many green men among the former. Overall, perhaps a third of Blucher's army was composed of unseasoned men. A little over 80 percent of the Prussian troops were infantry, a much higher proportion than in either the Allied or the French armies, while only a little more than 12 percent was composed of cavalry, far lower than in either of the other armies.

The Other Fronts:

The French and Allied forces deployed on the other fronts are given in outline only, clockwise from the north east around the perimeter of France, with garrisons given after field forces.

The French

The Army of the Rhine [V Corps] (Rapp)
(24,400 with 52 pieces)

15th Div (Rottembourg) (4,700 in 12 Bns & 1 Btty, with 8 pieces)
16th Div (Albert) (6,400 in 16 Bns & 1 Btty, with 8 pieces)
17th Div (Grandjean) (5,400 in 14 Bns & 1 Btty, with 8 pieces)
7th Cav Div (Merlin) (1,500 in 12 Sqns & 1 Btty, with 6 pieces)
Res NGd Bde (Berckheim)(3,100 in 6 Bns & 1 Btty, with 8 pieces)
Art Res (?) (300 in 2 Bttys, with 14 pieces)

I Corps of Observation [of the Jura] (LeCourbe)
(14,800 with 46 pieces)

18th Div (St.Abbe) (2,900 in 7 Bns & 1 Btty, with 8 pieces)
3rd NGd Div (Meunier) (5,000 in 8 Bns)
4th NGd Div (Laplane) (5,400 in 9 Bns & 1 Btty, with 8 pieces)
8th Cav Div (Carter) (900 in 9 Sqns)
Art Res (?) (400 in 3 Bttys, with 22 pieces)

The Army of the Alps [VII Corps] (Suchet)
(25,100 with 46 pieces)

22nd Div (Pacthod) (5,400 in 10 Bns & 1 Btty, with 8 pieces)
23rd Div (Dessaix) (2,800 in 7 Bns & 1 Btty, with 8 pieces)
5th NGd Div (Chabert) (5,100 in 12 Bns)
6th NGd Div (Pannetier) (3,700 in 8 Bns)
7th NGd Div (Maransin) (2,700 in 6 Bns)
15th Cav Div (Quesnel) (1,800 in 12 Sqns & 1 Btty, with 6 pieces)
Art Res (?) (400 in 3 Bttys, with 24 pieces)
Garrisons (3,300 in 14 Bns)

II Corps of Observaton [of the Var]
(Brune) (10,000 with 22 pieces)

24th Div (St. Merle) (5,000 in 10 Bns & 1 Btty, with 8 pieces)
25th Div (Dalton) (2,500 in 6 Bns & 1 Btty, with 8 pieces)
6th-bis NGd Div (Dufresse) (1,500 in 6 Bns)
14th Chasseurs a Cheval Rgt (?)(500 in 3 Sqns)
Art Res (?) (100 in 1 Btty, with 6 pieces)

III Corps of Observaton [of the Eastern Pyrennes]
(Decaen) (15,000 with 24 pieces)

26th Div (Harispe) (5,600 in 11 Bns, with 8 pieces)
NGd (8,500 in 16 Bns)
15th Chasseurs Rgt (?)(500 in 3 Sqns)
Art Res (?) (300 in 2 Bttys, with 16 pieces)

IV Corps of Observation [of the Western Pyrennes or of
the Gironde] (Clausel) (15,000 with 24 pieces)

27th Div (Fressinet) (5,100 in 10 Bns, with 8 pieces)
NGd (8,500 in 16 Bns)
5th Chasseurs Rgt (?)(500 in 3 Sqns)
Art Res (?) (300 in 2 Bttys, with 16 pieces)

The Army of the West [Loire, Vendee] (Lamarque)
(15,000 with 16 pieces)

1st Div (Brayer) (3,400 in 8 Bns, with 8 pieces)
2nd Div (Travot) (3,950 in 11 Bns, with 8 Pieces)
Attachments (7,000 in 17 Bns and 8 Sqns)

Marching Battalions of L'Armee du Nord
(7,200 with 24 pieces)

II Corps (1,250 in 3 Bns)

III Corps (1,200 in 3 Bns)

IV Corps (900 in 2 Bns)

VI Corps (2,300 in 5 Bns)

Imperial Guard (1,500 in 3 Bns & 3 Bttys, with 24 pieces)

Principal Garrisons, Reserves, Parks, and Depots
(156,000 with 600+ pieces)

Alsatian Fortresses (20,500 with ? pieces)
Avignon (8,000 with ? pieces)
Gendarmerie Mobile **(Savary) (45,000)**
LaFere (7,000 with 200 pieces)
Lyons (15,000 with ? pieces)
Paris (Davout) (50,000 with 400 pieces)
Thionville: *2nd NGd Div* **(Rouyer) (5,600 in 10 Bns)**
Verdun-Givet-Sedan: *1st NGd Div* **(Leclerc des Essarts) (5,200 in 6**
Bns & 1 Btty, with 8 pieces)

The Allies

Br 7th Div (McKenzie) (3,600 in 6 Bns)
Br 7th Bde (McKenzie) (1,200 in 3 Bns)
　　　2nd Bn, 25th Ln (388) Antwerp
　　　2nd Bn, 37th Ln (491) Antwerp
　　　2nd Bn, 78th Ln (337) Nieuport
Attached (2,000 in 3 Bns)
　　　1st K.G.L. Foreign Bn (595) Antwerp
　　　2nd Garrison Bn (739) Tournai
　　　13th Veteran Bn (683) Ostend

Note: Technically forming part of Wellington's reserve, these troops, along with some others not originally intended as such, performed occupation duties during the campaign.

French Royal "Army of Alost" (Berry)
(2100 in 4 Bns, 5 Sqns, and 1 Half-Btty, with 3 pieces).

　　　Gardes du Corps (40 in 1 sqn)
　　　Grenadiers a Cheval (2 Sqns)
　　　Chasseurs a Cheval du Roi (2 sqns)
　　　Regiment de la Couronne (2 Bns)
　　　Regiment du Nord (2 Bns)
　　　? Btty (3 pieces)

Note: Upon fleeing from France, Louis XVIII ended up establishing an elaborate court at Ghent, where, by 27 March his "army" comprised about 450 troops, some 300 cavalrymen and 150 infantry, mostly members of the *Maison militaire du Roi* plus some volunteers. This force was shortly entrusted to the Duc de Berry, the king's nephew, who established a camp of instruction at nearby Alost and laid plans for a all-arms force of 10,000 men, equipment for which was ordered in England. Recruiting proceeded rather slowly. On 22 April there were only about 820 men under arms, and by 1 June, when a "grand review" of the army was held, only some 2,100. However, had the war lasted into the Autumn it is possible that the goal of 10,000 men might have been attained, there being considerable sentiment for the Bourbons in many areas of France. Louis XVIII attempted to get Wellington to make use of his "army" in the coming campaign, but the Duke does not appear to have regarded its military prowess very highly, remarking "I wish to have no association with those people."

North German Corps (Kleist) (26,200 with 24 pieces)
Hesse-Cassel Div (Engelhardt) (? in 13 Bns, with 6 pieces)
Anhalt-Thuringian Bde (Eglossein)(? in 12 Bns, with 12 pieces)
Mecklenburg Bde (Mecklenburg-Strelitz)(? in 6 Bns, with 6 pieces)
Cav Bde (Mecklenburg-Schwerin)(? in 12 Sqns)

Austro-Allied Army of the Rhine (Schwarzenberg) (250,000 with 534 pieces)

[Right Wing (Wrede) (250,000 with 534 pieces)]

III [South German] Corps (Wurttemburg I) (43,800 with 64 pieces)
Austrian Div (Palombini)(18,000 in 14 Bns, 12 Sqn, & 3 Bttys, with 24 pieces)
Hesse-Darmstadt Div (Hesse-Darmstadt)(8,200 in 10 Bns)
Wurttemburg Div (Koch) (? in 11 Bns)
Wurttemburg Cav Div (Wurttemburg II) (? in 20 Sqns)
Wurttemburg LW Bde (?) (? in 9 Bns)
Art Res (Brand) (600 in 5 Bttys, with 40 pieces)

IV [Bavarian] Corps (Wrede) (57,000 and 120 pieces)
1st Div (Ragliovich) (10,300 in 10 Bns & 2 Bttys, with 8 pieces)
2nd Div (Beckers) (10,300 in 10 Bns & 2 Bttys, with 8 pieces)
3rd Div (Lamotte) (10,300 in 10 Bns & 2 Bttys, with 8 pieces)
4th Div (Zollern) (10,300 in 10 Bns & 2 Bttys, with 8 pieces)
1st Cav Div (Bavaria) (3,000 in 24 Sqns & 1 Btty, with 8 pieces)

2nd Cav Div (Preising) (3,000 in 24 Sqns & 1 Btty, with 8 pieces)
Res Inf Bde (Maillot) (6,100 in 6 Bns & 1 Btty, with 8 pieces)
Res Inf Bde (Seidow) (2,200 in 18 Sqns)
Art Res (Cologne) (500 in 4 Bttys, with 32 pieces)
Rus Advanced Guard (Lambert) (10,000 with 36 pieces)
9th Div (Udom) (8000 in 12 Bns & 2 Bttys, with 24 pieces)
1st Bde/2nd Hussar Div (?) (1000 in 12 Sqns & 1 Btty, with 6 pieces)

Left Wing (Ferdinand) (104,000 with 230 pieces)

I Austrian Corps (Colloredo) (24,500 with 64 pieces)
Lt Div (Lederer) (5,600 in 4 Bns, 16 Sqns, & 1 Btty, with 8 pieces)
1st Div (Marschall) (8,900 in 11 Bns & 1 Btty, with 8 pieces)
2nd Div (Marciani) (8,900 in 11 Bns & 1 Btty, with 8 pieces)
Art (?) (1,000 in 5 Bttys, with 40 pieces)

II Austrian Corps (Hohenzollern-Heckingen) (34,300 with 88 pieces)
Lt Div (Klebelsberg) (5,600 in 4 Bns, 16 Sqns, & 1 Btty, with 8 pieces)
1st Div (Mazzuchelli) (8,900 in 11 Bns & 1 Btty, with 8 pieces)
2nd Div (?) (8,900 in 11 Bns & 1 Btty, with 8 pieces)
Baden Div (Schafer) (9,100 in 10 Bns, 10 Sqns, & 3 Bttys, with 24 pieces)
Art (?) (1,000 in 5 Bttys, with 40 pieces)

Austrian Res Corps (Ferdinand) (45.000 with 80 pieces)
Lt Div (Wartensleben) (6,100 in 5 Bns, 12 Sqns, & 2 Bttys, with 16 pieces)
Mixed Div (A. Lichtenstein) (12,000 in 15 Bns & 2 Bttys, with 16 pieces)
1st Grenadier Div (Deitrich) (6,500 in 8 Bns)
2nd Grenadier Div (d'Este) (6,500 in 8 Bns)
Cav Div (Stutterheim) (2,400 in 14 Sqns & 1 Btty, with 8 pieces)
Hussar Div (M. Lichtenstein) (3,900 in 26 Sqns)
Cuirassier Div (Moritz) (5,100 in 34 Sqns)
Art (?) (1,000 in 5 Bttys, with 40 pieces)

General Res (Schwarzenburg) (50,100 with 96 pieces)
Austrian Blockade Corps (Meerfeld) (33,300 with 48 pieces)
Lt Div (Hardegg) (4,600 in 3 Bns, & 12 Sqns, & 1 Btty, with 8 pieces)

Mixed Cav Div (Rinstern) (3,600 in 24 Sqns)
1st Mixed Bde (Mumb) (9,500 in 9 Bns & 1 Btty, with 8 pieces)
2nd Mixed Bde (Hecht) (9,500 in 9 Bns & 1 Btty, with 8 pieces)
Mixed LW Bde (?) (5,500 in 6 Bns)
Art (?) (500 in 3 Bttys, with 24 pieces)
Saxon Corps (Coburg) (16,800 with 48 pieces)
1st Bde (Norris) (9,200 in 12 Bns)
2nd Bde (Einstebel) (4,600 in 6 Bns)
Cav Bde (Lenser) (1,500 in 10 Sqns)
Art (Meabe) (1,200 in 6 Bttys, with 48 pieces)

The Swiss Army (Bachman)
(35,000 with 48 pieces)

1st Div (Gasn) (8,400 in 12 Bns & 1 Btty, with 8 pieces)
2nd Div (Fulz) (8,400 in 12 Bns & 1 Btty, with 8 pieces)
3rd Div (d'Affry) (8,400 in 12 Bns & 1 Btty, with 8 pieces)
Res Bearnaise Bde (Giradrd) (5,200 in 8 Bns)
Frontier Gd Bde (Corzelles) (4,000 in 6 Bns)

The Austro-Piemontese Army of Upper Italy
(Frimont) (62,000 with 64 pieces)

I Austrian Corps (Radivojevich) (23,000 with 24 pieces)
Lt Div (Greenville) (4,800 in 2 Bns, 18 Sqns, & 1 Btty, with 8 pieces)
1st Bde (Bluger) (8,500 in 9 Bns & 1 Btty, with 8 pieces)
2nd Bde (Tolfeis) (8,500 in 9 Bns & 1 Btty, with 8 pieces)
II Austrian Corps (Bubna) (25,000 with 24 pieces)
Lt Div (Brettschneider) (11,300 in 9 Bns, 12 Sqns, & 1 Btty, with 8 pieces)
1st Bde (Trent) (5,900 in 6 Bns & 1 Btty, with 8 pieces)
2nd Bde (Klaustein) (5,900 in 6 Bns & 1 Btty, with 8 pieces)
III Piedmontese Corps (Latour) (13,000 with 16 pieces)
Lt Bde (di Salmour) (3000 in 5 Bns)
1st Div (Gislenga) (5,000 in 8 Bns & 1 Btty, with 8 pieces)
2nd Div (d'Artezzia) (5,000 in 8 Bns & 1 Btty, with 8 pieces)

The Spanish Army of the Pyrenees (Castaños)
(24,000 in c. 50 Bns, 20 Sqns, & 6 Bttys, with 36 pieces)

Note: Not yet ready for operations by the time Napoleon abdicated.

Allied "Second Echelon" Forces

The Russian Army (Barclay de Tollay)
(157,000 with 384 pieces)

Right Wing (Docturov) (59,000 in 60 Bns, 30 Sqns, & 11 Bttys, with 132 pieces)

III Corps (Docturov)
    7th Div (Kapzewitz) (12 Bns & 2 Bttys, with 24 pieces)
    24th Div (Rodt) (12 Bns & 2 Bttys, with 24 pieces)
    27th Div (Sabanejew) (12 Bns & 2 Bttys, with 24 pieces)
    3rd Dragoon Div(+) (Alerciam) (30 Sqns & 1 Btty, with 12 peces)
    Grenadier Corps (Jermolov)
    2nd Grenadier Div (Bastiewitz) (12 Bns & 2 Bttys, with 24 pieces)
    3rd Gren Div (Roth) (12 Bns & 2 Bttys, with 24 pieces)

[Center (Sachsen) (46,000 in 36 Bns, 81 Sqns, & 9 Bttys, with 108 pieces)

V Corps (Sachsen)
    12th Div (Woronzoff) (12 Bns & 2 Bttys, with 24 pieces)
    25th Div (Marsov) (12 Bns & 2 Bttys, with 24 pieces)
    26th Div (Emme) (12 Bns & 2 Bttys, with 24 pieces)
    2rd Dragoon Div (Korff) (24 Sqns & 1 Btty, with 12 pieces)

III Cav Corps (Pahlen)
    3rd Uhlan Div (Liffanowitz) (24 Sqns & 1 Btty, with 12 pieces)
    3rd Cuirrasier Div (Dusa) (24 Sqns & 1 Btty, with 12 pieces)
    Cossack Bde (?) (9 Sqns)

[Main Body (Langeron) (50,000 in 48 Bns, 96 Sqns, & 12 Bttys, with 144 pieces)

IV Corps (Rajewtsky)
    11th Div (?) (12 Bns & 2 Bttys, with 24 pieces)

17th Div (?) (12 Bns & 2 Bttys, with 24 pieces)
3rd Hussar Div (?) (24 Sqns & 1 Btty, with 12 pieces)

VI Corps (Langeron)
8th Div (Essen) (12 Bns & 2 Bttys, with 24 pieces)
10th Div (Leimen) (12 Bns & 2 Bttys, with 24 pieces)
2nd Bde/2nd Hussar Div (12 Sqns & 1 Btty, with 6 pieces)

II Cav Corps (Minzingerd)
2nd Uhlan Div (?) (24 Sqns & 1 Btty, with 12 pieces)
2nd Cuirassier Div (?) (24 Sqns & 1 Btty, with 12 pieces)
Cossack Bde (?) (12 Sqns)

Note: Making its way across southern Germany at the time the Napoleon began operations along the Sambre on 15 June. By the end of the month its leading elements were across the Rhine.

The Austro-Italian Army of Naples (Bianchi) (47,000 with 72 pieces)

I Austrian Corps (Neipperg) (14,000 with 24 pieces)
Adv Guard (Stahremberg) (2,700 in 3 Bns & 1 Btty, with 8 pieces)
Inf Div (Neipperg) (8,500 in 12 Bns & 2 Bttys, with 16 pieces)
Cav Bde (Ebhardt) (2,700 in 18 Sqns)

II Austrian Corps (Mohr) (13,000 with 24 pieces)
Adv Guard (?) (3,000 in 3 Bns & 1 Btty, with 8 pieces)
Inf Div (Mohr) (10,000 in 12 Bns & 2 Bttys, with 16 pieces)

III Austro-Italian Corps (Nugent) (19,000 with 24 pieces)

Adv Guard (Stefani) (2,800 in 4 Bns & 1 Btty, with 8 pieces)
Inf Div (Nugent) (11,600 in 13 Bns & 2 Bttys, with 16 pieces)
Tuscan Bde (?) (2,500 in 3 Bns)
Cav Bde (Taris) (1,800 in 12 Sqns)

Note: Performing occupation duties and besieging the fortress of Gaeta, which held out in the name of Murat until 8 August.

Other Allied Forces: In addition to the contingents shown, the Allies potentially had available, in varying states of readiness, further bodies of troops which were either being held in reserve or were designated for commitment to operations in France should the campaign there drag on into the autumn. The accompanying table summarizes these forces.

Other Allied Forces						
Contingent	Strength	Bns	Sqns	Bttys	guns	Note
Bremen-Hamburg	4,000	4	2	1	6	A
Denmark	17,000	10	16	4	24	B
Dutch-Belgian	12,500	45	1	11	88	C
Portugal	14,000	24	8	4	24	D
	6,000	12	4	2	12	E
Prussia	70,000	90	50	25	200	F
Spain	12,000	24	10	4	24	G

Notes:

A. At the time of the Waterloo Campaign this division was in the process of being formed for eventual service with Wellington's army

B. This division was designated for service with Wellington in Flanders. However, due primarily to the deliberate efforts of the pro-French Danes to delay its formation, the campaign was over before a single man marched.

C. Most of this force consisted of militia (c. 30 battalions' worth) or line troops not yet considered fit for active duty or assigned to garrisons in the Netherlands proper and as the Royal Guard.

D. This force was concentrating at Lisbon for shipment to Flanders and service with Wellington's army at the time the campaign ended.

E. At the time hostilities ended the Portuguese and British governments were in negotiation with the Spanish government for the movement of these forces to supplement Spanish efforts in the Pyrenees.

F. These forces comprised the V and VI Corps and the Royal Guard, all of which remained in Prussia throughout the campaign.

G. Had the campaign lasted through the autumn it is probable that Castaños' Army of the Pyrenees would have been enlarged by about 50 percent, at least on paper.

Index

Index